NOTE.

THESE Essays originally appeared in several American periodicals. To the seven papers represented by the title the Author has ventured to add five others which have much in common with the subjects of the former.

FRENCH POETS AND NOVELISTS.

FRENCH

POETS AND NOVELISTS.

BY
HENRY JAMES Jr.

Essay Index Reprint Series

BOOKS FOR LIBRARIES PRESS
FREEPORT, NEW YORK

First Published 1878
Reprinted 1972

Library of Congress Cataloging in Publication Data

James, Henry, 1843-1916.
   French poets and novelists.

   (Essay index reprint series)
   Reprint of the 1878 ed.
   CONTENTS: Alfred de Musset.--Théophile Gautier.
--Charles Baudelaire. [etc.]
   1. French literature--19th century--History and
criticism. 2. Authors, French--Biography. I. Title.
PQ286.J3   1972   840.9   70-38773
ISBN 0-8369-2660-9

PRINTED IN THE UNITED STATES OF AMERICA
BY
NEW WORLD BOOK MANUFACTURING CO., INC.
HALLANDALE, FLORIDA 33009

CONTENTS.

	PAGE
ALFRED DE MUSSET	1
THEOPHILE GAUTIER	39
CHARLES BAUDELAIRE	72
HONORÉ DE BALZAC	84
BALZAC'S LETTERS	151
GEORGE SAND	190
CHARLES DE BERNARD AND GUSTAVE FLAUBERT	237
IVAN TURGÉNIEFF	269
THE TWO AMPÈRES	321
MADAME DE SABRAN	359
MÉRIMÉE'S LETTERS	390
THE THÉÂTRE FRANÇAIS	403

FRENCH POETS AND NOVELISTS.

ALFRED DE MUSSET.

IT had been known for some time that M. Paul de Musset was preparing a biography of his illustrious brother, and the knowledge had been grateful to Alfred de Musset's many lovers; for the author of "Rolla" and the "Lettre à Lamartine" has lovers. The book has at last appeared—more than twenty years after the death of its hero.[1] It is probably not unfair to suppose that a motive for delay has been removed by the recent death of Madame Sand. M. Paul de Musset's volume proves, we confess, rather disappointing. It is a careful and graceful but at the same time a very slight performance, such as was to be expected from the author of "Lui et Elle" and of the indignant

[1] "Biographie de Alfred de Musset: sa Vie et ses Œuvres." Par Paul de Musset. Paris: Charpentier.

refutation (in the biographical notice which accompanies the octavo edition of Alfred de Musset's works) of M. Taine's statement that the poet was addicted to walking about the streets late at night. As regards this latter point, M. Paul de Musset hastened to declare that his brother had no such habits—that his customs were those of a *gentilhomme;* by which the biographer would seem to mean that when the poet went abroad after dark it was in his own carriage, or at least in a hired cab, summoned from the nearest stand. M. Paul de Musset is a devoted brother and an agreeable writer; but he is not, from the critic's point of view, the ideal biographer. This, however, is not seriously to be regretted, for it is little to be desired that the ideal biography of Alfred de Musset should be written, or that he should be delivered over, bound hand and foot, to the critics. Those who really care for him would prefer to judge him with all kinds of allowances and indulgences—sentimentally and imaginatively. Between him and his readers it is a matter of affection, or it is nothing at all; and there is something very happy, therefore, in M. Paul de Musset's fond fraternal reticences and extenuations. He has related his brother's life as if it were a pretty "story;" and indeed there is enough that was pretty in it to justify him. We should decline to profit by any information that might be offered us in regard to its prosaic, its possibly shabby side. To make the story complete, however, there appears simultaneously with M. Paul de Musset's volume a publication of a quite different sort—a biography of the poet by a clever German writer, Herr Paul Lindau.[1] Herr Lindau is highly appreciative, but he is also critical, and he says a great many things that M. Paul de Musset leaves unsaid. As becomes a German biographer, he is very minute and exhaustive, and a stranger who should desire a "general idea" of the poet would probably get more instruction from his pages than from the French memoir. Their fault is indeed that they are apparently addressed to persons whose mind is supposed to be a blank with regard to the author of "Rolla." The exactions of bookmaking alone can explain the long analyses and prose paraphrases of Alfred de Musset's comedies and tales to which Herr Lindau treats his readers—the dreariest kind of reading when an author is not in himself essentially inaccessible. Either one has not read Alfred de Musset's comedies or not felt the charm of them—in which case one will not be likely to resort to Herr Lindau's memoirs—or one has read them in the charming original, and can therefore dispense with an elaborate German summary.

[1] "Alfred de Musset." Von Paul Lindau. Berlin: Hofmann.

In saying just now that M. Paul de Musset's biography of his brother is disappointing, we meant more particularly to express our regret that he has given us no letters—or given us at least but two or three. It is probable, however, that he had no more in his hands. Alfred de Musset lived in a very compact circle; he spent his whole life in Paris, and his friends lived in Paris near him. He was little separated from his brother, who appears to have been his best friend (M. Paul de Musset was six years Alfred's senior) and much of his life was passed under the same roof with the other members of his family. Seeing his friends constantly, he had no occasion to write to them; and as he saw little of the world (in the larger sense of the phrase) he would have had probably but little to write about. He made but one attempt at travelling—his journey to Italy, at the age of twenty-three, with George Sand. "He made no important journeys," says Herr Lindau, "and if one excepts his love affairs, he really had no experiences." But his love affairs, as a general thing, could not properly be talked about. M. de Musset shows good taste in not pretending to narrate them. He mentions two or three of the more important episodes of this class, and with regard to the others he says that when he does not mention them they may always be taken for granted. It is perhaps indeed in a limited sense that Alfred de Musset's love affairs may be said to have been in some cases more important than in others. It was his own philosophy that in this matter one thing is about as good as another—

"Aimer est le grand point ; qu'importe la maîtresse ?
Qu'importe le flacon pourvu qu'on ait l'ivresse ? "

Putting aside the "ivresse," which was constant, Musset's life certainly offers little material for narration. He wrote a few poems, tales, and comedies, and that is all. He *did* nothing, in the sterner sense of the word. He was inactive, indolent, idle; his record has very few dates. Two or three times the occasion to do something was offered him, but he shook his head and let it pass. It was proposed to him to accept a place as *attaché* to the French embassy at Madrid, a comfortable salary being affixed to the post. But Musset found no inspiration in the prospect. He had written about Spain in his earlier years—he had sung in the most charming fashion about Juanas and Pepitas, about señoras in mantillas stealing down palace staircases that look " blue " in the starlight. But the desire to see the picturesqueness that he had dreamt of proved itself to have none of the force of a motive. This is the fact in Musset's life which the writer of these lines finds most regrettable—the fact of his contented smallness of horizon—the fact that on his own line he should not have cared to go farther. There is something really exasperating in the sight of a picturesque poet wantonly slighting an opportunity to go to Spain—the Spain of forty years ago. It does violence even to that minimum of intellectual eagerness which is the portion of a contemplative mind. It is annoying to think that Alfred de Musset should have been meagrely contemplative. This is the weakness that tells against him, more than the weakness of what would be called his excesses. From the point of view of his own peculiar genius it was a good fortune for him to be susceptible and tender, sensitive and passionate. The trouble was not that he was all this, but that he was lax and soft; that he had too little energy and curiosity. Shelley was at least equally tremulous and sensitive—equally a victim of his impressions, and an echo, as it were, of his temperament. But even Musset's fondest readers must feel that Shelley had within him a firm, divinely-tempered spring, against which his spirit might rebound indefinitely. As regards intense sensibility—that fineness of feeling which is the pleasure and pain of the poetic nature—M. Paul de Musset tells two or three stories of his brother which remind one of the anecdotes recorded of the author of the "Ode to the West Wind." "One of the things that he loved best in the world was a certain exclamation of

Racine's Phædra, which expresses by its *bizarrerie* the trouble of her sickened heart:

> 'Ariane, ma sœur, de quel amour blessée,
> Vous mourûtes aux bords où vous fûtes laissée!'

When Rachel used to murmur forth this strange, unexpected plaint, Alfred always took his head in his two hands and turned pale with emotion."

The author describes the poet's early years, and gives several very pretty anecdotes of his childhood. Alfred de Musset was born in 1810, in the middle of old Paris, on a spot familiar to those many American visitors who wander across the Seine, better and better pleased as they go, to the museum of the Hôtel de Cluny. The house in which Musset's parents lived was close to this beautiful monument—a happy birthplace for a poet; but both the house and the street have now disappeared. M. Paul de Musset does not relate that his brother began to versify in his infancy; but Alfred was indeed hardly more than an infant when he achieved his first success. The poems published under the title of "Contes d'Espagne et d'Italie" were composed in his eighteenth and nineteenth years; he had but just completed his nineteenth when the volume into which they had been gathered was put forth. There are certainly—if we consider the quality of the poems—few more striking examples of literary precocity. The cases of Chatterton and Keats may be equally remarkable but they are not more so. These first boyish verses of Musset have a vivacity, a brilliancy, a freedom of feeling and of fancy which may well have charmed the little *cénacle* to which he read them aloud—the group of littérateurs and artists which clustered about Victor Hugo, who, although at this time very young, was already famous. M. Paul de Musset intimates that if his brother was at this moment (and as we may suppose, indeed, always) one of the warmest admirers of the great author of "Hernani" and those other splendid productions which project their violent glow across the threshold of the literary era of 1830, and if Victor Hugo gave kindly audience to "Don Paez" and "Mardoche," this kindness declined in proportion as the fame of the younger poet expanded. Alfred de Musset was certainly not fortunate in his relations with his more distinguished contemporaries. Victor Hugo "dropped" him; it would have been better for him if George Sand had never taken him up; and Lamartine, to whom, in the shape of a passionate epistle, he addressed the most beautiful of his own, and one of the most beautiful of all, poems, acknowledged the compliment only many years after it was paid. The *cénacle* was all for Spain, for local colour, for serenades, and daggers, and Gothic arches. It was nothing if not audacious (it was in the van of the Romantic movement), and it was partial to what is called in France the "humoristic" as well as to the ferociously sentimental. Musset produced a certain "Ballade à la Lune" which began—

> "C'était dans la nuit brune
> Sur le clocher jauni
> La lune
> Comme un point sur un i!"

This assimilation of the moon suspended above a church spire to a dot upon an *i* became among the young Romanticists a sort of symbol of what they should do and dare; just as in the opposite camp it became a by-word of horror. But this was only playing at poetry, and in his next things, produced in the following year or two, Musset struck a graver and more resonant chord. The pieces published under the title of "Un Spectacle dans un Fauteuil" have all the youthful grace and gaiety of those that preceded them; but they have beyond this a suggestion of the quality which gives so high a value to the author's later and best verses—the accent of genuine passion. It is hard to see what, just yet, Alfred de Musset had to be passionate about; but passion, with a poet, even when it is most genuine, is very much an affair of the imagination and the personal temperament (independently, we mean, of strong provoking causes) and the sensibilities of this young man were already exquisitely active. His poems found a great many admirers, and these admirers were often women. Hence for the young poet, says M. Paul de Musset, a great many romantic and "*Boccaciennes*" adventures. "On several occasions I was awaked in the middle of the night to give my opinion on some question of high prudence. All these little stories having been confided to me under the seal of secrecy, I have been obliged to forget them; but I may affirm that more than one of them would have aroused the envy of Bassompierre and Lauzun. Women at that time were not wholly absorbed in their care for luxury and dress. To hope to please, young men had no need to be rich; and it served a purpose to have at nineteen years of age the prestige of talent and glory." This is very pretty, as well as very Gallic; but it is rather vague, and we may without offence suspect it to be, to a certain extent, but that conventional *coup de chapeau* which every self-respecting Frenchman renders to actual or potential, past, present, or future gallantry. Doubtless, however, Musset was, in the native phrase, *lancé*. He lived with his father and mother, his brother and sister; his purse was empty; Seville and Granada were very far away; and these "Andalusian passions," as M. Paul de Musset says, were mere reveries and boyish visions. But they were the visions of a boy who was all ready to compare reality with romance, and who, in fact, very soon acceded to a proposal which appeared to offer a peculiar combination of the two. It is noticeable, by the way, that from our modest Anglo-Saxon point of view these same "Andalusian passions," dealing chiefly with ladies tumbling about on disordered couches, and pairs of lovers who take refuge from an exhausted vocabulary in *biting* each other, are an odd sort of thing for an ingenuous lad, domiciled in the manner M. Paul de Musset describes, and hardly old enough to have a latch-key, to lay on the family breakfast-table. But this was very characteristic all round the circle. Musset was not a didactic poet, and he had no time to lose in going through the preliminary paces of one. His business was to talk about love in unmistakable terms, to proclaim its pleasures and pains with all possible eloquence; and he would have been quite at a loss to understand why he should have blushed or stammered in preluding to so beautiful a theme. Herr Lindau thinks that even in the germ Musset's inspiration is already vicious—that "his wonderful talent was almost simultaneously ripe and corrupted." But Herr Lindau speaks from the modest Saxon point of view; a point of view, however, from which, in such a matter, there is a great deal to be said.

The great event in Alfred de Musset's life, most people would say, was his journey to Italy with George Sand. This event has been abundantly—superabundantly—described, and Herr Lindau, in the volume before us, devotes a long chapter to it and lingers over it with peculiar complacency. Our own sentiment would be that there is something extremely displeasing in the publicity which has attached itself to the episode; that there is indeed a sort of colossal indecency in the way it has passed into the common fund of literary gossip. It illustrates the base, the weak, the trivial side of all the great things that were concerned in it—fame, genius and love. Either the Italian journey was in its results a very serious affair for the remarkable couple who undertook it—in which case it should be left in that quiet place in the history of the development of the individual into which public intrusion can bring no light, but only darkness—or else it was a piece of levity and conscious self-display; in which case the attention of the public has been invited to it on false grounds. If there ever was an affair it should be becoming to be silent about, it was certainly this one; but neither the actors nor the spectators have been of this way of thinking; one may almost say that there exists a whole literature on the subject. To this literature Herr Lindau's contribution is perhaps the most ingenious.

He has extracted those pages from Paul de Musset's novel of "Lui et Elle" which treat of the climax of the relations of the hero and heroine, and he has printed the names of George Sand and Alfred de Musset instead of the fictitious names. The result is perhaps of a nature to refresh the jaded vision of most lovers of scandal.

We must add that some of his judgments on the matter happen to have a certain felicity. M. Paul de Musset has narrated the story more briefly—having, indeed, by the publication of "Lui et Elle," earned the right to be brief. He mentions two or three facts, however, the promulgation of which he may have thought it proper, as we said before, to postpone to Madame Sand's death. One of them is sufficiently dramatic. Musset had met George Sand in the summer of 1833, about the time of the publication of "Rolla"—seeing her for the first time at a dinner given to the contributors of the "Revue des Deux Mondes," at the restaurant of the Trois Frères Provençaux. George Sand was the only woman present. Sainte-Beuve had already endeavoured to bring his two friends together, but the attempt had failed, owing to George Sand's reluctance, founded on an impression that she should not like the young poet. Alfred de Musset was twenty-three years of age; George Sand, who had published "Indiana," "Valentine," and "Lélia,"was close upon thirty. Alfred de Musset, as the author of "Rolla," was a very extraordinary young man—quite the young man of whom Heinrich Heine could say "he has a magnificent past before him." Upon his introduction to George Sand, an intimacy speedily followed—an intimacy commemorated by the lady in expansive notes to Sainte-Beuve, whom she kept informed of its progress. When the winter came the two intimates talked of leaving Paris together, and, as an experiment, paid a visit to Fontainebleau. The experiment succeeded, but this was not enough, and they formed the project of going to Italy. To this project, as regarded her son, Madame de Musset refused her consent. (Alfred's father, we should say, had died before the publication of "Rolla," leaving his children without appreciable property, though during his lifetime, occupying a post in a government office, he had been able to maintain them comfortably.) His mother's opposition was so vehement that Alfred gave up the project and countermanded the preparations that had already been made for departure.

"That evening toward nine o'clock," say M. Paul de Musset, "our mother was alone with her daughter by the fireside, when she was informed that a lady was waiting for her at the door in a hired carriage and begged urgently to speak with her. She went down accompanied by a servant. The unknown lady named herself; she besought this deeply grieved mother to confide her son to her, saying that she would have for him a maternal affection and care. As promises did not avail, she went so far as sworn vows. She used all her eloquence, and she must have had a great deal, since her enterprise succeeded. In a moment of emotion the consent was given." The author of "Lélia" and the author of "Rolla" started for Italy together. M. Paul de Musset mentions that he accompanied them to the mail coach " on a sad, misty evening, in the midst of circumstances that boded ill." They spent the winter at Venice, and M. Paul de Musset and his mother continued to hear regularly from Alfred. But toward the middle of February his letters suddenly stopped, and for six weeks they were without news. They were on the point of starting for Italy, to put an end to their suspense, when they received a melancholy epistle informing them that their son and brother was on his way home. He was slowly recovering from an attack of brain fever, but as soon as he should be able to drag himself along he would seek the refuge of the paternal roof.

On the 10th of April he reappeared alone. A quarter of a century later, and a short time after his death, Madame Sand gave to the world, in the guise of a novel, an account of the events which had occupied this interval. The account was highly to her own advantage and much to the discredit of her companion. Paul de Musset immediately retorted with a little book which is decidedly poor as fiction, but tolerably good, probably, as history. As a devoted brother, given all the circumstances, it was perhaps the best thing he could do. It is believed that his reply was more than, in the vulgar phrase, Madame Sand had bargained for; inasmuch as he made use of documents of whose existence she had been ignorant. Alfred de Musset, suspecting that her version of their relations would be given to the world, had, in the last weeks of his life, dictated to his brother a detailed statement of those incidents to which misrepresentation would chiefly address itself, and this narrative Paul de Musset simply incorporated in his novel. The gist of it is that the poet's companion took advantage of his being seriously ill, in Venice, to be flagrantly unfaithful, and that, discovering her infidelity, he relapsed into a brain fever which threatened his life, and from which he rose only to make his way home with broken wings and a bleeding heart. Madame Sand's version of the story is that his companion's infidelity was a delusion of the fever itself and the charge was but the climax of a series of intolerable affronts and general fantasticalities.

Fancy the great gossiping, vulgar-minded public, deliberately invited to ponder this delicate question ! The public should never have been appealed to ; but once the appeal made, it administers perforce a rough justice of its own. According to this rough justice, the case looks badly for Musset's fellow-traveller. She was six years older than he (at that time of life a grave fact); she had drawn him away from his mother, taken him in charge, assumed a responsibility. Their two literary physiognomies were before the world, and she was, on the face of the matter, the riper, stronger, more reasonable nature. She had made great pretensions to reason, and it is fair to say of Alfred de Musset that he had made none whatever. What the public sees is that the latter, unreasonable though he may have been, comes staggering home, alone and forlorn, while his companion remains quietly at Venice and writes three or four highly successful romances. Herr Lindau, who analyzes the affair, comes to the same conclusion as the gross, synthetic public; and he qualifies certain sides of it in terms of which observant readers of George Sand's writings will recognise the justice. It is very happy to say "she was something of a Philistine;" that at the bottom of all experience with her was the desire to turn it to some economical account ; and that she probably irritated her companion in a high degree by talking too much about loving him as a mother and a sister. (This, it will be remembered, is the basis of action with Thérèse, in " Elle et Lui." She becomes the hero's mistress in order to retain him in the filial relation, after the fashion of Rousseau's friend, Madame de Warens). On the other hand, it seems hardly fair to make it one of Musset's grievances that his comrade was industrious, thrifty and methodical ; that she had, as the French say, *de l'ordre ;* and that, being charged with the maintenance of a family, she allowed nothing to divert her from producing her daily stint of " copy."

It is easy to believe that Musset may have tried the patience of a tranquil associate. George Sand's Jacques Laurent in " Elle et Lui," is a sufficiently vivid portrait of a highly endowed, but hopelessly petulant, unreasonable and dissipated egotist. We are far from suspecting that the portrait is perfectly exact; no portrait by George Sand is perfectly exact. Whatever point of view she takes, she always abounds too much in her own sense. But it evidently has a tolerably solid foundation in fact. Herr Lindau holds that Alfred de Musset's life was literally blighted by the grief that he suffered in Italy, and that the rest of his career was a long, erratic, unprofitable effort to drown the recollection of it.

Our own inclination would be to judge him at once with more and with less indulgence. Whether deservedly or no, there is no doubt that his suffering was great; his brother quotes a passage from a document written five years after the event, in which Alfred affirms that, on his return to Paris, he spent four months shut up in his room in incessant tears—tears interrupted only by a "mechanical" game of chess in the evening. But Musset, like all poets, was essentially a creature of impressions; as with all poets, his sentimental faculty needed constantly to renew itself. He found his account in sorrow, or at least in emotion, and we may say, in differing from Herr Lindau, that he was not a man to let a grievance grow stale. To feel permanently the need of smothering sorrow is in a certain sense to be sobered by it. Musset was never sobered (a cynical commentator would say he was never sober). Emotions bloomed again lightly and brilliantly on the very stem on which others had withered. After the catastrophe at times his imagination saved him, distinctly, from permanent depression; and on a different line, this same imagination helped him into dissipation.

M. Paul de Musset mentions that in 1837 his brother conceived a "passion sérieuse" for an attractive young lady, and that the *liaison* lasted two years—"two years during which there was never a quarrel, a storm, a cooling-off; never a pretext for umbrage or jealousy. This is why," he adds, "there is nothing to be told of them. Two years of love without a cloud cannot be narrated." It is noticeable that this is the third "passion sérieuse" that M. Paul de Musset alludes to since the dolorous weeks which followed the return from Venice. Shortly after this period another passion had come to the front, a passion which, like that which led him to Italy, was destined to have a tragical termination. This particular love affair is commemorated, in accents of bitter melancholy, in the "Nuit de Décembre," just as the other, which had found its catastrophe at Venice, figures, by clear allusion, in the "Nuit de Mai," published a few months before. It may provoke a philosophic smile to learn, as we do from M. Paul de Musset—candid biographer!— that the "motives" of these two poems are not identical, as they have hitherto been assumed to be. It had never occurred to the reader that one disillusionment could follow so fast upon the heels of another. When we add that a short time afterward—as the duration of great intimacies of the heart is measured—Alfred de Musset was ready to embark upon "two years of love without a cloud" with still another object—to say nothing of the brief interval containing another sentimental episode of which our biographer gives the prettiest account—we seem to be justified in thinking that, for a "blighted" life, that of Alfred de Musset exhibited a certain germinal vivacity.

During his stay in Italy he had written nothing; but the five years which followed his return are those of his most active and brilliant productiveness. The finest of his verses, the most charming of his tales, the most original of his comedies, belong to this relatively busy period. Everything that he wrote at this time has a depth and intensity that distinguish it from the jocosely sentimental productions of his commencement and from the somewhat mannered and vapidly elegant compositions which he put forth, at wide intervals, during the last fifteen years of his life. This was the period of Musset's intellectual virility. He was very precocious, but he was at the same time, at first, very youthful. On the other hand, his decline began early; in most of his later things, especially in his verses (they become very few in number) the inspiration visibly runs thin. "Mon verre n'est pas grand, mais je bois dans mon verre," he had said, and both clauses of the sentence are true. His glass held but a small quantity; the best of his verses —those that one knows by heart and never wearies of repeating—are very soon counted. We have named them when we have mentioned "Rolla," the "Nuit de Mai," the "Nuit d'Août," and the "Nuit d'Octobre"; the "Lettre à Lamartine," and the "Stances à la

Malibran." These, however, are perfection ; and if Musset had written nothing else he would have had a right to say that it was from his own glass that he drank. The most beautiful of his comedies, "Il ne faut pas badiner avec l'Amour," dates from 1834, and to the same year belongs the "Lorenzaccio," the strongest, if not the most exquisite, of his dramatic attempts. His two most agreeable *nouvelles*, " Emmeline " and " Fréderic et Bernerette," appeared about the same time. But we have not space to enumerate his productions in detail. During the fifteen last years of his life, as we have said, they grew more and more rare ; the poet had, in a certain sense, out-lived himself. Of these last years Herr Lindau gives a rather realistic and unflattered sketch ; picturing him especially as a figure publicly familiar to Parisian loungers, who were used to observe him as " an unfortunate with an interesting face, dressed with extreme care," with the look of youth and the lassitude of age, seated in a corner of a café and gazing blankly over a marble table on which " a half empty bottle of absinthe and a quite empty glass" stood before him. M. Paul de Musset, in describing his brother's later years, is mindful of the rule to glide, not to press ; with a very proper fraternal piety, he leaves a great many foibles and transgressions in the shade. He mentions, however, Alfred's partiality for stimulants—a taste which had defined itself in his early years. Musset made an excessive use of liquor; in plain English, he got drunk. Sainte-Beuve, somewhere in one of his merciless, but valuable foot-notes, alludes to the author of "Rolla" coming tipsy to the sittings of the French Academy. Herr Lindau repeats a pun which was current on such occasions. "Musset s'absente trop," said some one. "Il s'absinthe trop," replied some one else. He had been elected to the Academy in 1852. His speech on the occasion of his reception was a disappointment to his auditors. Herr Lindau attributes the sterility of his later years to indolence and perversity; and it is probable that there is not a little justice in the charge. He was unable to force himself; he belonged to the race of gifted people who must do as it pleases them. When a literary task was proposed to him and he was not in the humour for it, he was wont to declare that he was not a maid-of-all-work but an artist. He must write when the fancy took him; the fancy took him, unfortunately, less and less frequently. With a very uncertain income and harassed constantly by his debts, he scorned to cultivate a pecuniary inspiration. He died in the arms of his brother in the spring of 1857.

He was beyond question one of the first poets of our day. If the poetic force is measured by the *quality* of the inspiration—by its purity, intensity, and closely personal savour—Alfred de Musset's place is surely very high. He was, so to speak, a thoroughly *personal* poet. He was not the poet of nature, of the universe, of reflection, of morality, of history; he was the poet simply of a certain order of personal emotions, and his charm is in the frankness and freedom, the grace and harmony, with which he expresses these emotions. The affairs of the heart—these were his province; in no other verses has the heart spoken more characteristically. Herr Lindau says very justly that if he was not the greatest poet among his contemporaries, he was at any rate the most poetically constituted nature. A part of the rest of Herr Lindau's judgment is worth quoting:

"He has remained the poet of youth. No one has sung so truthfully and touchingly its aspirations and its sensibilities, its doubts and its hopes. No one has comprehended and justified its follies and its amiable idiosyncrasies with a more poetic irony, with a deeper conviction. His joy was young, his sorrow was young, and young was his song. To youth he owed all happiness, and in youth he sang his brightest chants. But the weakness of youth was his fatal enemy, and with youth faded away his joy in existence and in creation."

This is exactly true. Half the beauty of Musset's writing is its simple suggestion of youthfulness—of something fresh and fair, slim and tremulous, with a tender epidermis. This quality, with some readers may seem to deprive him of a certain proper dignity;

and it is very true that he was was not a Stoic. You
may even call him unmanly. He cries out when he
is hurt; he resorts frequently to tears, and he talks
much about his tears. (We have seen that after his
return from Venice they formed, for four months, his
principal occupation). But his defence is that if he
does not bear things like a man, he at least, according
to Shakespeare's distinction, feels them like a man.
What makes him valuable is just this gift for the
expression of that sort of emotion which the conven-
tions and proprieties of life, the dryness of ordinary
utterance, the stiffness of most imaginations, leave
quite in the vague, and yet which forms a part of human
nature important enough to have its exponent. If
the presumption is against the dignity of deeply lyric
utterance, poor Musset is, in the vulgar phrase, nowhere—he is a mere grotesque sound of lamentation.
But if in judging him you do not stint your sympathy,
you will presently perceive him to have an extraordinarily precious quality—a quality equally rare in
literature and in life. He has passion. There is in
most poetry a great deal of reflection, of wisdom, of
grace, of art, of genius; but (especially in English
poetry) there is little of this peculiar property of
Musset's. When it occurs we feel it to be extremely
valuable; it touches us beyond anything else. It

was the great gift of Byron, the quality by which he will live in spite of those weaknesses and imperfections which may be pointed out by the dozen. Alfred de Musset in this respect resembled the poet whom he appears most to have admired—living at a time when it had not begun to be the fashion to be ashamed to take Byron seriously. Mr. Swinburne in one of his prose essays speaks of him with violent scorn as Byron's "attendant dwarf," or something of that sort. But this is to miss the case altogether. There is nothing diminutive in generous admiration, and nothing dwarfish in being a younger brother; Mr. Swinburne's charge is too coarse a way of stating the position. Musset resembles Byron in the fact that the beauty of his verse is somehow identical with the feeling of the writer—with his immediate, sensible warmth— and not dependent upon that reflective stage into which, to produce its great effects, most English poetic expression instantly passes, and which seems to chill even while it nobly beautifies. Musset is talked of nowadays in France very much as Byron is talked of among ourselves; it is noticed that he often made bad verses, and he is accused of having but half known his trade. This sort of criticism is eminently just, and there is a weak side of the author of "Rolla" which it is easy to attack.

Alfred de Musset, like Mr. Murray's fastidious correspondent, wrote poetry as an amateur—wrote it, as they say in France, *en gentilhomme*. It is the fashion, I believe, in some circles, to be on one's guard against speaking foreign tongues too well (the precaution is perhaps superfluous) lest a marked proficiency should expose one to be taken for a teacher of languages. It was a feeling of this kind, perhaps, that led Alfred de Musset to a certain affectation of negligence and laxity : though he wrote for the magazine she could boast a long pedigree, and he had nothing in common with the natives of Grub Street. Since his death a new school of poets has sprung up—of which, indeed, his contemporary, Théophile Gautier, may be regarded as the founder. These gentlemen have taught French Poetry a multitude of paces of which so sober-footed a damsel was scarcely to have been supposed capable; they have discovered a great many secrets that Musset appears never to have suspected, or (if he did suspect them) to have thought not worth finding out. They have sounded the depths of versification, and beside their refined, consummate *facture* Musset's simple devices and good-natured prosody seem to belong to a primitive stage of art. It is the difference between a clever performer on the tight rope and a gentleman strolling along on soft

turf with his hands in his pockets. If people care
supremely for form, Musset will merely but half satisfy
them. It is very pretty, they will say; but it is
confoundedly unbusinesslike. His verse is not chiselled
and pondered, and in spite of an ineffable natural
grace it lacks the positive qualities of cunning work-
manship—those qualities which are found in such
high perfection in Théophile Gautier. To our own
sense Musset's exquisite feeling more than makes up
for one-half the absence of "chiselling," and the ineffable grace we spoke of just now makes up for the
other half. His sweetness of passion, of which the
poets who have succeeded him have so little, is a
more precious property than their superior science.
His grace is often something divine; it is in his
grace that we must look for his style. Herr Lindau
says that Heine speaks of "truth, harmony, and
grace" being his salient qualities. (By the first, we
take it, he meant what we have called Musset's
passion). His harmony, from the first, was often
admirable; the rhythm of even some of his earliest
verses makes them haunt the ear after one has murmured them aloud.

> Ulric, des mers nul œil n'a mesuré l'abîme,
> Ni les hérons plongeurs, ni les vieux matelots;
> Le soleil vient briser ses rayons sur leur cime,
> Comme un soldat vaincu brise ses javelots.

Musset's grace, in its suavity, freedom, and unaffectedness, is altogether peculiar; though it must be said that it is only in the poems of his middle period that it is at its best. His latest things are, according to Sainte-Beuve, *colifichets*—baubles; they are too much in the rococo, the Dresden china, style. But as we have said before, with his youth Musset's inspiration failed him. It failed him in his prose as well as in his verse. "Il faut qu'une Porte soit ouverte ou fermée," one of the last of his dramatic proverbs, is very charming, very perfect in its way; but compared with the tone of the "Caprices de Marianne," the "Chandelier," "Fantasio," the sentiment is thin and the style has rather a simper. It is what the French call *marivaudage*. There can, however, be no better example of the absoluteness of the poetic sentiment, of its justifying itself as it goes, of lyrical expression being as it were not only a means, but an end, than the irresistible beauty of such effusions as the "Lettre à Lamartine" and the "Nuit d'Août."

Poëte, je t'écris pour te dire que j'aime!

—that is all, literally, that Musset has to say to the "amant d'Elvire"; and it would be easy to make merry at the expense of so simply candid a piece of "gush." But the confidence is made with a transparent ardour, a sublime good faith, an audible, touching tremour of voice, which, added to the enchanting harmony of the verse, make the thing one of the most splendid poems of our day.

> Ce ne sont pas des chants, ce ne sont que des larmes,
> Et je ne te dirai que ce que Dieu m'a dit!

Musset has never risen higher. He has, in strictness, only one idea—the idea that the passion of love and the act of loving are the divinest things in a miserable world; that love has a thousand disappointments, deceptions, and pangs, but that for its sake they are all worth enduring, and that as Tennyson has said, more curtly and reservedly,

> 'Tis better to have loved and lost
> Than never to have loved at all.

Sometimes he expresses this idea in the simple epicurean fashion, with gaiety and with a more or less cynical indifference to the moral side of the divine passion. Then he is often pretty, picturesque, fanciful, but he remains essentially light. At other times he feels its relation to the other things that make up man's destiny, and the sense of aspiration mingles with the sense of enjoyment or of regret. Then he is at his best; then he seems an image of universally sentient youth.

> Je ne puis ; malgré moi, l'infini me tourmente,
> Je n'y saurais songer sans crainte et sans espoir ;
> Et quoiqu'on en ait dit, ma raison s'épouvante
> De ne pas le comprendre, et pourtant de le voir.

While we may suspect that there is something a little over-coloured in M. Paul de Musset's account of the degree to which his brother was haunted by the religious sentiment—by the impulse to grope for some philosophy of life—we may also feel that with the poet's sense of the "divineness" of love there went a conviction that ideal love implies a divine object. This is the feeling expressed in the finest lines of the "Lettre à Lamartine"—in lines at least which, if they are not the finest, are fine enough to quote :

> Eh bien, bon ou mauvais, inflexible ou fragile,
> Humble ou gai, triste ou fier, mais toujours gémissant,
> Cet homme, tel qu'il est, cet être fait d'argile,
> Tu l'a vu, Lamartine, et son sang est ton sang.
> Son bonheur est le tien ; sa douleur est la tienne ;
> Et des maux qu'ici bas il lui faut endurer,
> Pas un qui ne te touche et qui ne t'appartienne ;
> Puisque tu sais chanter, ami, tu sais pleurer.
> Dis-moi, qu'en penses-tu dans tes jours de tristesse ?
> Que t'a dit le malheur quand tu l'as consulté ?
> Trompé par tes amis, trahi par ta maîtresse,
> Du ciel et de toi-même as-tu jamais douté ?
> Non, Alphonse, jamais. La triste expérience
> Nous apporte la cendre et n éteint pas le feu.

> Tu respectes le mal fait par la Providence ;
> Tu le laisses passer et tu crois à ton Dieu.
> Quelqu'il soit c'est le mien ; il n'est pas deux croyances.
> Je ne sais pas son nom : j'ai regardé les cieux ;
> Je sais qu'ils sont à lui, je sais qu'ils sont immenses,
> Et que l'immensité ne peut pas être à deux.
> J'ai connu, jeune encor, de sévères souffrances ;
> J'ai vu verdir les bois et j'ai tenté d'aimer.
> Je sais ce que la terre engloutit d'espérances,
> Et pour y recueillir ce qu'il y faut semer.
> Mais ce que j'ai senti, ce que je veux t'écrire,
> C'est ce que m'ont appris les anges de douleur ;
> Je le sais mieux encor et puis mieux te le dire,
> Car leur glaive, en entrant, l'a gravé dans mon cœur.

And the rest of the poem is a lyrical declaration of belief in immortality.

We have called the "Lettre à Lamartine" Musset's highest flight, but the "Nuit de Mai" is almost as fine a poem—full of imaginative splendour and melancholy ecstasy. The series of the "Nuits" is altogether superb ; with an exception made, perhaps, for the "Nuit de Décembre," which has a great deal of sombre beauty, but which is not, like the others, in the form of dialogue between the Muse and the poet—the Muse striving to console the world-wounded bard for his troubles and urging him to take refuge in hope and production.

> Poëte, prends ton luth et me donne un baiser ;
> La fleur de l'églantier sent ses bourgeons éclore.
> Le printemps naît ce soir ; les vents vont s'embraser ;

Et la bergeronnette, en attendant l'aurore,
Aux premier buissons verts commence à se poser.
Poëte, prends ton luth et me donne un baiser.

That is impregnated with the breath of a vernal night. The same poem (the "Nuit de Mai") contains the famous passage about the pelican—the passage beginning—

Les plus désespérés sont les chants les plus beaux,
Et j'en sais d'immortels qui sont de purs sanglots—

in which the legend of the pelican opening his breast to feed his starving young is made an image of what the poet does to entertain his readers:

Poëte, c'est ainsi que font les grands poëtes.
Ils laissent s'égayer ceux qui vivent un temps ;
Mais les festins humains qu'ils servent à leurs fêtes
Ressemblent la plupart à ceux des pélicans.

This passage is perhaps—unless we except the opening verses of "Rolla"—Musset's noblest piece of poetic writing. We must place next to it—next to the three "Nuits"—the admirably passionate and genuine "Stanzas to Malibran"—a beautiful characterization of the artistic disinterestedness of the singer who suffered her genius to consume her—who sang herself to death. The closing verses of the poem have a wonderful purity; to rise so high, and yet in form, in accent, to remain so still and temperate, belongs only to great poetry; as it would be well to remind the critic who thinks the author of the "Stanzas to Malibran" dwarfish. There is another sort of verse in which violence of movement is more sensible than upwardness of direction.

So far in relation to Musset's lyric genius—though we have given but a brief and inadequate account of it. He had besides a dramatic genius of the highest beauty, to which we have left ourself space to devote only a few words. It is true that the drama with Musset has a decidedly lyrical element, and that though his persons always talk prose, they are constantly saying things which would need very little help to fall into the mould of a stanza or a sonnet. In his dramas as in his verses his weakness is that he is amateurish; they lack construction; their merit is not in their plots, but in what, for want of a better term, we may call their sentimental perfume. The earliest of them failed upon the stage, and for many years it was supposed they could not be played. Musset supposed so himself, and took no trouble to encourage the experiment. He made no concessions to contemporary "realism." But at last they were taken up—almost by accident—and it was found that, in the hands of actors whose education enabled them to appreciate their delicacy, this delicacy might become wonderfully effective. If feeling is the great quality in his verses, the case is the same in his strange, fantastic, exquisite little *comédies;* comedies in the literal English sense of the word we can hardly call them, for they have almost always a melancholy or a tragical termination. They are thoroughly sentimental; he puts before us people who convince us that they really feel; the drama is simply the history of their feeling. In the emotions of Valentin and Perdican, of Fantasio and Fortunio, of Célio and Octave, of Carmosine and Bettine, there is something contagious, irresistibly touching. But the great charm is Musset's dramatic world itself, the atmosphere in which his figures move, the element they breathe.

It seems at first a reckless thing to say, but we will risk it: in the *quality* of his fancy Musset always reminds us of Shakespeare. His little dramas go forward in the country of "As You Like It" and the "Winter's Tale"; the author is at home there, like Shakespeare himself, and he moves with something of the Shakespearean lightness and freedom. His fancy loves to play with human life, and in the tiny mirror that it holds up we find something of the depth and mystery of the object. Musset's dialogue, in its mingled gaiety and melancholy, its sweetness and irony, its allusions to real things and its kinship with a romantic world, has an altogether indefinable magic. To utter it on the stage is almost to make it coarse. Once Musset attempted a larger theme than usual; in "Lorenzaccio" he wrote an historical drama on the scale of Shakespeare's histories; that is, with multitudes of figures, scenes, incidents, illustrations. He laid his hand on an admirable subject—the story of a certain Lorenzino de' Medici, who played at being a debauchee and a poltroon in order better to put the tyrant of Florence (his own cousin) off his guard, and serve his country by ridding her of him. The play shows an extraordinary abundance and vivacity of imagination, and really, out of those same "histories" of Shakespeare, it is hard to see where one should find an equal spontaneity in dealing with the whole human furniture of a period. Alfred de Musset, in "Lorenzaccio," has the air of being as ready to handle a hundred figures as a dozen—of having imagination enough for them all. The thing has the real creative inspiration, and if it is not the most perfect of his productions it is probably the most vigorous.

We have not spoken of his tales; their merit is the same as of the *comédies*—that of spontaneous feeling, and of putting people before us in whose feelings

we believe. Besides this, they have Musset's grace
and delicacy in a perhaps excessive degree ; they are
the most mannered of his productions. Two or three
of them, however—" Emmeline," " Les Deux Maî-
tresses," " Frédéric et Bernerette "—are masterpieces ;
this last epithet is especially to be bestowed upon the
letter written by the heroine of the last-mentioned
tale (an incorrigibly *volage* grisette) to her former
lover on the occasion of his marrying and settling.
The incoherency, the garrulity, the mingled resignation and regret of an amiable flirt of the lower orders,
divided between the intensity of her emotion and the
levity of her nature, are caught in the act. And yet
it is not fair to say of anything represented by Musset
that it is caught in the act. Just the beauty and
charm of it is that it is not the exact reality, but a
something seen by the imagination—a tinge of the
ideal, a touch of poetry. We must try to see Musset
himself in the same way ; his own figure needs to a
certain extent the help of our imagination. And yet,
even with such help taken, we cannot but feel that he
is an example of the wasteful way in which nature and
history sometimes work—of their cruel indifference to
our personal standards of economy—of the vast amount
of material they take to produce a little result.

Alfred de Musset's superfine organization, his exaltations and weaknesses, his pangs and tears, his passions and debaucheries, his intemperance and idleness, his years of unproductiveness, his innumerable mistresses (with whatever pangs and miseries it may seem proper to attribute to *them*) his quarrel with a woman of genius, and the scandals, exposures, and recriminations that are so ungracefully bound up with it—all this was necessary in order that we should have the two or three little volumes into which his *best* could be compressed. It takes certainly a great deal of life to make a little art! In this case, however, we must remember, that little is exquisite.

THEOPHILE GAUTIER.

THERE very recently died in Paris a man of genius whom his eulogists all made haste to proclaim a true poet. Many of them, indeed, spoke of Théophile Gautier as a great poet, and one, we remember, mentioned his last little volume, "Tableaux de Siége," as the crowning glory of the resistance to the Prussians. Gautier was indeed a poet and a strongly representative one—a French poet in his limitations even more than in his gifts; and he remains an interesting example of how, even when the former are surprisingly great, a happy application of the latter may produce the most delightful works. Completeness on his own scale is to our mind the idea he most instantly suggests. Such as his finished task now presents him, he is almost sole of his kind. He has had imitators who have imitated everything but his spontaneity and his temper; and as they have therefore failed to equal him, we doubt whether the literature of our day presents so naturally perfect a genius. We say this with no desire to transfer Gautier to a higher pedestal than he has fairly earned —a poor service, for the pedestal sometimes sadly dwarfs the figure. His great merit was that he understood himself so perfectly and handled himself so skilfully. Even more than Alfred de Musset (with whom the speech had a shade of mock-modesty) he might have said that, if his glass was not large, at least it was all his own glass. As an artist, he never knew an hour's weakness or failed to strike the note that should truly render his idea. He was, indeed, of literary artists the most accomplished. He was not of the Academy, but he completes not unworthily the picturesque group, gaining relief from isolation, of those eminent few—Molière, Pascal, Balzac, Béranger, George Sand—who have come near making it the supreme literary honour in France not to be numbered among the Forty. There are a host of reasons why we should not compare Gautier with such a poet as Browning; and yet there are several why we should. If we do so, with all proper reservations, we may wonder whether we are the richer, or, at all events, the better entertained, as a poet's readers should before all things be, by the clear, undiluted strain of Gautier's minor key, or by the vast, grossly commingled volume of utterance of the author of "Men and Women." This, perhaps, is an idle question ; and the artificer of " Émaux et Camées " was presumably of opinion that it is idle at all times to point a moral. But if there are sermons in stones, there are profitable reflections to be made even on Théophile Gautier ; notably this one—that a man's supreme use in the world is to master his intellectual instrument and play it in perfection.

There is, perhaps, scant apparent logic in treating a closed career more tenderly than an open one ; but we suspect it belongs to the finer essence of good criticism to do so, and, at any rate, we find our judgment of the author of the " Voyage en Espagne " and the " Capitaine Fracasse " turning altogether to unprotesting kindness. We had a vague consciousness of lurking objections ; but on calling them to appear they gave no answer. Gautier's death, indeed, in the nature of things could not but be touching and dispose one to large allowances. The world he left was the sum of the universe for him, and upon any other his writings throw but the dimmest light— project, indeed, that contrasted darkness which surrounds the edges of a luminous surface. The beauty and variety of our present earth and the insatiability of our earthly temperament were his theme, and we doubt whether these things have ever been placed in a more flattering light. He brought to his task a sort of pagan *bonhomie* which makes most of the descriptive and pictorial poets seem, by contrast, a group of shivering ascetics or muddled metaphysicians. He excels them by his magnificent good temper and the unquestioning serenity of his enjoyment of the great spectacle of nature and art. His style certainly is one of the latest fruits of time; but his mental attitude before the universe has an almost Homeric simplicity. His world was all material, and its outlying darkness hardly more suggestive, morally, than a velvet canopy studded with silver nails. To close his eyes and turn his back on it must have seemed to him the end of all things; de th, for him, must have been as the sullen dropping of a stone into a well. His faculty of visual discrimination was extraordinary. His observation was so penetrating and his descriptive instinct so unerring, that one might have fancied grave Nature, in a fit of coquetry, or tired of receiving but half-justice, had determined to construct a genius with senses of a finer strain than the mass of the human family. Gautier, as an observer, often reminds us of those classic habitués of the opera who listen with a subtler sense than their neighbours and register with a murmured *brava* the undistinguishable shades of merit in a prima donna's execution. He was for many years a diligent theatrical critic, faithful to his post in all dramatic weathers, so that one has only to extend the image a little to conceive him as always in an orchestra-stall before the general stage, watching a lamplit performance—flaring gas in one case, the influence of his radiant fancy in the other. "Descriptive" writing, to our English taste, suggests nothing very enticing—a respectable sort of padding, at best, but a few degrees removed in ponderosity from downright moralizing. The prejudice, we admit, is a wholesome one, and the limits of verbal portraiture of all sorts should be jealously guarded. But there is no better proof of Gautier's talent than that he should have triumphantly reformed this venerable abuse and, in the best sense, made one of the heaviest kinds of writing one of the lightest. Of his process and his success we could give an adequate idea only by a long series of citations, and these we lack the opportunity to collect. The reader would conclude with us, we think, that Gautier is an inimitable model. He would never find himself condemned to that thankless task of pulling the cart up hill—retouching the picture—which in most descriptions is fatal to illusion. The author's manner is so light and true, so really creative, his fancy so alert, his taste so happy, his humour so genial, that he makes illusion almost as contagious as laughter; the image, the object, the scene, stands arrested by his phrase with the wholesome glow of truth overtaken. Gautier's native gift of expression was extremely rich, and he cultivated and polished it with a diligence that may serve to give the needed balance of gravity to his literary character. He enriched his picturesque vocabulary from the most recondite sources; it has a most robust comprehensiveness. His favourite reading, we have somewhere seen, was the dictionary; he loved words for themselves—for their look, their aroma, their colour, their fantastic intimations. He kept a supply of the choicest constantly at hand and introduced them at effective points. In this respect he was a sort of immeasurably lighter-handed Rabelais, whom, indeed, he resembled in that sensuous exuberance of temperament which his countrymen are fond of calling peculiarly "Gaulois." He had an almost Rabelaisian relish for enumerations, lists, and catalogues —a sort of grotesque delight in quantity. We need hardly remind the reader that these are not the tokens of a man of thought, and Gautier was none. In the line of moral expression his phrase would have halted sadly; and when occasionally he emits a reflection he is a very Philistine of Philistines. In his various records of travel, we remember, he never takes his seat in a railway train without making a neat little speech on the marvels of steam and the diffusion of civilization. If it were not in a Parisian *feuilleton* it might proceed from Mr. Barlow, and be addressed to Harry Sandford and Tommy Merton. These genial commonplaces are Gautier's only tributes to philosophy. It seems as absurd to us as that very puerile performance itself that the philosophic pretensions of the famous preface to " Mademoiselle de Maupin " should have provoked any other retort than a laugh. Gautier was incapable of looking, for an appreciable duration of time, at any other than the superficial, the picturesque, face of a question. If you find him glancing closer, you may be sure, with all respect, that the phenomenon will last just as long as a terrier will stand on his hind-legs.

To raise on such a basis so large a structure was possible only to a Frenchman, and to a Frenchman inordinately endowed with the national sense of form and relish for artistic statement. Gautier's structure is composed of many pieces. He began, in his early youth, with "Mademoiselle de Maupin." It has seemed to us rather a painful exhibition of the prurience of the human mind that, in most of the recent notices of the author's death (those, at least, published in England and America) this work alone should have been selected as the critic's text. It is Gautier's one disagreeable performance; how it came to be written it is of small profit at this time to inquire. In certain lights the book is almost ludicrously innocent, and we are at a loss what to think of those critics who either hailed or denounced it as a serious profession of faith. With faith of any sort Gautier strikes us as slenderly furnished. Even his æsthetic principles are held with a good-humoured laxity that allows him, for instance, to say in a hundred places the most delightfully sympathetic and pictorial things about the romantic or Shakespearean drama, and yet to describe a pedantically classical revival of the "Antigone" at Munich with the most ungrudging relish. The only very distinct statement of intellectual belief that we remember in his pages is the singularly perfect little poem which closes the collection of chiselled and polished verses called "Émaux et Camées." It is a charming example of Gautier at his best, and we shall be pardoned for quoting it.

L'ART.

> Oui, l'œuvre sort plus belle
> D'une forme au travail
>   Rebelle,
> Vers, marbre, onyx, émail.
>
> Point de contraintes fausses !
> Mais que pour marcher droit
>   Tu chausses,
> Muse, un cothurne étroit.

Fi du rhythme commode,
Comme un soulier trop grand,
   Du mode
Que tout pied quitte et prend !

Statuaire, repousse
L'argile que pétrit
   Le pouce,
Quand flotte ailleurs l'esprit ;

Lutte avec le carrare,
Avec le paros dur
   Et rare,
Gardiens du contour pur ;

Emprunte à Syracuse
Son bronze où fermement
   S'accuse
Le trait fier et charmant ;

D'une main délicate
Poursuis dans un filon
   D'agate
Le profil d'Apollon.

Peintre, fuis l'aquarelle,
Et fixe la couleur
   Trop frêle
Au four de l'émailleur ;

Fais les sirènes bleues,
Tordant de cent façons
   Leurs queues ;
Les monstres des blasons ;

Dans son nimbe trilobe
La Vierge et son Jésus ;
　Le globe
Avec la croix dessus.

Tout passe.—L'art robuste
Seul a l'éternité.
　Le buste
Survit à la cité.

Et la médaille austère
Que trouve un laboreur
　Sous terre
Révèle un empereur.

Les dieux eux-mêmes meurent,
Mais les vers souverains
　Demeurent
Plus forts que les airains.

Sculpte, lime, cisèle ;
Que ton rêve flottant
　Se scelle
Dans le bloc résistant.

These admirable verses seem to us to be almost tinged with intellectual passion. It is a case of an æsthetic, an almost technical, conviction, glowing with a kind of moral fervour. They vividly reflect, in our opinion, the great simplicity of the author's mind. We doubt whether life often addressed him a more puzzling question than the one he has so gracefully answered here. He had, of course, his likes and dislikes; and, as the poet of the luxuries of life, he naturally preferred those paternal governments which pay heavy subventions to opera-houses, order palace frescos by the half-mile, and maintain various picturesque sinecures. He was sensuously a conservative; although, after all, as an observer and describer, he was the frankest of democrats. He had a glance for everything and a phrase for everything on the broad earth, and all that he asked of an object, as a source of inspiration, was that it should have length, breadth and colour. Much of Gautier's poetry is of the same period as "Mademoiselle de Maupin," and some of it of the same quality; notably the frantically picturesque legend of "Albertus," written in the author's twenty-first year, and full of the germs of his later flexibility of diction. "Émaux et Camées," the second volume of his collected verses, contains, evidently, his poetic bequest. In this chosen series every poem is a masterpiece; it has received the author's latest and fondest care; all, as the title indicates, is goldsmiths' work. In Gautier's estimation, evidently, these exquisite little pieces are the finest distillation of his talent; not one of them but ought to have outweighed a dozen Academic blackballs. Gautier's best verse is neither sentimental, satirical, narrative, nor even lyrical. It is always pictorial and plastic—a matter of images, "effects,' and colour. Even when the motive is an idea—of course, a slender one—the image absorbs and swallows it, and the poem becomes a piece of rhythmic imitation. What is this delightful little sonnet—the "Pot de Fleurs"—but a piece of self-amused imagery?

Parfois un enfant trouve une petite graine,
Et tout d'abord, charmé de ses vives couleurs,
Pour la planter, il prend un pot de porcelaine
Orné de dragons bleus et de bizarres fleurs.

Il s'en va. La racine en couleuvres s'allonge,
Sort de terre, fleurit et devient arbrisseau ;
Chaque jour, plus avant, son pied chevelu plonge
Tant qu'il fasse éclater le ventre du vaisseau.

L'enfant revient ; surpris, il voit la plante grasse
Sur les débris du pot brandir ses verts poignards ;
Il la veut arracher, mais la tige est tenace ;
Il s'obstine, et ses doigts s'ensanglantent aux dards.

Ainsi germa l'amour dans mon âme surprise ;
Je croyais ne semer qu'une fleur de printemps :
C'est un grand aloès dont la racine brise
Le pot de porcelaine aux dessins éclatants.

We may almost fancy that the whole sonnet was written for the sake of the charming line we have marked—a bit of Keats Gallicized. Gautier's first and richest poetry, however, is to be found in his prose— the precious, artistic prose which for forty years he lavished in newspaper feuilletons and light periodicals. Here the vivid, plastic image is his natural, constant formula; he scatters pictures as a fine singer roulades; every paragraph is the germ of a sonnet, every sentence a vignette. "It is pure Lacrima-Christi," as Sainte-Beuve says, "*qu'on vous verse au coin d'une borne.*" The twenty-five volumes or so into which this long daily labour has been gathered—feuilletons and sketches, novels and tales, records of travel, reports of "damned" plays and unsold pictures—form a great treasury of literary illustration. When Gautier, according to present promise, begins to be remembered mainly as the author of an indecent novel whose title is circulated in the interest of virtue, needy poets may deck their wares for the market with unmissed flowers of description from his blooming plantations. He has commemorated every phase and mood and attribute of nature and every achievement and possibility of art; and you have only to turn his pages long enough to find the perfect presentment of your own comparatively dim and unshaped vision.

Early in life he began to travel—to travel far for a Frenchman—and, of course, to publish his impressions. They relate altogether to the *look* of the countries he visited—to landscape, art-collections, street-scenery and costume. On the "institutions" of foreign lands he is altogether silent. His delightful vividness on his chosen points is elsewhere unapproached, and his " Voyage en Espagne," his " Constantinople," his " Italia," and his " Voyage en Russie," seem to us his most substantial literary titles. No other compositions of the same kind begin to give us, in our chair, under the lamp, the same sense of standing under new skies, among strange scenes. With Gautier's readers the imagination travels in earnest and makes journeys more profitable in some respects than those we really undertake. He has the broad-eyed, universal, almost innocent gaze at things of a rustic at a fair, and yet he discriminates them with a shrewdness peculiarly his own. We renew over his pages those happiest hours of youth when we have strolled forth into a foreign town, still sprinkled with the dust of travel, and lost ourselves deliciously in the fathomless sense of local difference and mystery. Gautier had a passion for material detail, and he vivifies, illuminates, interprets it, woos it into relief, resolves it into pictures, with a joyous ingenuity which makes him the prince of *ciceroni*. His " Voyage en Espagne " is, in this respect, a masterpiece and model. It glows, from beginning to end, with an overcharged verisimilitude in which we seem to behold some intenser essence of Spain —of her light and colour and climate, her expression and personality. All this borrows a crowning vivacity from the author's genial unpretentiousness, his almost vainglorious triviality. A "high standard" is an excellent thing; but we sometimes fancy it takes away more than it gives, and that an untamed natural faculty of enjoying at a venture is a better conductor of æsthetic light and heat. Gautier's superbly appreciative temperament makes him, at the least, as solid an observer as the representative German doctor in spectacles, bristling with critical premises. It is signally suggestive to compare his lusty tribute to San Moïsè at Venice, in his "Italia," with Ruskin's stern dismissal of it in his "Stones of Venice"— Ruskin so painfully unable to see the "joke" of it and Gautier, possibly, so unable to see anything but the joke. We may, in strictness, agree with Ruskin, but we envy Gautier. It was to be expected of such a genius that he should enjoy the East; and Gautier professed a peculiar devotion to it. He was fond of pretending that he was really an Oriental come astray into our Western world. He has described Eastern scenery and manners, Eastern effects of all kinds, with incomparable gusto; and, on reading the *libretti* to the three or four ballets included in the volume we have named, we wonder whether his natural attitude was not to recline in the perfumed dusk of a Turkish divan, puffing a chibouque and forecasting the successive episodes of a Mohammedan immortality. This pretension, however, did him injustice: and such a book as the "Voyage en Russie;" such chapters as his various notes on the Low Countries, their landscape and their painters; such a sketch, indeed, as his wonderful *humoristique* history of a week in London, in his "Caprices et Zigzags"—prove abundantly that he had more than one string to his bow. He shot equally far with them all. Each of his chapters of travel has a perfect tone of its own and that unity of effect which is the secret of the rarest artists. The "Voyage en Espagne" is a masterly mixture of hot lights and warm shadows; the "Constantinople" is an immense verbal Decamps, as one may say; and the "Voyage en Russie," compounded of effects taken from the opposite end of the scale, is illuminated with the cold blue light of the North. Gautier's volumes abound in records of the most unadventurous excursions—light sketches of a feuilletonist's holidays. His fancy found its account in the commonest things as well as the rarest—in Callot as well as in Paul Veronese—and these immediate notes are admirable in their multicoloured reflections of the perpetual entertainment of Nature. Gautier found Nature supremely entertaining; this seems to us the shortest description of him. She had no barren places for him, for he rendered her poverty with a *brio* that made it as picturesque as her wealth. He professed always to care for nothing but beauty. "Fortunio," he says, in the preface to this grotesquely meretricious production, "is a hymn to Beauty, Wealth, and Happiness—the only three divinities we recognise. It celebrates gold, marble, and purple." But, in fact, he was too curious an artist not to enjoy ugliness very nearly as much, and he drew from it some of his most striking effects. We recommend to the reader the account of a stroll among the slaughter-houses and the asylums of lost dogs and cats in the Paris *banlieue*, in the "Caprices et Zigzags;" his elaborate pictures, several times repeated, of Spanish bull-fights (which show to what lengths *l'art pour l'art* can carry the kindliest tempered of men), and a dozen painful passages in his "Tableaux de Siége." This little volume, the author's last, is a culminating example of his skill. It is a common saying with light littérateurs, that to describe a thing you must not know it too well. Gautier knew Paris—picturesque Paris—with a forty years' knowledge; yet he has here achieved the remarkable feat of suppressing the sense of familiarity and winning back, for the sake of inspiration, a certain freshness of impression. The book was written in evil days; but nothing from Gautier's hand is pleasanter; and the silvery strain of his beautiful rhetoric, after so long a season of thunderous bulletins and proclamations, suggests the high, clear note of some venerable nightingale after a summer storm. Deprived of his customary occupation he became a forced observer of certain vulgarly obvious things, and discovered that they, too, had their poetry, and that, if you only look at it closely, everything is remunerative. He found poetry in the poor rawboned lions and tigers of the Jardin des Plantes; in the hungry dogs in the street, hungrily eyed; in a trip on a circular railway and on the penny steamers on the Seine; in that delicacy of vanished seasons, a pat of fresh butter in Chevet's window. Beneath his touch these phenomena acquire the finely detailed relief of the accessories and distances in a print of Albert Dürer's; we remember no better example of the magic of style. But the happiest performance in the book is a series of chapters on Versailles, when the whirligig of time had again made its splendid vacancy an active spot in the world's consciousness. No one should go there now without Gautier's volume in his pocket. It was his good fortune that his autumn was as sound as his summer and his last writing second to none before it. The current of diction in this final volume is as full and clear as in the "Voyage en Espagne."

Gautier's stories and novels belong, for the most part, to his prime; he reached his climax as a story-teller ten years ago, with "Le Capitaine Fracasse." His productions in this line are not numerous, for dramatic invention with him was evidently not abundant. As was to be supposed, the human interest in his tales is inferior to the picturesque. They remind us of those small cabinet paintings of the contemporary French school, replete with archæological details as to costume and furniture, which hang under glass in immense gilt frames and form the delight of connoisseurs. Gautier's figures are altogether pictorial; he cared for nothing and knew nothing in men and women but the epidermis. With this, indeed, he was marvellously acquainted, and he organized in its service a phraseology as puzzlingly various as the array of pots and brushes of a coiffeur. His attitude towards the human creature is, in a sublimated degree, that of a barber or tailor. He anoints and arranges and dresses it to perfection; but he deals only in stuffs and colours. His fable is often pretty enough; but one imagines it always written in what is called a studio light—on the corner of a table littered with brushes and frippery. The young woman before the easel, engaged at forty sous a sitting to take off her dress and let down her hair, is obviously the model for the heroine. His stories are always the measure of an intellectual need to express an ideal of the exquisite in personal beauty and in costume, combined with that of a certain serene and full-blown sensuality in conduct, and accompanied with gorgeous visions of upholstery and architecture. Nothing classifies Gautier better, both as to the individual and the national quality of his genius, than the perfect frankness of his treatment of the human body. We of English speech pass (with the French) for prudish on this point; and certain it is that there is a limit to the freedom with which we can comfortably discourse of hair and skin, and teeth and nails, even to praise them. The French, on the other hand, discuss their physical texture as complacently as we discuss that of our trousers and boots. The Parisians profess, we believe, to have certain tendencies in common with the old Athenians; this unshrinking contemplation of our physical surfaces might be claimed as one of them. Practically, however, it gives one a very different impression from the large Greek taste for personal beauty; for the French type, being as meagre as the Greek was ample, has been filled out with the idea of "grace," which, by implying that the subject is conscious, makes modesty immediately desirable and the absence of it vicious. Gautier, in this respect, is the most eloquent of our modern Athenians, and pays scantiest tribute to our English scruples. Flesh and blood, noses and bosoms, arms and legs were a delight to him, and it was his mission to dilate upon them. For any one who has glanced at the dusky background of Parisian life, with its sallow tones and close odours, among which no Athenian sky makes a blue *repoussoir* either for statues or mortals, there is something almost touchingly heroic in Gautier's fixed conception of sublime good looks. He invents unprecedented attributes, and it is nothing to say of his people that they are too good to live. In "Une Nuit de Cléopâtre," the hero, inflamed with a hopeless passion for the Egyptian queen, has been pursuing her barge in a little skiff, and rowing so fast, under an Egyptian sun, that he has overtaken her fifty oarsmen. "He was a beautiful young man of twenty, with hair so black that it seemed blue, a skin blond as gold, and proportions so perfect that he might have been taken for a bronze of Lysippus. Although he had been rowing some time, he betrayed no fatigue, and *had not on his brow a single drop of sweat.*" Gautier's heroines are always endowed with transparent finger tips. These, however, are his idler touches. His real imaginative power is shown in his masterly evocation of localities, and in the thick-coming fancies that minister to his inexhaustible conception of that pictorial "setting" of human life which interested him so much more than human life itself. In the "Capitaine Fracasse," the "Roman de la Momie," "Le Roi Candaule," "Une Nuit de Cléopâtre," and "Aria Marcella" he revels in his passion for scenic properties and backgrounds. His science, in so far as it is archæological, is occasionally at fault, we suspect, and his facts slightly fantastic; but it all sounds very fine and his admirable pictorial instinct makes everything pass. He reconstructs the fabulous splendours of old Egypt with a magnificent audacity of detail, and rivals John Martin, of mezzotinto fame, in the energy with which he depicts the light of torches washing the black basalt of palace stairs. If the portrait is here and there inaccurate, so much the worse for the original. The works we have just mentioned proceed altogether by pictures. No reader of the "Roman de la Momie" will have forgotten the portentous image of the great Pharaoh, who sits like a soulless idol upon his palace roof and watches his messengers swim across the Nile and come and lie on their faces (some of them dying) at his feet. Such a picture as the following, from "Une Nuit de Cléopâtre," may be rather irresponsible archæology, but it is admirable imagery :—

Le spectacle changeait à chaque instant ; tantôt c'était de gigantesques propylées qui venaient mirer au fleuve leurs murailles en talus, plaquées de larges panneaux de figures bizarres ; des pylônes aux chapiteaux évasés, des rampes côtoyées de grands sphinx accroupis, coiffés du bonnet à barbe cannelée, et croisant sous leurs mamelles aiguës leurs pattes de basalte noir ; des palais démesurés, faisant saillir sur l'horizon les lignes horizontales et sévères de leur entablement, où le globe emblématique ouvrait les ailes mystérieuses comme un aigle à l'envergure démesurée ; des temples aux colonnes énormes, grosses comme des tours, où se détachait sur un fond d'éclatante blancheur des processions des figures hieroglyphiques ; toutes les prodigiosités de cette architecture de Titans ; tantôt des passages d'une aridité désolante ; des collines formées par des petits éclats de pierre provenant des fouilles et des constructions, miettes de cette gigantesque débauche de granit qui dura plus de trente siècles ; des montagnes exfoliées de chaleur, déchiquetées et zébrées de rayures noires, semblables aux cautérizations d'une incendie ; des tertres bossus et difformes, accroupis comme le creocéphale des tombeaux, et découpant au bord du ciel leur attitude contrefaite ; des marnes verdâtres, des ochres roux, des tufs d'un blanc farineux, et, de temps à autre, quelque escarpement de marbre couleur rose-sèche, où bâillaient les bouches noires des carrières.

If, as an illustration, we could transfuse the essence of one of Gautier's best performances into this colourless report, we should choose the " Capitaine Fracasse." In this delightful work Gautier surpassed himself, and produced the model of picturesque romances. The story was published, we believe, some twenty-five years after it was announced—and announced because the author had taken a fancy to the title and proposed to write "up" to it. We cannot say how much of the long interval was occupied with this endeavour; but certainly the "Capitaine Fracasse" is as good as if a quarter of a century had been given to it. Besides being his most ambitious work it bears more marks of leisure and meditation than its companions. M. Meissonier might have written it, if, with the same talent and a good deal more geniality, he had chosen to use the pen rather than the brush. The subject is just such a one as Gautier was born to appreciate—a subject of which the pictorial side emphasizes itself as naturally as that of "Don Quixote." It is borrowed, indeed, but as great talents borrow—for a use that brings the original into fashion again. Scarron's "Roman Comique," which furnished Gautier with his starting-point, is as barren to the eye as "Gil Blas" itself, besides being a much coarser piece of humour. The sort of memory one retains of the "Capitaine Fracasse" is hard to express, save by some almost physical analogy. We remember the perusal of most good novels as an intellectual pleasure —a pleasure which varies in degree, but is as far as it goes an affair of the mind. The hours spent over the "Capitaine Fracasse" seem to have been an affair of the senses, of personal experience, of observation and contact as illusory as those of a peculiarly vivid dream. The novel presents the adventures of a company of strolling players of Louis XIII.'s time, —their vicissitudes collective and individual, their miseries and gayeties, their loves and squabbles, and their final apportionment of worldly comfort—very much in that symmetrical fashion in which they have so often stood forth to receive it at the fall of the curtain. It is a fairy-tale of Bohemia, a triumph of the picaresque. In this case, by a special extension of his power, the author has made the dramatic interest as lively as the pictorial, and lodged good human hearts beneath the wonderfully-painted rusty doublets and tarnished satins of his maskers. The great charm of the book is a sort of combined geniality of feeling and colouring, which leaves one in doubt whether the author is the most joyous of painters or the cleverest of poets. It is a masterpiece of good-humour—a good-humour sustained by the artist's indefatigable relish for his theme. In artistic "bits," of course, the book abounds; it is a delightful gallery of portraits. The models, with their paint and pomatum, their broken plumes and threadbare velvet, their false finery and their real hunger, their playhouse manners and morals, are certainly not very choice company; but the author handles them with an affectionate, sympathetic jocosity of which we so speedily feel the influence that, long before we have finished, we seem to have drunk with them one and all out of the playhouse goblet to the confusion of respectability and life before the scenes. If we incline to look for deeper meanings, we can fancy the work in the last analysis an expression of that brotherly sympathy with the social position of the comedian which Gautier was too much what the French call an *homme de théâtre* not to entertain as an almost poetic sentiment. The "Capitaine Fracasse" ranks, in our opinion, with the first works of imagination produced in our day.

Of Gautier as a critic there is not much to say that we have not said of him as a traveller and storyteller. Rigid critic he was none; it was not in his nature to bring himself to fix a standard. The things he liked he spoke well of; of the things he disliked, a little less well. His brother critics, who would have preferred to count on him to substantiate their severities, found him unpardonably "genial." We imagine that, in the long run, he held a course nearer the truth than theirs, and did better service. His irresistible need for the positive in art, for something describable—phrasable, as we may say—often led him to fancy merit where it was not, but more often, probably, to detect it where it lurked. He was a constructive commentator; and if the work taken as his text is often below his praise, the latter, with its magical grasp of the idea, may serve as a sort of generous lesson. His work as a critic is very abundant and has been but partially collected. For many years he reported elaborately on the annual Salon and produced a weekly review of the theatre. His accounts of the Salon, which have yet to be republished, form, probably, the best history—if also the least didactic—of modern French art. When pictures and statues have passed out of sight, it is rather meagre entertainment to peruse amendments to their middle distance and to the finer points in their anatomy. Gautier's pages preserve what was best in them—the attempt, the image, the vision. His criticism illustrates more pointedly, perhaps, than his poems and tales, his native incapacity to moralize. Occasionally, we think, a promising subject comes near being sacrificed to it. We were lately struck, in reading the delightful "Correspondance" of Henri Regnault, whose herald-in-chief Gautier constituted himself, with the latter's fatally shallow conception of the duties of an æsthetic guide, philosopher and friend. Gautier, possibly, claimed no such office; but, at any rate, he spoke with authority; and the splendid, unmeasured flattery which he pours out on the young painter gives us something of the discomfort with which we should see an old man plying a young lad with strong wine. Regnault, fortunately, had a strong head; but the attitude, in Gautier, is none the less immoral. He repaints the young man's pictures, verbally, with almost superior power, and consecrates their more ominous eccentricities by his glowing rhetoric. To assure a youth of genius, by sound of trumpet, that his genius is infallible, is, doubtless, good comradeship, but, from a high point of view, it is poor æsthetics.

The first half of Gautier's theatrical feuilletons have been gathered into six volumes, under the ambitious title—a device, evidently, of the publishers rather than the author—of "L'Histoire de l'Art Dramatique en France." In the theatre, as at the Salon, he is the most good-natured of critics, and enjoys far less picking a feeble drama to pieces than sketching fine scenery and good acting. The book, however, is an excellent one; its tone is so easy, its judgments so happy and unpedantic, its good taste so pervasive, its spirit so wholesomely artistic. But we confess that what has most struck us, in turning it over, has been the active part played by the stage in France during these forty years, its incalculable fertility and its insatiable absorption of talent and ingenuity. Buried authors and actors are packed away in Gautier's pages as on the shelves of an immense mausoleum; and if, here and there, they exhibit the vivifying touch of the embalmer, the spectacle is on the whole little less lugubrious. It takes away one's breath to think of the immense consumption of witticisms involved in the development of civilization. Gautier's volumes seem an enormous monument to the shadowy swarm of jokes extinct and plots defunct—dim-featured ghosts, still haunting the lawless circumference of literature in pious confidence that the transmigration of souls will introduce them to the foot-lights again. Gautier's dealings with the theatre were altogether those of a spectator; for the little comedies collected in the volume which forms the text of our remarks are not of the sort approved by managers. They are matters of colour, not of structure, and masterpieces of style rather than of "effect." The best of them, the "Tricorne Enchanté, Bastonnade en un Acte, et en Vers, Mêlée d'un Couplet," has been represented since the author's death, but, we believe, with only partial success. The piece is a *pastiche*, suggested by various sources—Molière, Goldoni, the old prints of the figures in the conventional Italian farce. The style is a marvel of humorous ingenuity and exhales a delightful aroma of the grotesque stage-world of jealous guardians and light-fingered valets, saucy waiting-maids and modest *ingénues*. The verse occasionally emulates Molière with the happiest vivacity. Géronte, having lost his valet, determines to serve himself.

> Quel est donc le fossé, quelle est donc la muraille
> Où gît, cuvant son vin, cette brave canaille?
> O Champagne! es-tu mort? As-tu pris pour cercueil
> Un tonneau défoncé de brie ou d'argenteuil?
> Modèle des valets, perle des domestiques,
> Qui passais en vertu les esclaves antiques,
> Que le ciel avait fait uniquement pour moi,—
> Par qui remplacer, comment vivre sans toi?
> —Parbleu! Si j'essayais de me servir moi-même?
> Ce serait la façon de trancher le problème.
> Je me commanderais et je m'obéirais.
> Je m'aurais sous la main, et quand je me voudrais,
> Je n'aurais pas besoin de me pendre aux sonnettes.
> Nul ne sait mieux que moi que j'ai des mœurs honnêtes,
> Que je me suis toujours conduit loyalement.
> Ainsi donc je m'accepte avec empressement.
> Ah, Messieurs les blondins, si celui-là me trompe,
> Vous le pourrez aller crier à son de trompe:
> J'empocherai votre or, et me le remettrai:
> Vos billets pleins de musc, c'est moi qui les lirai.
> D'ailleurs, je prends demain, qu'on me loue ou me blâme,
> Mademoiselle Inez, ma pupille, pour femme.

Elle me soignera dans mes quintes de toux,
Et près d'elle couché, je me rirai de vous,
Les Amadis transis, les coureurs de fortune,
Gelant sous le balcon par un beau clair de lune !
Et, quand j'apercevrai mon coquin de neveu,
De deux ou trois seaux d'eau j'arroserai son feu !

The little piece called "Une Larme du Diable," to which the author has affixed the half-apologetic qualification of "Mystère," is one of his cleverest and most characteristic performances. None illustrates better, perhaps, what we have called the simplicity of his mind —the way in which he conceived the most exalted ideas as picturesque and picturesque only. "Une Larme du Diable" is a light *pastiche* of a mediæval miracle-play, just as the "Tricorne Enchanté" is an imitation of a seventeenth-century farce. The scene is alternately in heaven and on earth. *Satanas* is the hero, and *le Bon Dieu* and *Christus*, grotesquely associated with Othello and Desdemona, are among the minor characters. *Christus* himself, conversing in heaven, manifests a taste for the picturesque. *"Ce matin je me suis déguisé en mendiant, je leur* (the two heroines) *ai demandé l'aumône; elles ont déposé dans ma main lépreuse, chacune à leur tour, une grosse pièce de cuivre, toute glacée de vert-de-gris."* These copper coins, glazed with verdigris, are a sort of symbol of the drama—a drama in which the celestial mind has a turn for bric-à-brac. Shrewdly fantastic as is the whole composition, it is a capital example of the weakness of an imagination dependent wholly upon the senses. That Gautier's fancy should have prompted him to write "Une Larme du Diable" is up to a certain point to its credit; that it should have carried him through the task suggests unutterable things as to his profundity. He had evidently no associations with divine images that it cost him a moment's hesitation to violate; and one may say of him that he was incapable of blasphemy because he was incapable of respect. He is compounded of consistent levity. These are strange things to find one's self saying of a poet, and they bring us back to our first remark—that our author's really splendid development is inexorably circumscribed. Infinite are the combinations of our faculties. Some of us are awkward writers and yearning moralists; others are masters of a perfect style which has never reflected a spiritual spark. Gautier's disposition served him to the end, and enabled him to have a literary heritage perfect of its kind. He could look every day at a group of beggars sunning themselves on the Spanish Steps at Rome, against their golden wall of mouldering travertine, and see nothing but the fine brownness of their rags and their flesh-tints—see it and enjoy it for ever, without an hour's disenchantment, without a chance of one of those irresistible revulsions of mood in which the "mellowest" rags are but filth, and filth is poverty, and poverty a haunting shadow, and picturesque squalor a mockery. His unfaltering robustness of vision—of appetite, one may say—made him not only strong but enviable.

CHARLES BAUDELAIRE.

As a brief discussion was lately carried on [1] touching the merits of the writer whose name we have prefixed to these lines, it may not be amiss to introduce him to some of those readers who must have observed the contest with little more than a vague sense of the strangeness of its subject. Charles Baudelaire is not a novelty in literature; his principal work [2] dates from 1857, and his career terminated a few years later. But his admirers have made a classic of him and elevated him to the rank of one of those subjects which are always in order. Even if we differ with them on this point, such attention as Baudelaire demands will not lead us very much astray. He is not, in quantity (whatever he may have been in quality), a formidable writer; having

---

[1] There had been an exchange of letters on the subject in an American journal.

[2] "Les Fleurs du Mal." Par Charles Baudelaire. Précédé d'une Notice par Thé phile Gautier. Paris: Michel Lévy.

died young, he was not prolific, and the most noticeable of his original productions are contained in two small volumes.

His celebrity began with the publication of "Les Fleurs du Mal," a collection of verses of which some had already appeared in periodicals. The "Revue des Deux Mondes" had taken the responsibility of introducing a few of them to the world—or rather, though it held them at the baptismal font of public opinion, it had declined to stand godfather. An accompanying note in the "Revue" disclaimed all editorial approval of their morality. This of course procured them a good many readers; and when, on its appearance, the volume we have mentioned was overhauled by the police a still greater number of persons desired to possess it. Yet in spite of the service rendered him by the censorship, Baudelaire has never become in any degree popular; the lapse of twenty years has seen but five editions of "Les Fleurs du Mal." The foremost feeling of the reader of the present day will be one of surprise, and even amusement, at Baudelaire's audacities having provoked this degree of scandal. The world has travelled fast since then, and the French censorship must have been, in the year 1857, in a very prudish mood. There is little in "Les Fleurs du Mal" to make the reader of either French or English prose and verse of the present day even open his eyes. We have passed through the fiery furnace and profited by experience. We are happier than Racine's heroine, who had not

<blockquote>Su se faire un front qui ne rougit jamais.</blockquote>

Baudelaire's verses do not strike us as being dictated by a spirit of bravado—though we have heard that, in talk, it was his habit, to an even tiresome degree, to cultivate the quietly outrageous—to pile up monstrosities and blasphemies without winking and with the air of uttering proper commonplaces.

"Les Fleurs du Mal" is evidently a sincere book—so far as anything for a man of Baudelaire's temper and culture could be sincere. Sincerity seems to us to belong to a range of qualities with which Baudelaire and his friends were but scantily concerned. His great quality was an inordinate cultivation of the sense of the picturesque, and his care was for how things looked, and whether some kind of imaginative amusement was not to be got out of them, much more than for what they meant and whither they led and what was their use in human life at large. The later editions of "Les Fleurs du Mal" (with some of the interdicted pieces still omitted and others, we believe, restored) contain a long preface by Théophile Gautier, which throws a curious side-light upon what the Spiritualist newspapers would call-Baudelaire's "mentality." Of course Baudelaire is not to be held accountable for what Gautier says of him, but we cannot help judging a man in some degree by the company he keeps. To admire Gautier is certainly excellent taste, but to be admired by Gautier we cannot but regard as rather compromising. He gives a magnificently picturesque account of the author of "Les Fleurs du Mal," in which, indeed, the question of pure exactitude is evidently so very subordinate that it seems grossly ill-natured for us to appeal to such a standard. While we are reading him, however, we find ourselves wishing that Baudelaire's analogy with the author himself were either greater or less. Gautier was perfectly sincere, because he dealt only with the picturesque and pretended to care only for appearances. But Baudelaire (who, to our mind, was an altogether inferior genius to Gautier) applied the same process of interpretation to things as regards which it was altogether inadequate; so that one is constantly tempted to suppose he cares more for his process—for making grotesquely-pictorial verse—than for the things themselves. On the whole, as we have said, this inference would be unfair. Baudelaire had a certain groping sense of the moral complexities of life, and if the best that he succeeds in doing is to drag them down into the very turbid element in which he himself plashes and flounders, and there present them to us much besmirched and bespattered, this was not a want of goodwill in him, but rather a dulness and permanent immaturity of vision. For American readers, furthermore, Baudelaire is compromised by his having made himself the apostle of our own Edgar Poe. He translated, very carefully and exactly, all of Poe's prose writings, and, we believe, some of his very valueless verses. With all due respect to the very original genius of the author of the "Tales of Mystery," it seems to us that to take him with more than a certain degree of seriousness is to lack seriousness one's self. An enthusiasm for Poe is the mark of a decidedly primitive stage of reflection. Baudelaire thought him a profound philosopher, the neglect of whose golden utterances stamped his native land with infamy. Nevertheless, Poe was vastly the greater charlatan of the two, as well as the greater genius.

"Les Fleurs du Mal" was a very happy title for Baudelaire's verses, but it is not altogether a just one. Scattered flowers incontestably do bloom in the quaking swamps of evil, and the poet who does not mind encountering bad odours in his pursuit of sweet ones is quite at liberty to go in search of them. But Baudelaire has, as a general thing, not plucked the flowers—he has plucked the evil-smelling weeds (we take it that he did not use the word flowers in a purely ironical sense) and he has often taken up mere cupfuls of mud and bog-water. He had said to himself that it was a great shame that the realm of evil and unclean things should be fenced off from the domain of poetry; that it was full of subjects, of chances and effects; that it had its light and shade, its logic and its mystery; and that there was the making of some capital verses in it. So he leaped the barrier and was soon immersed in it up to his neck. Baudelaire's imagination was of a melancholy and sinister kind, and, to a considerable extent, this plunging into darkness and dirt was doubtless very spontaneous and disinterested. But he strikes us on the whole as passionless, and this, in view of the unquestionable pluck and acuteness of his fancy, is a great pity. He knew evil not by experience, not as something within himself, but by contemplation and curiosity, as something outside of himself, by which his own intellectual agility was not in the least discomposed, rather, indeed (as we say his fancy was of a dusky cast) agreeably flattered and stimulated. In the former case, Baudelaire, with his other gifts, might have been a great poet. But, as it is, evil for him begins outside and not inside, and consists primarily of a great deal of lurid landscape and unclean furniture. This is an almost ludicrously puerile view of the matter. Evil is represented as an affair of blood and carrion and physical sickness—there must be stinking corpses and starving prostitutes and empty laudanum bottles in order that the poet shall be effectively inspired.

A good way to embrace Baudelaire at a glance is to say that he was, in his treatment of evil, exactly what Hawthorne was not—Hawthorne, who felt the thing at its source, deep in the human consciousness. Baudelaire's infinitely slighter volume of genius apart, he was a sort of Hawthorne reversed. It is the absence of this metaphysical quality in his treatment of his favourite subjects (Poe was his metaphysician, and his devotion sustained him through a translation of "Eureka!") that exposes him to that class of accusations of which M. Edmond Schérer's accusation of feeding upon *pourriture* is an example; and, in fact, in his pages we never know with what we are dealing. We encounter an inextricable confusion of sad emotions and vile things, and we are at a loss to know whether the subject pretends to appeal to our conscience or— we were going to say—to our olfactories. "Le Mal?" we exclaim; "you do yourself too much honour. This is not Evil; it is not the wrong; it is simply the nasty!" Our impatience is of the same order as that which we should feel if a poet, pretending to pluck "the flowers of good," should come and present us, as specimens, a rhapsody on plumcake and *eau du Cologne.* Independently of the question of his subjects, the charm of Baudelaire's verse is often of a very high order. He belongs to the class of geniuses in whom we ourselves find but a limited pleasure— the laborious, deliberate, economical writers, those who fumble a long time in their pockets before they bring out their hand with a coin in the palm. But the coin, when Baudelaire at last produced it, was often of a high value. He had an extraordinary verbal instinct and an exquisite felicity of epithet. We cannot help wondering, however, at Gautier's extreme admiration for his endowment in this direction; it is the admiration of the writer who gushes for the writer who trickles. In one point Baudelaire is extremely remarkable—in his talent for suggesting associations. His epithets seem to have come out of old cupboards and pockets; they have a kind of magical mustiness. Moreover, his natural sense of the superficial picturesqueness of the miserable and the unclean was extremely acute; there may be a difference of opinion as to the advantage of possessing such a sense; but whatever it is worth Baudelaire had it in a high degree. One of his poems— "To a Red-haired Beggar Girl"—is a masterpiece in the way of graceful expression of this high relish of what is shameful :—

> Pour moi, poëte chétif,
> Ton jeune corps maladif,
> Plein de taches de rousseur,
> A sa douceur.

Baudelaire repudiated with indignation the charge that he was what is called a realist, and he was doubtless right in doing so. He had too much fancy to adhere strictly to the real; he always embroiders and elaborates—endeavours to impart that touch of strangeness and mystery which is the very *raison d'être* of poetry. Baudelaire was a poet, and for a poet to be a realist is of course nonsense. The idea that Baudelaire imported into his theme was, as a general thing, an intensification of its repulsiveness, but it was at any rate ingenious. When he makes an invocation to "la Débauche aux bras immondes" one may be sure he means more by it than is evident to the vulgar—he means, that is, an intenser perversity. Occasionally he treats agreeable subjects, and his least sympathetic critics must make a point of admitting that his most successful poem is also his most wholesome and most touching; we allude to "Les Petites Vieilles"—a really masterly production. But if it represents the author's maximum, it is a note that he very rarely struck.

Baudelaire, of course, is a capital text for a discussion of the question as to the importance of the morality—or of the subject-matter in general—of a work of art; for he offers a rare combination of technical zeal and patience and of vicious sentiment. But even if we had space to enter upon such a discussion, we should spare our words; for argument on this point wears to our sense a really ridiculous aspect. To deny the relevancy of subject-matter and the importance of the moral quality of a work of art strikes us as, in two words, ineffably puerile. We do not know what the great moralists would say about the matter—they would probably treat it very good-humouredly; but that is not the question. There is very little doubt what the great artists would say. These geniuses feel that the whole thinking man is one, and that to count out the moral element in one's appreciation of an artistic total is exactly as sane as it would be (if the total were a poem) to eliminate all the words in three syllables, or to consider only such portions of it as had been written by candle-light. The crudity of sentiment of the advocates of "art for art" is often a striking example of the fact that a great deal of what is called culture may fail to dissipate a well-seated provincialism of spirit. They talk of morality as Miss Edgeworth's infantine heroes and heroines talk of " physic "—they allude to

G

its being put into and kept out of a work of art, put into and kept out of one's appreciation of the same, as if it were a coloured fluid kept in a big-labelled bottle in some mysterious intellectual closet. It is in reality simply a part of the essential richness of inspiration—it has nothing to do with the artistic process and it has everything to do with the artistic effect. The more a work of art feels it at its source, the richer it is; the less it feels it, the poorer it is. People of a large taste prefer rich works to poor ones and they are not inclined to assent to the assumption that the process is the whole work. We are safe in believing that all this is comfortably clear to most of those who have, in any degree, been initiated into art by production. For them the subject is as much a part of their work as their hunger is a part of their dinner. Baudelaire was not so far from being of this way of thinking as some of his admirers would persuade us; yet we may say on the whole that he was the victim of a grotesque illusion. He tried to make fine verses on ignoble subjects, and in our opinion he signally failed. He gives, as a poet, a perpetual impression of discomfort and pain. He went in search of corruption, and the ill-conditioned jade proved a thankless muse. The thinking reader, feeling himself, as a critic, all one, as we have said, finds the beauty perverted by the ugliness. What the poet wished, doubtless, was to seem to be always in the poetic attitude; what the reader sees is a gentleman in a painful-looking posture, staring very hard at a mass of things from which, more intelligently, we avert our heads.

HONORÉ DE BALZAC.

THE French in general do their duty by their great men; they render them a liberal tribute of criticism, commentary, annotation, biographical analysis. They do not, indeed, make them the subject of "memoirs" in the English sense; there are few French examples of that class of literature to which Boswell's "Johnson" and Lockhart's "Scott" belong. But there usually clusters about the image of a conspicuous writer an infinite number of *travaux*, as the French say, of every degree of importance. Many of these are very solid and serious; their authors are generally to be charged with attaching too absolute a value to their heroes. The departed genius is patiently weighed and measured; his works are minutely analysed; the various episodes of his life are made the object of exhaustive research; his letters are published, and his whole personality, physical, moral, intellectual, passes solemnly into literature. He is always in order as a "subject"; it is admitted that the last word can never be said about him. From this usual fate of eminent Frenchmen, one of the greatest has been strikingly exempted. Honoré de Balzac is weighted neither with the honours nor with the taxes of an accumulated commentary. The critic who proposes to study him, and who looks for extrinsic assistance in his task, perceives such aid to be very meagre. Balzac has been discussed with firstrate ability only by one writer. M. Taine's essay, incomplete as it is, may be said at any rate to be essentially worthy of its subject. Sainte-Beuve wrote upon Balzac two or three times, but always with striking and inexplicable inadequacy. There is a long article on the author of the "Comédie Humaine" by Théophile Gautier, which is admirably picturesque but not at all critical. M. Edmond Schérer, a writer upon whom an ample fold of Sainte-Beuve's mantle has fallen, lately published a few pages which are suggestive, but in which he affirms that Balzac is neither an artist, a master, nor a writer. The great novelist's countrymen, in a word, have taken him less seriously than was to be expected. If we desire biographical details we are reduced to consulting the very flimsy gossip of M. Léon Gozlan. Balzac has indeed what is called his *légende*, but it has been chiefly in the keeping of the mere tattlers of literature. The critic is forced to look for the man almost exclusively in his works; and it must be confessed that in the case of a writer so voluminous as Balzac such a field is ample. We should rather rejoice than regret that there are not more pages to turn. Balzac's complete works occupy twenty-three huge octavo volumes in the stately but inconvenient "édition définitive," lately published. There is a prospect of his letters being given to the world in a complementary volume.

I.

HONORÉ DE BALZAC was born at Tours in 1799; he died at Paris in 1850. Most first-rate men at fifty-one have still a good deal of work in them, and there is no reason to believe that, enormous as had been the demands he made upon it, Balzac's productive force was fully spent. His prefaces are filled with confident promises to publish novels that never appeared. Nevertheless it is impossible altogether to regret that Balzac died with work still in him. He had written enough; he had written too much. His novels, in spite of their extraordinary closeness of tissue, all betray the want of leisure in the author. It is true that shortly before his death he had encountered a change of fortune; he had married a rich woman and he was in a position to drive his pen no faster than his fancy prompted. It is interesting to wonder whether Balzac at leisure—Balzac with that great money-question which was at once the supreme inspiration and the æsthetic alloy of his life, placed on a relatively ideal basis—would have done anything essentially finer than "Les Parents Pauvres" or "Le Père Goriot." We can hardly help doubting it. M. Taine, looking as usual for formulas and labels, says that the most complete description of Balzac is that he was a man of business—a man of business in debt. The formula here is on the whole satisfactory; it expresses not only what he was by circumstances, but what he was by inclination. We cannot say how much Balzac liked being in debt, but we are very sure he liked, for itself, the process of manufacture and sale, and that even when all his debts had been paid he would have continued to keep his shop.

Before he was thirty years old he had published, under a variety of pseudonyms, some twenty long novels, veritable Grub Street productions, written in sordid Paris attics, in poverty, in perfect obscurity. Several of these "œuvres de jeunesse" have lately been republished, but the best of them are unreadable. No writer ever served a harder apprenticeship to his art, or lingered more hopelessly at the base of the ladder of fame. This early incompetence seems at first an anomaly, but it is only partially an anomaly. That so vigorous a genius should have learned his trade so largely by experiment and so little by divination; that in order to discover what he could do he should have had to make specific trial of each of the things he could not do—this is something which needs explanation. The explanation is found, it seems to us, simply in the folly of his attempting, at that age, to produce such novels as he aspired to produce. It was not that he could not use his wings; it was simply that his wings had not grown. The wings of great poets generally sprout very early; the wings of great artists in prose, great explorers of the sources of prose, begin to spread themselves only after the man is tolerably formed. Good observers, we believe, will confess to a general mistrust of novels written before thirty. Byron, Shelley, Keats, Lamartine, Victor Hugo, Alfred de Musset, were hardly in their twenties before they struck their fully resonant notes. Walter Scott, Thackeray, George Eliot, Madame Sand, waited till they were at least turned thirty, and then without prelude, or with brief prelude, produced a novel that was a masterpiece. If it was well for them to wait, it would have been infinitely better for Balzac. Balzac was to be preëminently a social novelist; his strength was to lie in representing the innumerable actual facts of the French civilization of his day—things only to be learned by patient experience. Balzac's inspiration, his stock, his *fonds*, was outside of him, in the complex French world of the nineteenth century. If, instead of committing to paper impossible imaginary tales, he could have stood for a while in some other relation to the society about him than that of a scribbler, it would have been a very great gain. The great general defect of his manner, as we shall see, is the absence of fresh air, of the trace of disinterested observation ; he had from his earliest years, to carry out our metaphor, an eye to the shop. In every great artist who possesses taste there is a little—a very little—of the amateur ; but in Balzac there is absolutely nothing of the amateur, and nothing is less to be depended upon than Balzac's taste. But he was forced to write ; his family wished to make a lawyer of him, and he preferred to be a romancer. He mastered enough law to be able to incorporate the mysteries of legal procedure in the "Comédie Humaine," and then embarked upon the most prolific literary career, perhaps, that the world has seen. His family cut down his supplies and tried to starve him out; but he held firm, and in 1830 made his first step into success. Meanwhile he had engaged in several commercial ventures, each one of which failed, leaving him a ponderous legacy of debt. To the end of his life he was haunted with undischarged obligations and was constantly trying new speculations and investments. It is true, we believe, that he amused himself with representing this pecuniary incubus as far more mysteriously and heroically huge than it was. His incessant labour brought him a remuneration which at this day and in this country would be considered contemptible. M. Gozlan affirms that his annual income, in his successful years, rarely exceeded 12,000 francs. This appears incredible until we find the editor of the "Revue de Paris" crying out against his demand of 3,000 francs for the MS. of "Eugénie Grandet." There is something pitiful in the contrast between this meagre personal budget and his lifelong visions of wealth and of the ways of amassing wealth, his jovial, sensual, colossal enjoyment of luxury, and the great monetary architecture as it were of the "Comédie Humaine." Money is the most general element of Balzac's novels; other things come and go, but money is always there. His great ambition and his great pretension as a social chronicler was to be complete, and he was more complete in this direction than in any other. He rarely introduces a person without telling us in detail how his property is invested, and the fluctuations of his *rentes* impartially divide the writer's attention with the emotions of his heart.

Balzac never mentions an object without telling us what it cost, and on every occasion he mentions an enormous number of objects. His women, too, talk about money quite as much as his men, and not only his ignoble and mercenary women (of whom there are so many) but his charming women, his heroines, his great ladies. Madame de Mortsauf is intended as a perfect example of feminine elevation, and yet Madame de Mortsauf has the whole of her husband's agricultural economy at her fingers' ends; she strikes us at moments as an attorney in petticoats. Each particular episode of the "Comédie Humaine" has its own hero and heroine, but the great general protagonist is the twenty-franc piece.

One thing at any rate Balzac achieved during these early years of effort and obscurity; he had laid the foundations of that intimate knowledge of Paris which was to serve as the basis—the vast mosaic pavement—of the "Comédie Humaine." Paris became his world, his universe; his passion for the great city deserves to rank in literature beside Dr. Johnson's affection for London. Wherever in his novels Paris is not directly presented she is even more vividly implied; the great negative to this brilliant positive, that *vie de province* of which he produced such elaborate pictures, is always observed from the standpoint of the

Boulevard. If Balzac had represented any other country than France, if his imagination had ever left a footprint in England or Germany, it is a matter of course for those who know him that his fathomless Parisian cockneyism would have had on these occasions a still sharper emphasis. But there is nothing to prove that he in the least "realized," as we say, the existence of England and Germany. That he had of course a complete theory of the British constitution and the German intellect makes little difference; for Balzac's theories were often in direct proportion to his ignorance. He never perceived with any especial directness that the civilized world was made up of something else than Paris and the provinces; and as he is said to have been able to persuade himself, by repeating it a few times, that he had done various things which he had not done—made a present of a white horse, for instance, to his publisher—so he would have had only to say often enough to himself that England was a mythic country to believe imperturbably that there was in fact, three hundred miles away, no magnificent far-spreading London to invalidate his constant assumption that Paris is the pivot of human history. Never was a great genius more essentially local. Shakespeare, Scott, Goethe, savour of their native soil; but they have a glance that has only to fix itself a moment to call up easily other horizons. Balzac's power of creation gains perhaps in intensity what it loses in reach; it is certain at any rate that his conception of the stage on which the "Comédie Humaine" is perpetually being acted is surrounded by a Chinese wall. Never was an imagination more in sympathy with the French theory of centralization.

When his letters are published it will be interesting to learn from them, in so far as we may, how his life was spent during these first ten years of his manhood. He began very early to write about countesses and duchesses; and even after he had become famous, the manner in which he usually portrays the denizens of the Faubourg St. Germain obliges us to believe that the place they occupy in his books is larger than any that they occupied in his experience. Did he go into society? did he observe manners from a standpoint that commanded the field? It was not till he became famous that he began to use the aristocratic prefix; in his earlier years he was plain M. Balzac. I believe it is more than suspected that the pedigree represented by this *de* was as fabulous (and quite as ingenious) as any that he invented for his heroes. Balzac was profoundly and essentially *roturier;* we shall see that the intrinsic evidence of his plebeian origin is abundant. He may very well, like his own Eugène de Rastignac, have lived at a Maison Vauquer; but did he, like Rastignac, call upon a Madame de Beauséant and see her receive him as a kinsman? We said just now that we had to look for Balzac almost altogether in his books; and yet his books are singularly void of personal revelations. They tell us a vast deal about his mind, but they suggest to us very little about his life. It is hard to imagine a writer less autobiographic. This is certainly a proof of the immense sweep of his genius—of the incomparable vividness of his imagination. The things he invented were as real to him as the things he knew, and his actual experience is overlaid with a thousand thicknesses, as it were, of imaginary experience. The person is irrecoverably lost in the artist. There is sufficient evidence, however, that the person led a rather hungry and predatory life during these early years, and that he was more familiar with what went on in the streets than with what occurred in the *salons*. Whatever he encountered, however, he observed. In one of his tales he describes a young man who follows people in the street to overhear what they say. This at least is autobiographic, and the young man is Honoré de Balzac, " devoured by his genius and by the consiousness of his genius," as M. Taine says—with all the unwritten "Comédie Humaine" within him. "In listening to these people I could espouse their life.

I felt their rags upon my back; I walked with my feet in their tattered shoes; their desires, their wants —everything passed into my soul, and my soul passed into theirs; it was the dream of a waking man." This glimpse of Balzac laying up data is especially interesting because it is singularly rare. It must be that for years he spent many an hour in silent, instinctive contemplation, for his novels imply a period of preparatory research, of social botanizing, geologizing, palæontologizing, just as Humboldt's "Cosmos" implies a large amount of travel. It happens that most of the anecdotes about Balzac pertain to his productive period, and present him to us in his white friar's dress, getting out of bed at midnight to work, in a darkened room, three weeks at a sitting. The open-air Balzac, as we may call it, has been little commemorated. White Dominican robes, darkened rooms, deep potations of coffee, form the staple of M. Gozlan's reminiscences. Every man works as he can and as he must; and if, in order to write the "Parents Pauvres," Balzac had had to dress himself in a bearskin, we trust he would not have hesitated. But it is nevertheless true that between the lines of the "Comédie Humaine" the reader too often catches a glimpse of the Dominican robe and the darkened room, and longs for an open window and a costume somewhat less capricious. A realistic novelist, he remembers, is not an astrologer or an alchemist.

In 1830 Balzac published the "Peau de Chagrin"— the first work of the series on which his reputation rests. After this, for twenty years, he produced without cessation. The quantity of his work, when we consider the quality, seems truly amazing. There are writers in the same line who have published an absolutely greater number of volumes. Alexandre Dumas, Madame Sand, Anthony Trollope, have all been immensely prolific; but they all weave a loose web, as it were, and Balzac weaves a dense one. The tissue of his tales is always extraordinarily firm and hard; it many not at every point be cloth of gold, but it has always a metallic rigidity. It has been worked over a dozen times, and the work can never be said to belong to light literature. You have only to turn the pages of a volume of Balzac to see that, whatever may be the purity of the current, it at least never runs thin. There is none of that wholesale dialogue, chopped into fragments, which Alexandre Dumas manufactures by the yard, and which bears the same relation to real narrative architecture as a chain of stepping-stones tossed across a stream does to a granite bridge. Balzac is always definite; you can say Yes or No to him as you go on; the story bristles with references that must be verified, and if sometimes it taxes the attention more than is thought becoming in a novel, we must admit that, being as hard reading in the way of entertainment as Hallam or Guizot, it may also have been very hard writing. This it is that makes Balzac's fertility so amazing—the fact that, whether we relish its results or not, we at least perceive that the process is not superficial. His great time was from 1830 to 1840; it was during these ten years that he published his most perfect works. " Eugénie Grandet," " La Recherche de l'Absolu," " Le Père Goriot," " Un Ménage de Garçon," " Le Cabinet des Antiques," belong to the earlier period. " Béatrix," " Modeste Mignon," " Une Ténébreuse Affaire," " Les Illusions Perdues," the " Mémoires de deux Jeunes Mariées," " La Muse du Département," " Le Député d'Arcis," belong to the latter. Balzac is never simple, and in a sense which it will be interesting to attempt to explain, he is always corrupt; but " La Recherche de Absolu " and " Le Père Goriot "—we will not mention " Eugénie Grandet," which was so praised for its innocence that the author found himself detesting it—have a certain relative simplicity and purity; whereas in the "Jeunes Mariées," " Béatrix," and " Modeste Mignon," we are up to our necks in sophistication. If, however, the works of the first half of Balzac's eminent period are, generally speaking, superior to those of the second half, it must be added that there are two or three incongruous transpositions. "Le Lys dans la Vallée," published in 1835, is bad enough to be coupled with "Béatrix"; and "Les Parents Pauvres" and "Les Paysans," finished shortly before the author's death, are in many respects his most powerful achievements. Most of Balzac's shorter tales are antecedent to 1840, and his readers know how many masterpieces the list contains. "Le Colonel Chabert" and "L'Interdiction" are found in it, as well as "La Femme Abandonnée," "La Grenadière" and "Le Message," and the admirable little stories grouped together (in the common duodecimo edition) with "Les Marana." The duration of Balzac's works will certainly not be in proportion to their length. "Le Curé de Tours," for all its brevity, will be read when "Le Député d'Arcis" lies unopened; and more than one literary adventurer will turn, outwearied, from "La Peau de Chagrin" and find consolation in "Un Début dans la Vie."

We know not how early Balzac formed the plan of the "Comédie Humaine"; but the general preface, in which he explains the unity of his work and sets forth that each of his tales is a block in a single immense edifice and that this edifice aims to be a complete portrait of the civilization of his

time—this remarkable manifesto dates from 1842.
(If we call it remarkable, it is not that we understand it; though so much as we have just expressed may easily be gathered from it. From the moment that Balzac attempts to philosophize, readers in the least sensible of the difference between words and things must part company with him.) He complains, very properly, that the official historians have given us no information about manners that is worth speaking of; that this omission is unpardonable; and that future ages will care much more for the testimony of the novel, properly executed, than for that of the writers who "set in order facts which are about the same in all nations, look up the spirit of laws which have fallen into disuse, elaborate theories which lead nations astray, or, like certain metaphysicians, endeavour to explain what is." Inspired by this conviction, Balzac proposed to himself to illustrate by a tale or a group of tales every phase of French life and manners during the first half of the nineteenth century. To be colossally and exhaustively complete—complete not only in the generals but in the particulars—to touch upon every salient point, to illuminate every typical feature, to reproduce every sentiment, every idea, every person, every place, every object, that has played a

part, however minute, however obscure, in the life of the French people—nothing less than this was his programme. The undertaking was enormous, but it will not seem at first that Balzac underestimated the needful equipment. He was conscious of the necessary talent and he deemed it possible to acquire the necessary knowledge. This knowledge was almost encyclopædic, and yet, after the vividness of his imagination, Blazac's strongest side is his grasp of actual facts. Behind our contemporary civilization is an immense and complicated machinery — the machinery of government, of police, of the arts, the professions, the trades. Among these things Balzac moved easily and joyously; they form the rough skeleton of his great edifice. There is not a little pedantry in his pretension to universal and infallible accuracy; but his accuracy, so far as we can measure it, is extraordinary, and in dealing with Balzac we must, in every direction, make our account with pedantry. He made his *cadres*, as the French say; he laid out his field in a number of broad divisions; he subdivided these, and then he filled up his moulds, pressing the contents down and packing it tight. You may read the categories on the back of the cover of the little common edition. There are the " Scènes de la Vie Privée "—" de la Vie de Province "—" de la Vie Parisienne "—" de la Vie Politique "—" de la Vie Militaire "—" de la Vie de Campagne "; and in a complementary way there are the " Études Philosophiques "—(this portentous category contains the picturesque " Recherche de l'Absolu ") — and the " Études Analytiques." Then, in the way of subdivisions, there are " Les Célibataires," " Les Parisiens en Province," " Les Rivalités," " Les Illusions Perdues," the " Splendeurs et Misères des Courtisanes," the " Parents Pauvres," the " Envers de l'Histoire Contemporaine." This goodly nomenclature had a retroactive effect; the idea of the " Comédie Humaine," having developed itself when the author was midway in his career, a number of its component parts are what we may call accomplices after the fact. They are pieces that dovetail into the vast mosaic as they best can. But even if the occasional disparities were more striking they would signify little, for what is most interesting in Balzac is not the achievement but the attempt. The attempt was, as he himself has happily expressed it, to " faire concurrence à l'état civil "—to start an opposition, as we should say in America, to the civil registers. He created a complete social system—an hierarchy of ranks and professions which should correspond with that of which the officers of the census have cognizance. Everything is there, as we find it in his pages—the king (in "Le Député d'Arcis" Louis XVIII. is introduced and makes witticisms quite *inédits*) the administration, the church, the army, the judicature, the aristocracy, the bourgeoisie, the prolétariat, the peasantry, the artists, the journalists, the men of letters, the actors, the children (a little girl is the heroine of "Pierrette," and an urchin the hero of "Un Début dans la Vie") the shopkeepers of every degree, the criminals, the thousand irregular and unclassified members of society. All this in Balzac's hands becomes an organic whole; it moves together; it has a pervasive life; the blood circulates through it; its parts are connected by sinuous arteries. We have seen in English literature, in two cases, a limited attempt to create a permanent stock, a standing fund, of characters. Thackeray has led a few of his admirable figures from one novel to another, and Mr. Trollope has deepened illusion for us by his repeated evocations of Bishop Proudie and Archdeacon Grantley. But these things are faint shadows of Balzac's extravagant thoroughness—his fantastic cohesiveness. A French brain alone could have persisted in making a system of all this. Balzac's "Comédie Humaine" is on the imaginative line very much what Comte's "Positive Philosophy" is on the scientific.

These great enterprises are equally characteristic of the French passion for completeness, for symmetry, for making a system as neat as an epigram—of its intolerance of the indefinite, the unformulated. The French mind likes better to squeeze things into a formula that mutilates them, if need be, than to leave them in the frigid vague. The farther limit of its power of arrangement (so beautiful as it generally is) is the limit of the knowable. Consequently we often see in the visions and systems of Frenchmen what may be called a conventional infinite. The civilization of the nineteenth century is of course not infinite, but to us of English speech, as we survey it, it appears so multitudinous, so complex, so far-spreading, so suggestive, so portentous—it has such misty edges and far reverberations—that the imagination, oppressed and overwhelmed, shrinks from any attempt to grasp it as a whole. The French imagination, in the person of Balzac, easily dominates it, as he would say, and, without admitting that the problem is any the less vast, regards it as practically soluble. He would be an incautious spirit who should propose hereupon to decide whether the French imagination or the English is the more potent. The one sees a vast number of obstacles and the other a vast number of remedies—the one beholds a great many shadows and the other a great many lights. If the human comedy, as Balzac pours it, condensed and solidified, out of his mould, is a very reduced copy of its original, we may nevertheless admit that the mould is of enormous dimensions. "Very good," the English imagination says; "call it large, but don't call it universal." The impartial critic may assent; but he privately remembers that it was in the convenient faculty of persuading himself that he could do everything that Balzac found the inspiration to do so much.

In addition to possessing an immense knowledge of his field, he was conscious that he needed a philosophy—a system of opinions. On this side too he equipped himself; so far as quantity goes no man was ever better provided with opinions. Balzac has an opinion on everything in heaven and on earth, and a complete, consistent theory of the universe, which was always ready for service. "The signs of a superior mind," says M. Taine, in speaking of him, "are *vues d'ensemble*—general views"; and judged by its wealth in this direction Balzac's should be the greatest mind the world has seen. We can think of no other mind that has stood ready to deliver itself on quite so many subjects. We doubt whether, on the whole, Aristotle had so many *vues d'ensemble* as Balzac. In Plato, in Bacon, in Shakespeare, in Goethe, in Hegel, there are shameful intermissions and lapses, ugly blank spots, ungraceful liabilities to be taken by surprise. But Balzac, as the showman of the human comedy, had measured his responsibilities unerringly and concluded that he must not only know what everything is, but what everything should be. He is thus *par excellence* the philosophic novelist; his pages bristle with axioms, moral, political, ethical, æsthetical; his narrative groans beneath the weight of metaphysical and scientific digression. The value of his philosophy and his science is a question to be properly treated apart; we mean simply to indicate that, formally, in this direction he is as complete as in the others. In the front rank, of course, stand his political and religious opinions. These are anchored to "the two eternal truths—the monarchy and the Catholic Church." Balzac is, in other words, an elaborate conservative —a Tory of the deepest dye. How well, as a picturesque romancer, he knew what he was about in adopting this profession of faith will be plain to the most superficial reader. His philosophy, his morality, his religious opinions have a certain picturesque correspondence with his political views. Speaking generally, it may be said that he had little belief in virtue and still less admiration for it. He is so large and various that you find all kinds of contradictory things in him; he has that sign of the few supreme geniuses that, if you look long enough he offers you a specimen of every possible mode of feeling. He has represented virtue, innocence and purity in the most vivid forms. César Birotteau, Eugénie Grandet, Mlle. Cormon, Mme. Graslin, Mme. Claes, Mme. de Mortsauf, Popinot, Genestas, the Cousin Pons, Schmucke, Chesnel, Joseph Bridau, Mme. Hulot—these and many others are not only admirably good people, but they are admirably successful figures. They live and move, they produce an illusion, for all their goodness, quite as much as their baser companions—Mme. Vauquer, Mme. Marneffe, Vautrin, Philippe Bridau, Mme. de Rochefide. Balzac had evidently an immense kindliness, a salubrious good nature which enabled him to feel the charm of all artless and helpless manifestations of life. That robustness of temperament and those high animal spirits which carried him into such fantastic explorations of man's carnal nature as the "Physiologie du Mariage" and the "Contes Drôlatiques"—that lusty natural humour which was not humour in our English sense, but a relish, sentimentally more dry but intellectually more keen, of all grotesqueness and quaintness and uncleanness, and which, when it felt itself flagging, had still the vigour to keep itself up a while as what the French call the "humoristic"—to emulate Rabelais, to torture words, to string together names, to be pedantically jovial and archaically hilarious—all this helped Balzac to appreciate the simple and the primitive with an intensity subordinate only to his enjoyment of corruption and sophistication. We do wrong indeed to say subordinate; Balzac was here as strong and as frank as he was anywhere. We are almost inclined to say that his profoundly simple people are his best—that in proportion to the labour expended upon them they are most lifelike. Such a figure as "big Nanon," the great, strapping, devoted maid-servant in "Eugénie Grandet," may stand as an example. (Balzac is full, by the way, of good servants; from Silvie and Christophe in "Le Père Goriot" to Chesnel the notary, whose absolutely canine fidelity deprives him even of the independence of a domestic, in "Le Cabinet des Antiques.") What he represents best is extremely simple virtue, and vice simple or complex, as you please. In superior virtue, intellectual virtue, he fails; when his superior people begin to reason they are lost—they become prigs and hypocrites, or worse. Madame de Mortsauf, who is intended to be at once the purest and cleverest of his good women, is a kind of fantastic monster; she is perhaps only equalled by the exemplary Madame de l'Estorade, who (in "Le Député d'Arcis") writes to a lady with whom she is but scantily acquainted a series of *pros* and *cons* on the question whether "it will be given" (as she phrases it) to a certain gentleman to make her "manquer à ses devoirs." This gentleman has snatched her little girl from under a horse's hoofs, and for a while afterward has greatly annoyed her by his importunate presence on her walks and drives. She immediately assumes that he has an eye to her "devoirs." Suddenly, however, he disappears, and it occurs to her that he is "sacrificing his fancy to the fear of spoiling his fine action." At this attractive thought her "devoirs" begin to totter, and she ingenuously exclaims, "But on this footing he would really be a man to reckon with, and, my dear M. de l'Estorade, you would have decidedly to look out!" And yet Madame de l'Estorade is given us as a model of the all-gracious wife and mother; she figures in the "Deux Jeunes Mariées" as the foil of the luxurious, passionate and pedantic Louise de Chaulieu—the young lady who, on issuing from the convent where she has got her education, writes to her friend that she is the possessor of a "virginité savante."

There are two writers in Balzac—the spontaneous one and the reflective one—the former of which is much the more delightful, while the latter is the more extraordinary. It was the reflective observer that aimed at colossal completeness and equipped himself with a universal philosophy : and it was of this one we spoke when we said just now that Balzac had little belief in virtue. Balzac's beliefs, it must be confessed, are delicate ground ; from certain points of view, perhaps, the less said about them the better. His sincere, personal beliefs may be reduced to a very compact formula ; he believed that it was possible to write magnificent novels, and that he was the man to do it. He believed, otherwise stated, that human life was infinitely dramatic and picturesque, and that he possessed an incomparable analytic perception of the fact. His other convictions were all derived from this and humbly danced attendance upon it ; for if being a man of genius means being identical with one's productive faculty, never was there such a genius as Balzac's. A monarchical society is unquestionably more picturesque, more available for the novelist than any other, as the others have as yet exhibited themselves ; and therefore Balzac was with glee, with gusto, with imagination, a monarchist. Of what is to be properly called religious feeling we do not remember a suggestion in all his many pages; on the other hand, the reader constantly encounters the handsomest compliments to the Catholic Church as a social *régime*. A hierarchy is as much more picturesque than a "congregational society" as a mountain is than a plain. Bishops, abbés, priests, Jesuits, are invaluable figures in fiction, and the morality of the Catholic Church allows of an infinite *chiaroscuro*. In "La Fille aux Yeux d'Or" there is a portrait of a priest who becomes preceptor to the youthful hero. "This priest, vicious but politic, sceptical but learned, perfidious but amiable, feeble in aspect, but as strong in body as in head, was so truly useful to his pupil, so complaisant to his vices, so good a calculator of every sort of force, so deep when it was necessary to play some human trick, so young at table, at the gaming house, at—I don't know where—that the only thing the grateful Henry de Marsay could feel soft-hearted over in 1814 was the portrait of his dear bishop—the single object of personal property he was able to inherit from this prelate, an admirable type of the men whose genius will save the Catholic Apostolic and Roman Church." It is hardly an exaggeration to say that we here come as near as we do at any point to Balzac's religious feeling. The reader will see that it is simply a lively assent to that great worldly force of the Catholic Church, the art of using all sorts of servants and all sorts of means. Balzac was willing to accept any morality that was curious and unexpected, and he found himself as a matter of course more in sympathy with a theory of conduct which takes account of circumstances and recognises the merits of duplicity, than with the comparatively colourless idea that virtue is nothing if not uncompromising. Like all persons who have looked a great deal at human life, he had been greatly struck with most people's selfishness, and this quality seemed to him the most general in mankind. Selfishness may go to dangerous lengths, but Balzac believed that it may somehow be regulated and even chastened by a strong throne and a brilliant court, with MM. de Rastignac and de Trailles as supports of the one and Mesdames de Maufrigneuse and d'Espard as ornaments of the other, and by a clever and impressive Church, with plenty of bishops of the pattern of the one from whose history a leaf has just been given. If we add to this that he had a great fancy for "electricity" and animal magnetism, we have touched upon the most salient points of Balzac's philosophy. This makes, it is true, rather a bald statement of a matter which at times seems much more considerable; but it may be maintained that an exact analysis of his heterogeneous opinions will leave no more palpable deposit. His imagination was so fertile, the movement of his mind so constant, his curiosity and ingenuity so unlimited, the energy of his phrase so striking, he raises such a cloud of dust about him as he goes, that the reader to whom he is new has a sense of his opening up gulfs and vistas of thought and pouring forth flashes and volleys of wisdom. But from the moment he ceases to be a simple dramatist Balzac is an arrant charlatan. It is probable that no equally vigorous mind was ever at pains to concoct such elaborate messes of folly. They spread themselves over page after page, in a close, dense verbal tissue, which the reader scans in vain for some little flower of available truth. It all rings false—it is all mere flatulent pretension. It may be said that from the moment he attempts to deal with an abstraction the presumption is always dead against him. About what the discriminating reader thus brutally dubs his charlatanism, as about everything else in Balzac, there would be very much more to say than this small compass admits of. (Let not the discriminating reader, by the way, repent of his brutality; Balzac himself was brutal, and must be handled with his own weapons. It would be absurd to write of him in semi-tones and innuendoes; he never used them himself.) The chief point is that he himself was his most perfect dupe; he believed in his own magnificent rubbish, and if he made it up, as the phrase is, as he went along, his credulity kept pace with his invention. This was, briefly speaking, because he was morally and intellectually so superficial. He paid himself, as the French say, with shallower conceits than ever before passed muster with a strong man. The moral, the intellectual atmosphere of his genius is extraordinarily gross and turbid; it is no wonder that the flower of truth does not bloom in it, nor any natural flower whatever. The difference in this respect between Balzac and the other great novelists is extremely striking. When we approach Thackeray and George Eliot, George Sand and Turgénieff, it is into the conscience and the mind that we enter, and we think of these writers primarily as great consciences and great minds. When we approach Balzac we seem to enter into a great temperament—a prodigious nature. He strikes us half the time as an extraordinary physical phenomenon. His robust imagination seems a sort of physical faculty and impresses us more with its sensible mass and quantity than with its lightness or fineness.

This brings us back to what was said just now touching his disbelief in virtue and his homage to the selfish passions. He had no natural sense of morality, and this we cannot help thinking a serious fault in a novelist. Be the morality false or true, the writer's deference to it greets us as a kind of essential perfume. We find such a perfume in Shakespeare; we find it, in spite of his so-called cynicism, in Thackeray; we find it, potently, in George Eliot, in George Sand, in Turgénieff. They care for moral questions; they are haunted by a moral ideal. This southern slope of the mind, as we may call it, was very barren in Balzac, and it is partly possible to account for its barrenness. Large as Balzac is, he is all of one piece and he hangs perfectly together. He pays for his merits and he sanctifies his defects. He had a sense of this present terrestrial life which has never been surpassed, and which in his genius overshadowed everything else. There are many men who are not especially occupied with the idea of another world, but we believe there has never been a man so completely detached from it as Balzac. This world of our senses, of our purse, of our name, of our *blason* (or the absence of it)—this palpable world of houses and clothes, of seven per cents and multiform human faces, pressed upon his imagination with an unprecedented urgency. It certainly is real enough to most of us, but to Balzac it was ideally real— charmingly, absorbingly, absolutely real. There is nothing in all imaginative literature that in the least resembles his mighty passion for *things*—for material objects, for furniture, upholstery, bricks and mortar. The world that contained these things filled his consciousness, and *being*, at its intensest, meant simply being thoroughly at home among them. Balzac possessed indeed a lively interest in the supernatural: "La Peau de Chagrin," "Louis Lambert," "Séraphita," are a powerful expression of it. But it was a matter of adventurous fancy, like the same quality in Edgar Poe; it was perfectly cold, and had nothing to do with his moral life. To get on in this world, to succeed, to live greatly in all one's senses, to have plenty of *things*—this was Balzac's infinite; it was here that his heart expanded. It was natural, therefore, that the life of mankind should seem to him above all an eager striving along this line—a multitudinous greed for personal enjoyment. The master-passion among these passions—the passion of the miser—he has depicted as no one else has begun to do. Wherever we look, in the "Comédie Humaine," we see a miser, and he—or she—is sure to be a marvel of portraiture. In the struggle and the scramble it is not the sweetest qualities that come uppermost, and Balzac, watching the spectacle, takes little account of these. It is strength and cunning that are most visible—the power to climb the ladder, to wriggle to the top of the heap, to clutch the money-bag. In human nature, viewed in relation to this end, it is force only that is desirable, and a feeling is fine only in so far as it is a profitable practical force. Strength of purpose seems the supremely admirable thing, and the spectator lingers over all eminent exhibitions of it. It may show itself in two great ways—in vehemence and in astuteness, in eagerness and in patience. Balzac has a vast relish for both, but on the whole he prefers the latter form as being the more dramatic. It admits of duplicity, and there are few human accomplishments that Balzac professes so explicit a respect for as this. He scatters it freely among his dear "gens d'église," and his women are all compounded of it. If he had been asked what was, for human purposes, the faculty he valued most highly, he would have said the power of dissimulation. He regards it as a sign of all superior people, and he says somewhere that nothing forms the character so finely as having had to exercise it in one's youth, in the bosom of one's family. In this attitude of Balzac's there is an element of affectation and of pedantry; he praises duplicity because it is original and audacious to do so. But he praises it also because it has for him the highest recommendation that anything can have—it is picturesque. Duplicity is more picturesque than honesty—just as the line of beauty is the curve and not the straight line. In place of a moral judgment of conduct, accordingly, Balzac usually gives us an æsthetic judgment. A magnificent action with him is not an action which is remarkable for its high motive, but an action with a great force of will or of desire behind it, which throws it into striking and monumental relief. It may be a magnificent sacrifice, a magnificent devotion, a magnificent act of faith; but the presumption is that it will be a magnificent lie, a magnificent murder, or a magnificent adultery.

II.

THIS overmastering sense of the present world was of course a superb foundation for the work of a realistic romancer, and it did so much for Balzac that one is puzzled to know where to begin to enumerate the things he owed to it. It gave him in the first place his background—his *mise en scéne*. This part of his story had with Balzac an importance—his rendering of it a solidity—which it had never enjoyed before, and which the most vigorous talents in the school of which Balzac was founder have never been able to restore to it. The place in which an event occurred was in his view of equal moment with the event itself; it was part of the action; it was not a thing to take or to leave, or to be vaguely and gracefully indicated; it imposed itself; it had a part to play; it needed to be made as definite as anything else. There is accordingly a very much greater amount of description in Balzac than in any other writer, and the description is mainly of towns, houses and rooms. Descriptions of scenery, properly so called, are rare, though when they occur they are often admirable. Almost all of his tales "de la vie de province" are laid in different towns, and a more or less minute portrait of the town is always attempted. How far in these cases Balzac's general pretension to be exact and complete was sustained we are unable to say; we know not what the natives of Limoges, of Saumur, of Angoulême, of Alençon, of Issoudun, of Guérande, thought of his presentation of these localities; but if the picture is not veracious, it is at least always definite and masterly. And Balzac did what he could, we believe, to be exact; he often made a romancer's pilgrimage to a town that he wished to introduce into a story. Here he picked out a certain number of houses to his purpose, lodged the persons of his drama in them, and reproduced them even to their local odours. Many readers find all this very wearisome, and it is certain that it offers one a liberal chance to be bored. We, for our part, have always found Balzac's houses and rooms extremely interesting; we often prefer his places to his people. He was a profound connoisseur in these matters; he had a passion for bric-à-brac, and his tables and chairs are always in character. It must be admitted that in this matter as in every other he had his right and his wrong, and that in his enumerations of inanimate objects he often sins by extravagance. He has his necessary houses and his superfluous houses: often when in a story the action is running thin he stops up your mouth against complaint, as it were, by a choking dose of brick and mortar. The power of his memory, his representative vision, as regards these things is something amazing; the reader never ceases to wonder at the promptness with which he can "get up" a furnished house—at the immense supply of this material that he carries about in his mind. He expends it with a royal liberality; where another writer makes an allusion Balzac gives you a Dutch picture. In "Le Cabinet des Antiques," on the verge of its close, Madame Camusot makes a momentary appearance. She has only twenty lines to speak, but immediately we are confronted with her domicile. "Leaning against the next house, so as to present its front to the court, it had on each floor but one window on the street. The court, confined in its width by two walls ornamented by rose-bushes and privet, had at its bottom, opposite the house, a shed supported upon two brick arches. A little half-door admitted you into this dusky house, made duskier still by a great walnut-tree planted in the middle of the court." We are told furthermore about the dining-room and the kitchen, about the staircase and the rooms on the first floor. We learn that the second floor was an attic, and that it had one room for the cook and another for the femme de chambre, who kept the children with her. We are informed that the woodwork, painted a dirty grey, was of the most melancholy aspect, and that Madame Camusot's bedroom had a carpet and blue and white ornaments. All this is entirely out of the current of the story, which pretends to be short and simple, and which is ostensibly hurrying towards its dénoûment. Some readers will always remember the two brick arches of Madame Camusot's shed, the dirty grey of her walls and the blue and white upholstery of her room; others will say that they care nothing about them, and these are not to be gainsaid.

Three or four descriptions of this kind stand out in the reader's memory. One is the picture of the dark and chill abode in which poor Eugénie Grandet blooms and fades; another is the elaborate and elegant portrait of the beautiful old house at Douai, half Flemish, half Spanish, in which the delusions of Balthazar Claës bring his family to ruin; the best of all is the magnificent account of the "pension bourgeoise des deux sexes et autres," kept by Madame Vauquer, *née* de Conflans, preceded by a glass door armed with a shrill alarm-bell, through which you see an arcade in green marble painted on a wall and a statue of Cupid with the varnish coming off in scales. In this musty and mouldy little boarding-house the Père Goriot is the senior resident. Certain students in law and medicine, from the Quartier Latin, hard by, subscribe to the dinner, where Maman Vauquer glares at them when she watches them cut their slice from the loaf. When the Père Goriot dies horribly, at the end of the tragedy, the kindest thing said of him, as the other boarders unfold their much-crumpled napkins, is, "Well, he won't sit and sniff his bread any more!" and the speaker imitates the old man's favourite gesture. The portrait of the Maison Vauquer and its inmates is one of the most portentous settings of the scene in all the literature of fiction. In this case there is nothing superfluous; there is a profound correspondence between the background and the action. It is a pity not to be able to quote the whole description, or even that of the greasy, dusky dining-room in which so much of the story goes forward. "This apartment is in all its lustre at the moment when, toward seven o'clock in the morning, Madame Vauquer's cat precedes his mistress, jumping on the sideboards, smelling at the milk contained in several basins covered with plates, and giving forth his matutinal purr. Presently the widow appears, decked out in her tulle cap, under which hangs a crooked band of false hair; as she walks she drags along her wrinkled slippers. Her little plump elderly face, from the middle of which protrudes a nose like a parrot's beak; her little fat dimpled hands, her whole person, rounded like a church-rat, the waist of her gown, too tight for its contents, which flaps over it, are all in harmony with this room, where misfortune seems to ooze, where speculation lurks in corners, and of which Madame Vauquer inhales the warm, fetid air without being nauseated. Her countenance, fresh as a first autumn frost, her wrinkled eyes, whose expression passes from the smile prescribed to *danseuses* to the acrid scowl of the discounter—her whole person, in short, is an explanation of the boarding-house, as the boarding-house is an implication of her person. . . . Her worsted petticoat, which falls below her outer skirt, made of an old dress, and with the wadding coming out of the slits in the stuff, which is full of them, resumes the parlour, the dining-room, the yard, announces the kitchen, and gives a presentiment of the boarders." But we must pause, for we are passing from the portraiture of places to that of people.

This latter is Balzac's strongest gift, and it is so strong that it easily distances all competition. Two other writers in this line have gone very far, but they suffer by comparison with him. Dickens often sets a figure before us with extraordinary vividness; but the outline is fantastic and arbitrary; we but half believe in it, and feel as if we were expected but half to believe in it. It is like a silhouette in cut paper, in which the artist has allowed great license to his scissors. If Balzac had a rival, the most dangerous rival would be Turgénieff. With the Russian novelist the person represented is equally definite—or meant to be equally definite; and the author's perception of idiosyncrasies is sometimes even more subtle. With Turgénieff as with Balzac the whole person springs into being at once; the character is never left shivering for its fleshly envelope, its face, its figure, its gestures, its tone, its costume, its name, its bundle of antecedents. But behind Balzac's figures we feel a certain heroic pressure that drives them home to our credence—a contagious illusion on the author's own part. The imagination that produced them is working at a greater heat; they seem to proceed from a sort of creative infinite and they help each other to be believed in. It is pictorially a larger, sturdier, more systematic style of portraiture than Turgénieff's. This is altogether the most valuable element in Balzac's novels; it is hard to see how the power of physical evocation can go farther. In future years, if people find his tales, as a whole, too rugged and too charmless, let them take one up occasionally and, turning the leaves, read simply the portraits. In Balzac every one who is introduced is minutely described; if the individual is to say but three words he has the honours of a complete portrait. Portraits shape themselves under his pen as if in obedience to an irresistible force; while the effort with most writers is to collect the material—to secure the model—the effort with Balzac is to disintegrate his visions, to accept only one candidate in the dozen. And it is not only that his figures are so definite, but that they are so plausible, so real, so characteristic, so recognisable. The fertility of his imagination in this respect was something marvellous.

When we think of the many hundred complete human creatures (he calls the number at least two thousand) whom he set in motion, with their sharp differences, their histories, their money-matters, their allotted place in his great machine, we give up the attempt to gauge such a lusty energy of fancy. In reading over Balzac, we have marked a great many portraits for quotation, but it is hard to know what to choose or where to begin. The appreciative reader may safely begin at hazard. He opens the little tale of "L'Interdiction," and finds the physiognomy of the excellent Judge Popinot thus depicted: "If nature, therefore, had endowed M. Popinot with an exterior but scantily agreeable, the magistracy had not embellished him. His frame was full of angular lines. His big knees, his large feet, his broad hands, contrasted with a sacerdotal face, which resembled vaguely the head of a calf, soft to insipidity, feebly lighted by two lateral eyes, altogether bloodless, divided by a straight flat nose, surmounted by a forehead without protuberance, decorated by two huge ears, which bent awkwardly forward. His hair, thin in quantity and quality, exposed his skill in several irregular furrows. A single feature recommended this countenance to the student of physiognomy. The man had a mouth on whose lips a divine goodness hovered. These were good big red lips, sinuous, moving, with a thousand folds, through which nature had never expressed any but high feelings—lips which spoke to the heart," &c.

That is certainly admirable for energy and vividness —closeness to the individual. But, after all, Popinot plays a part; he appears in several tales; he is the type of the upright judge, and there is a fitness in his figure being strongly lighted. Here is Madame de Kergarouet, who merely crosses the stage in " Béatrix," who rises in answer to a momentary need, and yet who is as ripe and complete, as thoroughly seen, felt and understood, as if she had been soaked, as it were, for years in the author's consciousness : " As for the Vicomtesse de Kergarouet, she was the perfect *provinciale*. Tall, dry, faded, full of hidden pretensions which showed themselves after they had been wounded; talking much and, by dint of talking, catching a few ideas, as one cannons at billiards, and which gave her a reputation for cleverness; trying to humiliate the Parisians by the pretended *bonhomie* of departmental wisdom, and by a make-believe happiness which she was always putting forward; stooping to get herself picked up and furious at being left on her knees; fishing for compliments, and not always taking them; dressing herself at once strikingly and carelessly; taking the want of affability for impertinence, and thinking to embarrass people greatly by paying them no attention; refusing what she wanted in order to have

it offered to her twice, and to seem to be urged beyond
resistance; occupied with the things that people have
ceased to talk about and greatly astonished at not
being in the current of fashion; finally, keeping quiet
with difficulty an hour without bringing up Nantes, and
the tigers of Nantes, and the affairs of the high society
of Nantes, and complaining of Nantes, and criticising
Nantes, and making a personal application of the
phrases extracted from the people whose attention
wandered, and who agreed with her to get rid of her.
Her manners, her language, her ideas, had all more or
less rubbed off on her four daughters." Here also, to
prove that Balzac's best portraits are not always his
harshest, is an admirably friendly portrait of an old
rustic gentlewoman, taken from the same novel: "Mademoiselle Zephirine, deprived of her sight, was ignorant of the changes which her eighty years had made
in her physiognomy. Her pale, hollow face, which
the immobility of her white, sightless eyes caused to
look like that of a dead person, which three or four
protruding teeth rendered almost threatening, in
which the deep orbit of the eyes was circled with
red tones, in which a few signs of virility, already
white, cropped up about the mouth and chin—this
cold, calm face was framed in a little nun-like cap
of brown calico, pricked like a counterpane, garnished

with a cambric frill, and tied under the chin by two strings which were always a trifle rusty. She wore a short gown of coarse cloth, over a petticoat of *piqué*, a real mattress which contained forty-franc pieces—as also a pair of pockets sewed to a belt which she put on and took off morning and night like a garment. Her body was fastened into the common jacket of Brittany, in stuff matching with that of her skirt, ornamented with a little collar of a thousand folds, the washing of which was the subject of the only dispute she ever had with her sister-in-law—she herself wishing to change it but once a week. From the great wadded sleeves of this jacket issued two desiccated but nervous arms, at the end of which moved two hands of a ruddy hue, which made her arms appear as white as the wood of the poplar. Her hands, with the fingers hooked and contracted by knitting, were like a stocking-loom for ever wound up; the phenomenon would have been to see them stop. From time to time she took a long knitting-needle that was planted in her bosom, and thrust it in between her cap and her head, while she rummaged in her white hair. A stranger would have laughed at the carelessness with which she stuck the needle back again, without the least fear of wounding herself. She was as straight as a belfry.

This columnar rectitude might have passed for one of those egotisms practised by old people, which prove that pride is a passion necessary to life. Her smile was gay."

One of the most striking examples of Balzac's energy and facility of conception and execution in this line is the great gallery of portraits of the people who come to the party given by Madame de Bargeton, in "Les Illusions Perdues." These people are all mere supernumeraries; they appear but on this occasion, and having been marshalled forth in their living grotesqueness, they stand there simply to deepen the local colour about the central figure of Madame de Bargeton. When it lets itself loose among the strange social types that vegetate in silent corners of provincial towns, and of which an old and complex civilization, passing from phase to phase, leaves everywhere so thick a deposit, Balzac's imagination expands and revels and rejoices in its strength. In these cases it is sometimes kindly and tender and sympathetic; but as a general thing it is merciless in its irony and contempt. There is almost always, to us English readers, something cruel and wounding in French irony—something almost sanguinary in French caricature. To be ridiculous is made to appear like a crime and to deprive the unhappy victim

of any right that an acute observer is bound to
respect. The Dodson family, in George Eliot's "Mill
on the Floss"—the illustrious stock from which
Mrs. Glegg and Mrs. Pullet issue—are apparently a
scantily mitigated mixture of the ridiculous and the
disagreeable; and yet every reader of that admirable
novel will remember how humanly, how generously
these ladies are exhibited, and how in the author's
treatment of them the highest sense of their absurdi-
ties never leads her to grudge them a particle of
their freedom. In a single word, the picture is not
invidious. Balzac, on the other hand, in correspond-
ing pictures—pictures of small middle-class ignorance,
narrowness, penury, poverty, dreariness, ugliness
physical and mental—is always invidious. He grudges
and hates and despises. These sentiments certainly
often give a masterly force to his touch; but they
deepen that sense, which he can so ill afford to have
deepened, of the meagreness of his philosophy. It is
very true that the "vie de province" of the "Comédie
Humaine" is a terribly dreary and sordid affair; but,
making every concession to the ignorant and self-
complacent stupidity of the small French bourgeoisie
during the Restoration and the reign of Louis Philippe,
it is impossible to believe that a chronicler with a
scent a little less rabidly suspicious of Philistinism

would not have shown us this field in a somewhat rosier light. Like all French artists and men of letters, Balzac hated the bourgeoisie with an immitigable hatred, and more than most of his class he hated the provincial. All the reasons for this general attitude it would take us too far to seek; two of them, we think, are near the surface. Balzac and his comrades hate the bourgeois, in the first place, because the bourgeois hates them, and in the second place, because they are almost always fugitives from the bourgeoisie. They have escaped with their lives, and once in the opposite camp they turn and shake their fists and hurl defiance. Provincial life, as Balzac represents it, is a tissue of sordid economies and ignoble jealousies and fatuous tittle-tattle, in cold, musty, unlovely houses, in towns where the grass grows in the streets, where the passage of a stranger brings grotesquely eager faces to the window, where one or two impotently pretentious salons, night after night, exhibit a collection of human fossils. Here and there a brighter thread runs through the dusky web—we remember Véronique Tascheron, Eugénie Grandet, Marguerite Claës, Ursule Mirouët, David and Eve Séchard. White has a high picturesque value when properly distributed, and Balzac's innocent people, who are always more or less tragical dupes and victims, serve admirably to deepen the general effect of dreariness, stinginess and ferocious venality. With what a grasp of the baser social realities, with what energy and pathos and pictorial irony he has moulded these miseries and vices into living figures, it would be interesting to be able to exhibit in detail. It is grim economy that is always in the foreground —it is the clutch of the five-franc piece that is the essence of every gesture. It is the miser Grandet, doling out the sugar lump by lump for the coffee of the household; it is that hideous she-wolf of thrift, Silvie Rogron, pinching and persecuting and starving little Pierrette Lorrain; it is the heirs male and female of Doctor Mirouët flocking to the reading of his will like vultures and hyenas.

Balzac's figures, as a general thing, are better than the use he makes of them; his touch, so unerring in portraiture and description, often goes wofully astray in narrative, in the conduct of a tale. Of all the great novelists, he is the weakest in talk; his conversations, if they are at all prolonged, become unnatural, impossible. One of his pupils, as they say in French, Charles de Bernard (who had, however, taken most justly the measure of his own talent, and never indiscreetly challenged comparison with the master)—this charming writer, with but a tenth of

Balzac's weight and genius, very decidedly excels him in making his figures converse. It is not meant by this, however, that the story in Balzac is not generally powerfully conceived and full of dramatic stuff. Afraid of nothing as he was, he attacked all the deepest things in life and laid his hand upon every human passion. He has even—to be complete—described one or two passions that are usually deemed unmentionable. He always deals with a strong feeling in preference to a superficial one, and his great glory is that he pretended to take cognizance of man's moral nature to its deepest, most unillumined and, as the French say, most *scabreux* depths—that he maintained that for a writer who proposes seriously to illustrate the human soul there is absolutely no forbidden ground. He has never, that we remember, described what we call in English a flirtation, but he has described ardent love in a thousand forms (sometimes very well, sometimes horribly ill), with its clustering attributes of sensuality and jealousy, exaltation and despair, good and evil. It is hard to think of a virtue or a vice of which he has not given some eminent embodiment. The subject, in other words, is always solid and interesting; through his innumerable fallacies of form and style, of taste and art, that is always valuable. Some of his novels rise much above the others in this dignity and pregnancy of theme; M. Taine, in his essay, enumerates the most striking cases, and his sonorous echo of Balzac's tragic note is a tribute to our author's power. Balzac's masterpiece, to our own sense, if we must choose, is "Le Père Goriot." In this tale there is most of his characteristic felicity and least of his characteristic infelicity. Shakespeare had been before him, but there is excellent reason to believe that beyond knowing that "King Lear" was the history of a doting old man, buffeted and betrayed by cruel daughters, Balzac had not placed himself in a position to be accused of plagiarism. He had certainly not read the play in English, and nothing is more possible than that he had not read it in such French translations as existed in 1835. It would please him to have his reader believe that he has read everything in the world; but there are limits to the reader's good nature. "Le Père Goriot" holds so much, and in proportion to what it holds is, in comparison with its companions, so simple and compact, that it easily ranks among the few greatest novels we possess. Nowhere else is there such a picture of distracted paternal love, and of the battle between the voice of nature and the constant threat of society that you shall be left to rot by the roadside if you drop out of the ranks. In every novel of Balzac's, on the artistic line, there are the great intentions that fructify and the great intentions that fail. In "Le Père Goriot" the latter element, though perceptible, comes nearest to escaping notice. Balzac has painted a great number of "careers"; they begin in one story and are unfolded in a dozen others. He has a host of young men whom he takes up on the threshold of life, entangles conspicuously in the events of their time, makes the pivots of contemporaneous history. Some of them are soldiers, some men of letters, some artists; those he handles with most complacency are young men predestined by high birth to politics. These latter are, as a class, Balzac's most conspicuous failures, but they are also his most heroic attempts. The reader will remember De Marsay, De Trailles, Rastignac, the two Vandenesses, D'Esgrignon, Baudenord, Des Lupeaulx, Tillet, Blondet, Bridau, Nathan, Bixiou, Rubempré, Lousteau, D'Arthez. The man whose career is most distinctly traced is perhaps Eugène de Rastignac, whose first steps in life we witness in "Le Père Goriot." The picture is to some extent injured by Balzac's incurable fatuity and snobbishness; but the situation of the young man, well born, clever, and proud, who comes up to Paris, equipped by his family's savings, to seek his fortune and find it at any cost, and who moves from the edge of one social abyss to the edge of another (finding abysses in every shaded place he looks into) until at last his nerves are steeled, his head steadied, his conscience cased in cynicism and his pockets filled—all this bears a deep imaginative stamp. The *donnée* of " Le Père Goriot " is typical; the shabby Maison Vauquer, becoming the stage of vast dramas, is a sort of concentrated focus of human life, with sensitive nerves radiating out into the infinite. Then there is Madame d'Espard's attempt to prove that her excellent husband is insane and to have him sequestrated; and the Countess Ferraud, who repudiates her husband, when he reappears, crippled and penniless, after having been counted among the slain at the battle of Eylau; and Philippe Bridau, who bullies, sponges, swindles, bleeds his family to death to pay for his iniquities; Madame Marneffe, who drags an honourable family into desolation and ruin by the rapacity of her licentiousness, and the Baron Hulot d'Ervy, who sees his wife and children beggared and disgraced, and yet cannot give up Madame Marneffe; Victurnien d'Esgrignon, who comes up from Alençon to see the world, and sees it with a vengeance, so that he has to forge a note to pay for his curiosity, and his doting family have to beggar themselves to pay for his note; Madame de La Baudraye, who leaves her husband, burns her ships, and comes to live in Paris with an ignoble journalist, partly for the love of letters and partly for the love of the journalist himself; Lucien de Rubempré, who tries to be a great poet, and to give an airing, in the highest places, to the poetic temperament, and who, after irrecordable alternations of delight and of misery, hangs himself in a debtors' prison; Marguerite Claës, who finds her father turning monomaniac and melting down her patrimony, and her motherless brother's and sister's, in the crucible of alchemy, and who fights for years a hand-to-hand duel with him, at great cost to her natural tenderness and her reputation; Madame de Mortsauf, who, after years of mysterious anguish, dies broken-hearted, between a brutal husband and a passionate lover, without ever having said a word to offend the one or, as she regards it, to encourage the other; poor Cousin Pons, the kindly virtuoso, who has made with years of patient labour a precious collection of pictures, and who is plundered, bullied, and morally murdered by rapacious relatives, and left without a penny to bury him.

It is the opinion of many of Balzac's admirers, and it was the general verdict of his day, that in all this the greatest triumphs are the characters of women. Every French critic tells us that his immense success came to him through women—that they constituted his first, his last, his fondest public. "Who rendered more deliciously than he," asks Sainte-Beuve, "the duchesses and viscountesses of the end of the Restoration—those women of thirty who, already on the stage, awaited their painter with a vague anxiety, so that when he and they stood face to face there was a sort of electric movement of recognition?" Balzac is supposed to have understood the feminine organism as no one had done before him—to have had the feminine heart, the feminine temperament, feminine nerves, at his fingers' ends—to have turned the feminine puppet, as it were, completely inside out. He has placed an immense number of women on the stage, and even those critics who are least satisfied with his most elaborate female portraits must at least admit that he has paid the originals the compliment to hold that they play an immense part in the world. It may be said, indeed, that women are the keystone of the "Comédie Humaine." If the men were taken out, there would be great gaps and fissures; if the women were taken out, the whole fabric would collapse. Balzac's superior handling of women seems to us to be both a truth and a fallacy; but his strength and weakness so intermingle and overlap that it is hard to keep a separate account with each.

His reader very soon perceives, to begin with, that he does not take that view of the sex that would commend him to the "female sympathizers" of the day. There is not a line in him that would not be received with hisses at any convention for giving women the suffrage, for introducing them into Harvard College, or for trimming the exuberances of their apparel. His restrictive remarks would be considered odious; his flattering remarks would be considered infamous. He takes the old-fashioned view —he recognises none but the old-fashioned categories. Woman is the female of man and in all respects his subordinate; she is pretty and ugly, virtuous and vicious, stupid and cunning. There is the great *métier de femme*—the most difficult perhaps in the world, so that to see it thoroughly mastered is peculiarly exhilarating. The *métier de femme* includes a great many branches, but they may be all summed up in the art of titillating in one way or another the senses of man. Woman has a "mission" certainly, and this is it. Man's capacity for entertainment fortunately is large, and he may be gratified along a far-stretching line; so that woman in this way has a very long rope and no reason to complain of want of liberty. Balzac's conception of what a woman may be and do is very comprehensive; there is no limit to her cleverness, her energy, her courage, her devotion; or, on the other hand, to her vices, her falsity, her meanness, her cruelty, her rapacity. But the great sign of Balzac's women is that in all these things the sexual quality is inordinately emphasized and the conscience on the whole inordinately sacrificed to it. It is an idea familiar to all novelists—it is indeed half their stock in trade—that women in good and in evil act almost exclusively from personal motives. Men do so often, the romancer says; women do so always. Balzac carries this idea infinitely farther than any other novelist, and imparts to the personal motive a peculiar narrowness and tenacity. It suggests the agility and the undulations, the claws and the vemon, of the cat and the serpent. That perfectly immoral view of what people do, which we spoke of as one of his great characteristics, is supremely conspicuous in Balzac's dealings with his heroines. " Leur gros libertin de père," M. Taine calls him in relation to certain of them; and the phrase really applies to him in relation to all, even the purest and most elevated. It is their personal, physical quality that he relishes—their attitudes, their picturesqueness, the sense that they give him of playing always, sooner or later, into the hands of man—*gros libertin* that he naturally and inevitably is. He has drawn a great many women's figures that are nobly pure in intention; he has even attempted three or four absolute saints. But purity in Balzac's hands is apt to play us the strangest tricks. Madame Graslin is a saint who has been privy to the murder of her lover and who allows an innocent man to suffer the penalty of the law; Madame Hulot is a saint who at fifty (being very well preserved) offers herself to a man she loathes in order to procure money for her daughter's marriage portion; Madame de Mortsauf is a saint familiar with the most cynical views of life (*vide* her letter of advice to Félix de Vandenesse on his entering upon his career, in which the tone is that of a politician and shrewd man of the world) who drives about with her lover late at night, kissing his head and otherwise fondling him. Balzac's women—and indeed his characters in general—are best divided into the rich and the poor, the Parisians and the rustics. His most ambitious female portraits are in the former class—his most agreeable, and on the whole his most successful, in the latter. Here the women, young and old, are more or less grotesque, but the absence of the desire to assimilate them to the type of the indescribable monster whom Balzac enshrines in the most sacred altitudes of his imagination as the Parisienne, has allowed them to be more human and more consonant to what we, at least, of the Anglo-Saxon race, consider the comfortable social qualities in the gentler sex. Madame Bridau, Madame Grandet, Mademoiselle Cormon, Madame Séchard—these, in Balzac, are the most natural figures of good women. His imagination has easily comprehended them; they are homely and pious and *naïves*, and their horizon is bounded by the walls of their quiet houses. It is when Balzac enters the field of the great ladies and the courtesans that he is supposed to have won his greatest triumphs, the triumphs that placed all the women on his side and made them confess that they had found their prophet and their master. To this view of the matter the writer of these lines is far from assenting. He finds it impossible to understand that the painter of Louise de Chaulieu and Madame d'Espard, of Madame de La Baudraye and Madame de Bargeton, of Lady Dudley and Madame de Maufrigneuse, should not have made all the clever women of his time his enemies.

It is not however, certainly, that here his energy, his force of colour, his unapproached power of what the French call in analytic portrayal "rummaging" —to *fouiller*—are not at their highest. Never is he more himself than among his coquettes and courtesans, among Madame Schontz and Joséphа, Madame

Marneffe and Madame de Rochefide. "Balzac loves his Valérie," says M. Taine, speaking of his attitude toward the horrible Madame Marneffe, the depths of whose depravity he is so actively sounding; and paradoxical as it sounds it is perfectly true. She is, according to Balzac's theory of the matter, a consummate Parisienne, and the depravity of a Parisienne is to his sense a more remunerative spectacle than the virtue of any *provinciale*, whether her province be Normandy or Gascony, England or Germany. Never does he so let himself go as in these cases—never does his imagination work so at a heat. Feminine nerves, feminine furbelows, feminine luxury and subtlety, intoxicate and inspire him; he revels among his innumerable heroines like Mahomet in his paradise of houris. In saying just now that women could not complain of Balzac's restrictions upon their liberty, we had in mind especially the liberty of telling lies. This exquisite and elaborate mendacity he considers the great characteristic of the finished woman of the world, of Mesdames d'Espard, de Sérisy, de Langeais, de Maufrigneuse. The ladies just enumerated have all a great many lovers, a great many intrigues, a great many jealousies, a terrible entanglement of life behind the scenes. They are described as irresistibly charming, as *grandes dames* in the supreme sense of the word; clever, cold, self-possessed, ineffably elegant, holding salons, influencing politics and letting nothing interfere with their ambition, their coquetry, their need for money. Above all they are at swords' points with each other; society for them is a deadly battle for lovers, disguised in a tissue of caresses. To our own sense this whole series of figures is fit only to have a line drawn through it as a laborious and extravagant failure—a failure on which treasures of ingenuity have been expended, but which is perhaps on that account only the more provocative of smiles. These ladies altogether miss the mark; they are vitiated by that familiar foible which Thackeray commemorated in so many inimitable pages. Allusion was made in the earlier part of these remarks to Balzac's strong plebeian strain. It is no reproach to him; if he was of the "people," he was magnificently so; and if the people never produced anything less solid and sturdy it would need to fear no invidious comparisons. But there is something ineffably snobbish in his tone when he deals with the aristocracy, and in the tone which those members of it who circulate through his pages take from him. They are so conscious, so fatuous, so *poseurs*, so perpetually alluding to their grandeurs and their quarterings, so determined to be impertinent, so afraid they shall not be impertinent enough, so addicted to reminding you that they are not bourgeois, that they do not pay their debts or practise the vulgar virtues, that they really seem at times to be the creatures of the dreams of an ambitious hairdresser who should have been plying his curling-irons all day and reading fashionable novels all the evening. The refinement of purpose in Balzac, in everything that relates to the emphasis of the aristocratic tone, is often extraordinary; and to see such heroic ingenuity so squandered and dissipated gives us an alarming sense of what a man of genius may sometimes do in the way of not seeing himself as others see him. Madame d'Espard, when she has decided to "take up" her provincial *cousine*, Madame de Bargeton, conveys her one night to the opera. Lucien de Rubempré comes into the box and, by his provincial dandyism and ingenuous indiscretions, attracts some attention. A rival who is acquainted with the skeleton in his closet goes and tells Madame d'Espard's friends and enemies that he is not properly a De Rubempré (this being only his mother's name), and that his father was M. Chardon, a country apothecary. Then the traitor comes and announces this fact to Madame d'Espard and intimates that her neighbours know it. This great lady hereupon finds the situation intolerable, and informs her companion that it will never do to be seen at the opera with the son of an apothecary. The ladies, accordingly, beat a precipitate retreat, leaving Lucien the master of the field. The caste of Vere de Vere in this case certainly quite forgot its repose. But its conduct is quite of a piece with that of the young men of high fashion who, after Madame de Bargeton has been a fortnight in Paris (having come very ill-dressed from Angoulême) are seen to compliment her on the "metamorphosis of her appearance." What is one to say about Madame de Rochefide, a person of the highest condition, who has by way of decoration of her drawing-room a series of ten water-colour pictures representing the different bedrooms she has successively slept in? What Balzac says is that this performance "gave the measure of a superior impertinence"; and he evidently thinks that he has bestowed the crowning touch upon a very crushing physiognomy. What is here indicated of Balzac's great ladies is equally true of his young dandies and lions—his De Marsays and De Trailles. The truly initiated reader of the "Comédie Humaine" will always feel that he can afford to skip the page when he sees the name of De Marsay. Balzac's dandies are tremendous fellows from a picturesque point of view; the account of De Marsay in "La Fille aux Yeux d'Or" is an

example of the "sumptuous" gone mad. Balzac
leaves nothing vague in the destinies he shapes for
these transcendant fops. Rastignac is prime minister
of France, and yet Rastignac in his impecunious youth
has been on those terms with Madame de Nücingen
which characterized the relations of Tom Jones with
Lady Bellaston. Fielding was careful not to make
his hero a rival of Sir Robert Walpole. Balzac's
young *gentilshommes*, as possible historical figures, are
completely out of the question. They represent,
perhaps, more than anything else, the author's extraordinary union of vigour and shallowness. In this,
however, they have much in common with several
other classes of characters that we lack space to
consider. There are the young girls (chiefly of the
upper class) like Modeste Mignon and Louise de
Chaulieu; there are the women of literary talent, like
Mademoiselle des Touches and Madame de La Baudraye; there are the journalists, like Lousteau and
Emile Blondet. In all these cases Balzac " rummages "
with extraordinary ardour; but his faults of taste
reach their maximum and offer us an incredible im-
broglio of the superb and the ignoble. Mademoiselle
de Chaulieu talks about her arms, her bosom, her
hips, in a way to make a trooper blush. Lousteau,
when a lady says a clever thing, tells her he will

steal it from her for his newspaper and get two dollars. As regards Rubempré and Canalis, we have specimens of their poetry, but we have on the whole more information about their coats and trousers, their gloves and shirts and cosmetics.

In all this it may seem that there has been more talk about faults than about merits, and that if it is claimed that Balzac did a great work we should have plucked more flowers and fewer thistles. But the greatest thing in Balzac cannot be exhibited by specimens. It is Balzac himself—it is the whole attempt —it is the method. This last is his unsurpassed, his incomparable merit. That huge, all-compassing, all-desiring, all-devouring love of reality which was the source of so many of his fallacies and stains, of so much dead-weight in his work, was also the foundation of his extraordinary power. The real, for his imagination, had an authority that it has never had for any other. When he looks for it in the things in which we all feel it, he finds it with a marvellous certainty of eye, and proves himself the great novelist that he pretends to be. When he tries to make it prevail everywhere, explain everything and serve as a full measure of our imagination—then he becomes simply the greatest of dupes. He is an extraordinary tissue of contradictions. He is at once one of the most corrupt of writers and one of the most naïf, the most mechanical and pedantic, and the fullest of *bonhomie* and natural impulse. He is one of the finest of artists and one of the coarsest. Viewed in one way, his novels are ponderous, shapeless, overloaded ; his touch is graceless, violent, barbarous. Viewed in another, his tales have more colour, more composition, more grasp of the reader's attention than any others. Balzac's style would demand a chapter apart. It is the least simple style, probably, that ever was written ; it bristles, it cracks, it swells and swaggers; but it is a perfect expression of the man's genius. Like his genius, it contains a certain quantity of everything, from immaculate gold to flagrant dross. He was a very bad writer, and yet unquestionably he was a very great writer. We may say briefly, that in so far as his method was an instinct it was successful, and that in so far as it was a theory it was a failure. But both in instinct and in theory he had the aid of an immense force of conviction. His imagination warmed to its work so intensely that there was nothing his volition could not impose upon it. Hallucination settled upon him, and he believed anything that was necessary in the circumstances. This accounts for all his grotesque philosophies, his heroic attempts to furnish specimens of things of which he was profoundly ignorant. He believed that he was about as creative as the Deity, and that if mankind and human history were swept away the "Comédie Humaine" would be a perfectly adequate substitute for them. M. Taine says of him very happily that, after Shakespeare, he is our great magazine of documents on human nature. When Shakespeare is suggested we feel rather his differences from Shakespeare—feel how Shakespeare's characters stand out in the open air of the universe, while Balzac's are enclosed in a peculiar artificial atmosphere, musty in quality and limited in amount, which persuades itself with a sublime sincerity that it is a very sufficient infinite. But it is very true that Balzac may, like Shakespeare, be treated as a final authority upon human nature; and it is very probable that as time goes on he will be resorted to much less for entertainment, and more for instruction. He has against him that he lacks that slight bu needful thing—charm. To feel how much he lacked it, you must read his prefaces, with their vanity, avidity, and garrulity, their gross revelation of his processes, of his squabbles with his publishers, their culinary atmosphere. But our last word about him is that he had incomparable power.

BALZAC'S LETTERS.

THE first feeling of the reader of the two volumes which have lately been published under the foregoing title is that he has almost done wrong to read them. He reproaches himself with having taken a shabby advantage of a person who is unable to defend himself. He feels as one who has broken open a cabinet or rummaged an old desk. The contents of Balzac's letters are so private, so personal, so exclusively his own affairs and those of no one else, that the generous critic constantly lays them down with a sort of dismay and asks himself in virtue of what peculiar privilege or what newly discovered principle it is that he is thus burying his nose in them. Of course he presently reflects that he has not broken open a cabinet nor violated a desk, but that these repositories have been very freely and confidently emptied into his lap. The two stout volumes of the " Correspondance de H. de

Balzac, 1819—1850,"[1] lately put forth, are remarkable, like many other French books of the same sort, for the almost complete absence of editorial explanation or introduction. They have no visible sponsor, only a few insignificant lines of preface and the scantiest possible supply of notes. Such as the book is, in spite of its abruptness, we are thankful for it; in spite, too, of our bad conscience. What we mean by our bad conscience is the feeling with which we see the last remnant of charm, of the graceful and the agreeable, removed from Balzac's literary physiognomy. His works had not left much of this favouring shadow, but the present publication has let in the garish light of full publicity. The grossly, inveterately professional character of all his activity, the absence of leisure, of contemplation, of disinterested experience, the urgency of his consuming money-hunger—all this is rudely exposed. It is always a question whether we have a right to investigate a man's life for the sake of anything but his official utterances—his results. The picture of Balzac's career which is given in these letters is a record of little else but painful processes, unrelieved by reflections or speculations, by any moral or intellectual emanation. To prevent

[1] Paris: Calmann Lévy. 1876.

misconception, however, we hasten to add that they tell no disagreeable secrets; they contain nothing for the lovers of scandal. Balzac was a very honest man, but he was a man almost tragically uncomfortable, and the unsightly underside of his discomfort stares us full in the face. Still, if his personal portrait is without ideal beauty, it is by no means without a certain brightness, or at least a certain richness, of colouring. Huge literary ogre as he was, he was morally nothing of a monster. His heart was capacious, and his affections vigorous; he was powerful, coarse and kind.

The first letter in the series is addressed to his elder sister, Laure, who afterward became Madame de Surville, and who, after her illustrious brother's death, published in a small volume some agreeable reminiscences of him. For this lady he had, especially in his early years, a passionate affection. He had in 1819 come up to Paris from Touraine, in which province his family lived, to seek his fortune as a man of letters. The episode is a strange and gloomy one. His vocation for literature had not been favourably viewed at home, where money was scanty; but the parental consent, or rather the parental tolerance, was at last obtained for his experiment. The future author of the "Père Goriot" was at this time but twenty years of age, and in the way of symptoms of genius had nothing but a very robust self-confidence to show. His family, who had to contribute to his support while his masterpieces were a-making, appear to have regretted the absence of farther guarantees. He came to Paris, however, and lodged in a garret, where the allowance made him by his father kept him neither from shivering nor from nearly starving. The situation had been arranged in a way very characteristic of French manners. The fact that Honoré had gone to Paris was kept a secret from the friends of the family, who were told that he was on a visit to a cousin in the South. He was on probation, and if he failed to acquire literary renown his excursion should be hushed up. This pious fraud did not contribute to the comfort of the young scribbler, who was afraid to venture abroad by day lest he should be seen by an acquaintance of the family. Balzac must have been at this time miserably poor. If he goes to the theatre, he has to pay for the pleasure by fasting. He wishes to see Talma (having, to go to the play, to keep up the fiction of his being in the South, in a latticed box). "I shall end by giving in. . . . My stomach already trembles." Meanwhile he was planning a tragedy of "Cromwell," which came to nothing, and writing the "Héritière de Birague," his first novel, which he sold for one hundred and sixty dollars. Through these early letters, in spite of his chilly circumstances, there flows a current of youthful ardour, gaiety, and assurance. Some passages in his letters to his sister are a sort of explosion of animal spirits : " Ah, my sister, what torments it gives us— the love of glory! Long live grocers! they sell all day, count their gains in the evening, take their pleasure from time to time at some frightful melodrama —and behold them happy! Yes, but they pass their time between cheese and soap. Long live rather men of letters! Yes, but these are all beggars in pocket, and rich only in conceit. Well, let us leave them all alone, and long live every one!"

Elsewhere he scribbles : "Farewell, *soror!* I hope to have a letter *sororis*, to answer *sorori*, then to see *sororem*," &c. Later, after his sister is married, he addresses her as "*the box that contains everything pleasing; the elixir of virtue, grace, and beauty; the jewel, the phenomenon of Normandy; the pearl of Bayeux, the fairy of St. Lawrence, the virgin of the Rue Teinture, the guardian angel of Caen, the goddess of enchantments, the treasure of friendship.*"

We shall continue to quote, without the fear of our examples exceeding, in the long run, our commentary. "Find me some widow, a rich heiress," he writes to his sister at Bayeux, whither her husband had taken her to live. " You know what I mean. Only brag about me. Twenty-two years old, a good fellow, good manners, a bright eye, fire, the best dough for a husband that heaven has ever kneaded. I will give you five per cent. on the dowry." "Since yesterday," he writes in another letter, " I have given up dowagers and have come down to widows of thirty. Send all you find to Lord Rhoone [this remarkable improvisation was one of his early *noms de plume*]; that's enough—he is known at the city limits. Take notice. They are to be sent prepaid, without crack or repair, and they are to be rich and amiable. Beauty isn't required. The varnish goes and the bottom of the pot remains ! "

Like many other young men of ability, Balzac felt the little rubs—or the great ones—of family life. His mother figures largely in these volumes (she survived her glorious son), and from the scattered reflection of her idiosyncrasies the attentive reader constructs a sufficiently vivid portrait. She was the old middle-class Frenchwoman whom he has so often seen—devoted, active, meddlesome, parsimonious, exacting veneration and expending zeal. Honoré tells his sister that "the other day, coming back from Paris much bothered, it never occurred to me to thank *maman* for a black coat which she had had made for me; at my age one isn't particularly sensitive to such a present. Nevertheless, it would not have cost me much to seem touched by the attention, especially as it was a sacrifice. But I forgot it. *Maman* began to pout, and you know what her aspect and her face amount to at those moments. I fell from the clouds, and racked my brain to know what I had done. Happily Laurence [his younger sister] came and notified me, and two or three words as fine as amber mended *maman's* countenance. The thing is nothing — a mere drop of water; but it's to give you an example of our manners. Ah, we are a jolly set of originals in our holy family. What a pity I can't put us into novels!"

His father wished to find him an opening in some profession, and the thought of being made a notary was a bugbear to the young man: "Think of me as dead if they cap me with that extinguisher." And yet, in the next sentence he breaks out into a cry of desolate disgust at the aridity of his actual circumstances: "They call this mechanical rotation living—this perpetual return of the same things. If there were only something to throw some charm or other over my cold existence! I have none of the flowers of life, and yet I am in the season in which they bloom. What will be the use of fortune and pleasures when my youth has departed? What need of the garments of an actor if one no longer plays a part? An old man is a man who has dined and who watches others eat; and I, young as I am—my plate is empty, and I am hungry. Laure, Laure, my two only and immense desires, *to be famous and to be loved*—will they ever be satisfied?"

These occasional bursts of confidence in his early letters to his sister are (with the exception of certain excellent pages addressed in the last years of his life to the lady he eventually married) Balzac's most delicate, most emotional utterances. There is a touch of the ideal in them. Later one wonders where he keeps his ideal. He has one of course, artistically, but it never peeps out. He gives up talking sentiment and he never discusses "subjects"; he only talks business. Meanwhile, however, at this period business was increasing with him. He agrees to write three novels for eight hundred and twenty dollars. Here begins the inextricable mystery of Balzac's literary promises, pledges, projects, contracts. His letters form a swarming register of schemes and bargains through which he passes like a hero of the circus, riding half a dozen piebald coursers at once. We confess that in this matter we have been able to keep no sort of account; the wonder is that Balzac should have accomplished the feat himself. After the first year or two of his career we never see him working upon a single tale; his productions dovetail and overlap, dance attendance upon each other in the most bewildering fashion. As soon as one novel is fairly on the stocks he plunges into another, and while he is rummaging in this with one hand he stretches out an heroic arm and breaks ground in a third. His plans are always vastly in advance of his performance; his pages swarm with titles of books that were never to be written. The title circulates with such an assurance that we are amazed to find, fifty pages later, that there is no more of it than of the cherubic heads. With this, Balzac was constantly paid in advance by his publishers—paid for works not begun, or barely begun; and the money was as constantly spent before the equivalent had been delivered. Meanwhile more money was needed, and new novels were laid out to obtain it; but prior promises had first to be kept. Keeping them, under these circumstances, was not an exhilarating process; and readers familiar with Balzac will reflect with wonder that these were yet the circumstances in which some of his best tales were written. They were written, as it were, in the fading light, by a man who saw night coming on and yet could not afford to buy candles. He could only hurry. But Balzac's way of hurrying was all his own; it was a sternly methodical haste and might have been mistaken, in a more lightly-weighted genius, for elaborate trifling. The close texture of his work never relaxed; he went on doggedly and insistently, pressing it down and packing it together, multiplying erasures, alterations, repetitions, transforming proof-sheets, quarrelling with editors, enclosing subject within subject, accumulating notes upon notes.

The letters make a jump from 1822 to 1827, during which interval he had established, with borrowed capital, a printing house, and seen his enterprise completely fail. This failure saddled him with a mountain of debt which pressed upon him crushingly for years, and of which he rid himself only toward the close of his life. Balzac's debts are another labyrinth in which we do not profess to hold a clue. There is scarcely a page of these volumes in which they are not alluded to, but the reader never quite understands why they should bloom so perennially. The liabilities incurred by the collapse of the printing-scheme can hardly have been so vast as not to have been for the most part cancelled by ten years of heroic work. Balzac appears not to have been extravagant; he had neither wife nor children (unlike many of his comrades, he had no known illegitimate offspring), and when he admits us to a glimpse of his domestic economy we usually find it to be of a very meagre pattern. He writes to his sister in 1827 that he has not the means either to pay the postage of letters or to use omnibuses, and that he goes out as little as possible, so as not to wear out his clothes. In 1829, however, we find him in correspondence with a duchess, Madame d'Abrantès, the widow of Junot, Napoleon's rough marshal, and author of those voluminous memoirs upon the imperial court which it was the fashion to read in the early part of the century. The Duchesse d'Abrantès wrote bad novels, like Balzac himself at this period, and the two became good friends.

The year 1830 was the turning-point in Balzac's career. Renown, to which he had begun to lay siege in Paris in 1820, now at last began to show symptoms of self-surrender. Yet one of the strongest expressions of discontent and despair in the pages before us belongs to this brighter moment. It is also one of the finest passages: "Sacredieu, my good friend, I believe that literature, in the day we live in, is no better than the trade of a woman of the town, who prostitutes herself for a dollar. It leads to nothing. I have an itch to go off and wander and explore, make of my life a drama, risk my life; for, as for a few miserable years more or less! . . . Oh, when one looks at these great skies of a beautiful night, one is ready to unbutton——." But the modesty of the English tongue forbids us to translate the rest of the phrase. Dean Swift might have related how Balzac aspired to express his contempt for all the royalties of the earth. Now that he is in the country, he goes on, "I have been seeing real splendours, such as fine sound fruit and gilded insects; I have been quite turning philosopher, and if I happen to tread upon an anthill, I say, like that immortal Bonaparte, 'These creatures or men: what is it to Saturn, or Venus, or the North Star?' And then my philosopher comes down to scribble 'items' for a newspaper. *Proh pudor!* And so it seems to me that the ocean, a brig, and an English vessel to sink, if you must sink yourself to do it, are rather better than a writing-desk, a pen, and the Rue St. Denis."

But Balzac was fastened to the writing-desk. In 1831 he tells one of his correspondents that he is working fifteen or sixteen hours a day. Later, in 1837, he describes himself repeatedly as working eighteen hours out of the twenty-four. In the midst of all this (it seems singular) he found time for visions of public life, of political distinction. In a letter written in 1830 he gives a succinct statement of his political views, from which we learn that he approved of the French monarchy possessing a constitution, and of instruction being diffused among the lower orders. But he desired that the people should be kept "under the most powerful yoke possible," so that in spite of their instruction they should not become disorderly. It is fortunate, probably, both for Balzac and for France, that his political rôle was limited to the production of a certain number of forgotten editorials in newspapers; but we may be sure that his dreams of statesmanship were brilliant and audacious. Balzac indulged in no dreams that were not.

Some of his best letters are addressed to Madame Zulma Carraud, a lady whose acquaintance he had made through his sister Laure, of whom she was an intimate friend, and whose friendship (exerted almost wholly through letters, as she always lived in the country) appears to have been one of the brightest and most salutary influences of his life. He writes to her thus in 1832 :—" There are vocations which we must obey, and something irresistible draws me on to glory and power. It is not a happy life. There is within me the worship of woman (*le culte de la femme*) and a need of love which has never been fully satisfied. Despairing of ever being loved and understood by such a woman as I have dreamed of, having met her only under one form, that of the heart, I throw myself into the tempestuous sphere of political passions and into the stormy and desiccating atmosphere of literary glory. I shall fail perhaps on both sides; but, believe me, if I have wished to live the life of the age itself, instead of running my course in happy obscurity, it is just because the pure happiness of mediocrity has failed me. When one has a fortune to make, it is better to make it great and illustrious; because, pain for pain, it is better to suffer in a high sphere than in a low one, and I prefer dagger-blows to pin-pricks." All this, though written at thirty years of age, is rather juvenile; there was to be much less of the "tempest" in Balzac's life than is here foreshadowed. He was tossed and shaken a great deal, as we all are, by the waves of the time, but he was too stoutly anchored at his work to feel the winds.

In 1832 "Louis Lambert" followed the "Peau de Chagrin," the first in the long list of his masterpieces. He describes "Louis Lambert" as "a work in which I have striven to rival Goethe and Byron, Faust and Manfred. I don't know whether I shall succeed, but the fourth volume of the 'Philosophical Tales' must be a last reply to my enemies and give the presentiment of an incontestable superiority. You must therefore forgive the poor artist his fatigue [he is writing to his sister] his discouragements, and especially his momen-

tary detachment from any sort of interest that does not belong to his subject. 'Louis Lambert' has cost me so much work! To write this book I have had to read so many books! Some day or other, perhaps, it will throw science into new paths. If I had made it a purely learned work, it would have attracted the attention of thinkers, who now will not drop their eyes upon it. But if chance puts it into their hands, perhaps they will speak of it!" In this passage there is an immense deal of Balzac—of the great artist who was so capable at times of self-deceptive charlatanism. "Louis Lambert," as a whole, is now quite unreadable; it contains some admirable descriptions, but the "scientific" portion is mere fantastic verbiage. There is something extremely characteristic in the way Balzac speaks of its having been optional with him to make it a "purely learned" work. His pretentiousness was simply colossal, and there is nothing surprising in his wearing even the mask *en famille* (the letter we have just quoted from is, as we have said, to his sister); he wore it during his solitary fifteen-hours sessions in his study. But the same letter contains another passage, of a very different sort, which is in its way as characteristic :—
"Yes, you are right. My progress is real, and my infernal courage will be rewarded. Persuade my mother of this too, dear sister; tell her to give me

her patience in charity; her devotion will be laid up in her favour. One day, I hope, a little glory will pay her for everything. Poor mother, that imagination of hers which she has given me throws her for ever from north to south and from south to north. Such journeys tire us; I know it myself! Tell my mother that I love her as when I was a child. As I write you these lines my tears start—tears of tenderness and despair; for I feel the future and I need this devoted mother on the day of triumph! When shall I reach it? Take good care of our mother, Laure, for the present and the future. . . . Some day, when my works are unfolded, you will see that it must have taken many hours to think and write so many things; and then you will absolve me of everything that has displeased you, and you will excuse, not the selfishness of the man (the man has none), but the selfishness of the worker."

Nothing can be more touching than that; Balzac's natural affections were as robust as his genius and his physical nature. The impression of the reader of his letters quite confirms his assurance that the man proper had no selfishness. Only we are constantly reminded that the man had almost wholly resolved himself into the worker, and we remember a statement of Sainte-Beuve's, in one of his malignant foot-notes, to the effect that Balzac was "the grossest, greediest example of literary vanity that he had ever known"—*l'amour-propre littéraire le plus avide et le plus grossier que j'aie connu*. When we think of what Sainte-Beuve must have known in this line these few words acquire a portentous weight.

By this time (1832) Balzac was, in French phrase, thoroughly *lancé*. He was doing, among other things, some of his most brilliant work, certain of the "Contes Drôlatiques." These were written, as he tells his mother, for relaxation, as a rest from harder labour. One would have said that no work could have been much harder than concocting the marvellously successful imitation of mediæval French in which these tales are written. He had, however, other diversions as well. In the autumn of 1832 he was at Aix-les-Bains with the Duchesse de Castries, a great lady and one of his kindest friends. He has been accused of drawing portraits of great ladies without knowledge of originals; but Madame de Castries was an inexhaustible fund of instruction upon this subject. Three or four years later, speaking of the story of the "Duchesse de Laugeais" to one of his correspondents, another *femme du monde*, he tells her that as a *femme du monde* she is not to pretend to find flaws in the picture, a high authority having read the proofs for the express purpose of removing them. The authority is evidently the Duchesse de Castries.

Balzac writes to Madame Carraud from Aix: "At Lyons I corrected 'Lambert' again. I licked my cub, like a she-bear. . . . On the whole, I am satisfied; it is a work of profound melancholy and of science. Truly, I deserve to have a mistress, and my sorrow at not having one increases daily; for love is my life and my essence. . . . I have a simple little room," he goes on, "from which I see the whole valley. I rise pitilessly at five o'clock in the morning and work before my window until half-past five in the evening. My breakfast comes from the club—an egg. Madame de Castries has good coffee made for me. At six o'clock we dine together and I pass the evening with her. She is the finest type (*le type le plus fin*) of woman; Madame de Beauséant [from "Le Père Goriot"] improved; only, are not all these pretty manners acquired at the expense of the soul?"

During his stay at Aix he met an excellent opportunity to go to Italy; the Duc de Fitz-James, who was travelling southward, invited him to become a member of his party. He discusses the economical problem (in writing to his mother) with his usual intensity, and throws what will seem to the modern traveller the light of enchantment upon that golden age of cheapness.

Occupying the fourth place in the carriage of the Duchesse de Castries, his quarter of the total travelling expenses from Geneva to Rome (carriage, beds, food, &c.) was to be fifty dollars! But he was ultimately prevented from joining the party. He went to Italy some years later.

He mentions, in 1833, that the chapter entitled "Juana," in the superb tale of "Les Marana," as also the story of "La Grenadière," was written in a single night. He gives at the same period this account of his habits of work: "I must tell you that I am up to my neck in excessive work. My life is mechanically arranged. I go to bed at six or seven in the evening, with the chickens; I wake up at one in the morning and work till eight; then I take something light, a cup of pure coffee, and get into the shafts of my cab until four; I receive, I take a bath, or I go out, and after dinner I go to bed. I must lead this life for some months longer, in order not to be overwhelmed by my obligations. The profit comes slowly; my debts are inexorable and fixed. Now, it is certain that I will make a great fortune; but I must wait for it, and work for three years. I must go over things, correct them again, put everything à l'état monumental; thankless work not counted, without immediate profit." He speaks of working at this amazing rate for three years longer;

in reality he worked for fifteen. But two years after the declaration we have just quoted it seemed to him that he should break down : " My poor sister, I am draining the cup to the dregs. It is in vain that I work my fourteen hours a day; I cannot do enough. While I write this to you I find myself so weary that I have just sent Auguste to take back my word from certain engagements that I had formed. I am so weak that I have advanced my dinner-hour in order to go to bed earlier; and I go nowhere." The next year he writes to his mother, who had apparently complained of his silence: " My good mother, do me the charity to let me carry my burden without suspecting my heart. A letter, for me, you see, is not only money, but an hour of sleep and a drop of blood."

We spoke just now of Balzac's sentimental consolations; but it appears that at times he was more acutely conscious of what he missed than of what he enjoyed. "As for the soul," he writes to Madame Carraud in 1833, "I am profoundly sad. My work alone sustains me in life. Is there then to be no woman for me in this world? My physical melancholy and ennui last longer and grow more frequent. To fall from this crushing labour to nothing—not to have near me that soft, caressing mind of woman, for whom I have done so much!" He had, however, a devoted feminine friend, to whom none of the letters in these volumes are addressed, but who is several times alluded to. This lady, Madame de Berny, died in 1836, and Balzac speaks of her ever afterward with extraordinary tenderness and veneration. But if there had been a passion between them it was only a passionate friendship. "Ah, my dear mother," he writes on New Year's day, 1836, " I am harrowed with grief. Madame de Berny is dying; it is impossible to doubt it. No one but God and myself knows what my despair is. And I must work—work while I weep!" He writes of Madame de Berny at the time of her death as follows. The letter is addressed to a lady with whom he was in correspondence more or less sentimental, but whom he never saw : " The person whom I have lost was more than a mother, more than a friend, more than any creature can be for another. The term *divinity* only can explain her. She had sustained me by word, by act, by devotion, during my worst weather. If I live, it is by her; she was everything for me. Although for two years illness and time had separated us, we were visible at a distance for each other. She reacted upon me; she was a moral sun. Madame de Mortsauf, in the 'Lys dans la Vallée,' is a pale expression of this person's slightest qualities." Three years afterward he writes to his sister : " I am alone against all my troubles, and formerly, to help me to resist them,

I had with me the sweetest and bravest person in the world; a woman who every day is born again in my heart, and whose divine qualities make the friendships that are compared with hers seem pale. I have now no adviser in my literary difficulties; I have no guide but the fatal thought, 'What would she say if she were living?'" And he goes on to enumerate some of his actual and potential friends. He tells his sister that she herself might have been for him a close intellectual comrade if her duties of wife and mother had not given her too many other things to think about. The same is true of Madame Carraud: "Never has a more extraordinary mind been more smothered: she will die in her corner unknown! George Sand," he continues, "would speedily be my friend; she has no pettiness whatever in her soul—none of the low jealousies that obscure so many contemporary talents. Dumas resembles her in this; but she has not the critical sense. Madame Hanska is all this; but I cannot weigh upon her destiny." Madame Hanska was the Polish lady whom he ultimately married and of whom we shall speak. Meanwhile, for a couple of years (1836 and 1837), he carried on an exchange of opinions, of the order that the French call *intimes*, with the unseen correspondent to whom we have alluded, and who figures in these volumes as "Louise." The letters, however, are not love-letters;

Balzac, indeed, seems chiefly occupied in calming the ardour of the lady, who was evidently a woman of social distinction. "Don't have any friendship for me," he writes; "I need too much. Like all people who struggle, suffer, and work, I am exacting, mistrustful, wilful, capricious. . . . If I had been a woman, I should have loved nothing so much as some soul buried like a well in the desert—discovered only when you place yourself directly under the star which indicates it to the thirsty Arab."

His first letter to Madame Hanska here given bears the date of 1835; but we are informed in a note that he had at that moment been for some time in correspondence with her. The correspondence had begun, if we are not mistaken, on Madame Hanska's side, before they met; she had written to him as a literary admirer. She was a Polish lady of great fortune, with an invalid husband. After her husband's death, projects of marriage defined themselves more vividly, but practical considerations kept them for a long time in the background. Balzac had first to pay off his debts, and Madame Hanska, as a Polish subject of the Czar Nicholas, was not in a position to marry from one day to another. The growth of their intimacy is, however, amply reflected in these volumes, and the dénoûment presents itself with a certain dramatic force. Balzac's letters to his future wife, as to every one else, deal almost exclusively with his financial situation. He discusses the details of this matter with all his correspondents, who apparently have—or are expected to have—his monetary entanglements at their fingers' ends. It is a constant enumeration of novels and tales begun or delivered, revised or bargained for. The tone is always profoundly sombre and bitter. The reader's general impression is that of lugubrious egotism. It is the rarest thing in the world that there is an allusion to anything but Balzac's own affairs, and the most sordid details of his own affairs. Hardly an echo of the life of his time, of the world he lived in, finds its way into his letters; there are no anecdotes, no impressions, no opinions, no descriptions, no allusions to things heard, people seen, emotions felt —other emotions, at least, than those of the exhausted or the exultant worker. The reason of all this is of course very obvious. A man could not be such a worker as Balzac and be much else besides. The note of animal spirits which we observed in his early letters is sounded much less frequently as time goes on; although the extraordinary robustness and exuberance of his temperament plays richly into his books. The "Contes Drôlatiques" are full of it and his conversation was also full of it. But the letters constantly show us a man with the edge of his spontaneity gone—a man groaning and sighing as from Promethean lungs, complaining of his tasks, denouncing his enemies, in complete ill humour, generally, with life. Of any expression of enjoyment of the world, of the beauties of nature, art, literature, history, human character, these pages are singularly destitute. And yet we know that such enjoyment—instinctive, unreasoning, essential—is half the inspiration of the poet. The truth is that Balzac was as little as possible of a poet; he often speaks of himself as one, but he deserved the name as little as his own Canalis or his own Rubempré. He was neither a poet nor a moralist, though the latter title in France is often bestowed upon him—a fact which strikingly helps to illustrate the Gallic lightness of soil in the moral region. Balzac was the hardest and deepest of *prosateurs*; the earth-scented facts of life, which the poet puts under his feet, he had put above his head. Obviously there went on within him a large and constant intellectual unfolding. His mind must have had a history of its own—a history of which it would be very interesting to have an occasional glimpse. But the history is not related here, even in glimpses. His books are full of ideas; his letters have almost none. It is probably not unfair to argue from this fact that there were few ideas that he greatly cared for. Making all allowance for the pressure and tyranny of circumstances, we may believe that if he had greatly cared to *se recueillir*, as the French say—greatly cared, in the Miltonic phrase, "to interpose a little ease"—he would sometimes have found an opportunity for it. Perpetual work, when it is joyous and salubrious, is a very fine thing; but perpetual work, when it is executed with the temper which more than half the time appears to have been Balzac's, has in it something almost debasing. We constantly feel that his work would have been greatly better if the Muse of "business" had been elbowed away by her larger-browed sister. Balzac himself, doubtless, often felt in the same way; but, on the whole, "business" was what he most cared for. The "Comédie Humaine" represents an immense amount of joy, of spontaneity, of irrepressible artistic life. Here and there in the letters this occasionally breaks out in accents of mingled exultation and despair. "Never," he writes in 1836, "has the torrent which bears me along been more rapid; never has a work more majestically terrible imposed 'itself upon the human brain. I go to my work as the gamester to the gaming-table; I am sleeping now only five hours and working eighteen; I shall arrive dead. . . . Write to me; be generous; take nothing in bad part, for you don't know how, at moments, I deplore this life of fire. But how can I jump out of the chariot?"

We have already had occasion in these pages to say that his great characteristic, far from being a passion for ideas, was a passion for *things*. We said just now that his books are full of ideas; but we must add that his letters make us feel that these ideas are themselves in a certain sense "things." They are pigments, properties, frippery; they are always concrete and available. Balzac cared for them only if they would fit into his inkstand.

He never jumped out of his chariot; but as the years went on he was able at times to let the reins hang more loosely. There is no evidence that he made the great fortune he had looked forward to; but he must have made a great deal of money. In the beginning his work was very poorly paid, but after his reputation was solidly established he received large sums. It is true that they were swallowed up in great part by his "debts"—that dusky, vaguely outlined, insatiable maw which we see grimacing for ever behind him, like the face on a fountain which should find itself receiving a stream instead of giving it out. But he travelled (working all the while en route). He went to Italy, to Germany, to Russia; he built houses, he bought pictures and pottery. One of his journeys illustrates his singular mixture of economic and romantic impulses. He made a breathless pilgrimage to the island of

Sardinia to examine the scoriæ of certain silver mines, anciently worked by the Romans, in which he had heard that the metal was still to be found. The enterprise was fantastic and impracticable; but he pushed his excursion through night and day, as he had written the "Père Goriot." In his relative prosperity, when once it was established, there are strange lapses and stumbling-places. After he had built and was living in his somewhat fantastical villa of Les Jardies at Sèvres, close to Paris, he invites a friend to stay with him on these terms: "I can take you to board at forty sous a day, and for thirty-five francs you will have firewood enough for a month." In his jokes he is apt to betray the same preoccupation. Inviting Charles de Bernard and his wife to come to Les Jardies to help him to arrange his books, he adds that they will have fifty sous a day and their wine. He is constantly talking of his expenses, of what he spends in cab-hire and postage. His letters to the Countess Hanska are filled with these details. "Yesterday I was running about all day; twenty-five francs for carriages!" The man of business is never absent. For the first representations of his plays he arranges his audiences with an eye to effect, like an *impresario* or an agent. In the boxes, for "Vautrin," "I insist upon there being handsome women." Presenting a copy of the

"Comédie Humaine" to the Austrain ambassador, he accompanies it with a letter calling attention, in the most elaborate manner, to the typographical beauty and the cheapness of the work; the letter reads like a prospectus or an advertisement.

In 1840 (he was forty years old) he thought seriously of marriage—with this remark as the preface to the announcement : "*Je ne veux plus avoir de cœur !* . . . If you meet a young girl of twenty-two," he goes on, "with a fortune of 200,000 francs, or even of 100,000, provided it can be used in business, you will think of me. I want a woman who shall be able to be what the events of my life may demand of her—the wife of an ambassador or a housewife at Les Jardies. But don't speak of this; it's a secret. She must be an ambitious, clever girl." This project, however, was not carried out; Balzac had no time to marry. But his friendship with Madame Hanska became more and more absorbing, and though their project of marriage, which was executed in 1850, was kept a profound secret until after the ceremony, it is apparent that they had had it a long time in their thoughts.

For this lady Balzac's esteem and admiration seem to have been unbounded; and his letters to her, which in the second volume are very numerous, contain many noble and delicate passages. "You know too well,"

he says to her somewhere, with a happy choice of words
—for his diction was here and there as felicitous as it
was generally intolerable—"*Vous savez trop bien que
tout ce qui n'est pas vous n'est que surface, sottise et vains
palliatifs de l'absence.*" "You must be proud of your
children," he writes to his sister from Poland: "such
daughters are the recompense of your life. You must
not be unjust to destiny; you may now accept many
misfortunes. It is like myself with Madame Hanska.
The gift of her affection explains all my troubles, my
weariness and my toil; I was paying to evil, in
advance, the price of such a treasure. As Napoleon
said, we pay for everything here below; nothing is
stolen. It seems to me that I have paid very little.
Twenty-five years of toil and struggle are nothing
as the purchase-money of an attachment so splendid,
so radiant, so complete."

Madame Hanska appears to have come rarely to
Paris, and, when she came, to have shrouded her
visits in mystery; but Balzac arranged several meetings with her abroad and visited her at St. Petersburg
and on her Polish estates. He was devotedly fond
of her children, and the tranquil, opulent family life
to which she introduced him appears to have been
one of the greatest pleasures he had known. In
several passages which, for Balzac, may be called

graceful and playful, he expresses his homesickness for her chairs and tables, her books, the sight of her dresses. Here is something, in one of his letters to her, that is worth quoting : "In short, this is the game that I play; four men will have had, in this century, an immense influence—Napoleon, Cuvier, O'Connell. I should like to be the fourth. The first lived on the blood of Europe ; *il s'est inoculé des armées ;* the second espoused the globe; the third became the incarnation of a people ; I—I shall have carried a whole society in my head. But there will have been in me a much greater and much happier being than the writer—and that is your slave. My feeling is finer, grander, more complete, than all the satisfactions of vanity or of glory. Without this plenitude of the heart I should never have accomplished the tenth part of my work ; I should not have had this ferocious courage." During a few days spent at Berlin, on his way back from St. Petersburg, he gives his impressions of the "capital of Brandenburg" in a tone which almost seems to denote a prevision of the style of allusion to this locality and its inhabitants which was to become fashionable among his countrymen thirty years later. Balzac detested Prussia and the Prussians. "It is owing to this charlatanism [the spacious distribution of the streets, &c.] that Berlin has a more populous look than Petersburg; I would have said "more animated" look if I had been speaking of another people; but the Prussian, with his brutal heaviness, will never be able to do anything but crush. To produce the movement of a great European capital you must have less beer and bad tobacco and more of the French or Italian spirit; or else you must have the great industrial and commercial ideas which have produced the gigantic development of London; but Berlin and its inhabitants will never be anything but an ugly little city, inhabited by an ugly big people."

"I have seen Tieck *en famille*," he says in another letter. "He seemed pleased with my homage. He had an old countess, his contemporary in spectacles, almost an octogenarian—a mummy with a green eye-shade, whom I supposed to be a domestic divinity. . . . I am at home again; it is half-past six in the evening, and I have eaten nothing since this morning. Berlin is the city of ennui; I should die here in a week. Poor Humboldt is dying of it; he drags with him everywhere his nostalgia for Paris."

Balzac passed the winter of 1848–'49 and several months more at Vierzschovnia, the Polish estate of Madame Hanska and her children. His health had been gravely impaired, and the doctors had absolutely forbidden him to work. His inexhaustible and indefatigable brain had at last succumbed to fatigue. But the prize was gained; his debts were paid; he was looking forward to owning at last the money that he made. He could afford—relatively speaking at least—to rest. His fame had been solidly built up; the public recognised his greatness. Already, in 1846, he had written:—" You will learn with pleasure, I am sure, that there is an immense reaction in my favour. At last I have conquered! Once more my protecting star has watched over me. . . . At this moment the public and the papers turn toward me favourably; more than that, there is a sort of acclammation, a general consecration. . . . It is a great year for me, dear Countess."

To be ill and kept from work was, for Balzac, to be a chained Prometheus; but there was much during these last months to alleviate his impatience. His letters at this period are easier, less painfully preoccupied than at any other; and he found in Poland better medical advice than he deemed obtainable in Paris. He was preparing a house in Paris to receive him as a married man—preparing it apparently with great splendour. At Les Jardies the pictures and divans and tapestries had mostly been nominal—had been present only in grand names, chalked grotesquely upon the empty walls. But during the last years of his life Balzac appears to have been a great collector.

He bought many pictures and other objects of value; in particular there figures in these letters a certain set of Florentine furniture which he was willing to sell again, but to sell only to a royal purchaser. The King of Holland appears to have been in treaty for it. Readers of the "Comédie Humaine" have no need to be reminded of the author's passion for furniture; nowhere else are there such loving or such invidious descriptions of it. "Decidedly," he writes once to Madame Hanska, "I will send to Tours for the Louis XVI. secretary and bureau; the room will then be complete. It's a matter of a thousand francs; but for a thousand francs what can one get in modern furniture? ' *Des platitudes bourgeoises, des misères sans valeur et sans goût.*"

Old Madame de Balzac was her son's factotum and universal agent. His letters from Vierzschovnia are filled with prescriptions of activity for his mother, accompanied always with the urgent reminder that she is to use cabs *ad libitum*. He goes into the minutest details (she was overlooking the preparation of his house in the Rue Fortunée, which must have been converted into a very picturesque residence):—"The carpet in the dining-room must certainly be readjusted. Try and make M. Henry send his carpet-layer. I owe that man a good *pour-boire:* he laid all the carpets, and I once was rough with him. You must tell him that in September he can come and get his present. I want particularly to give it to him myself."

His mother occasionally annoyed him by unreasonable exactions and untimely interferences. There is an episode of a letter which she writes to him at Verzschovnia, and which, coming to Madame Hanska's knowledge, endangers his prospect of marriage. He complains bitterly to his sister that his mother cannot get it out of her head that he is still fifteen years old. But there is something very touching in his constant tenderness toward her—as well as something very characteristically French—very characteristic of the French sentiment of family consistency and solidarity—in the way in which, by constantly counting upon her practical aptitude and zeal, he makes her a fellow-worker toward the great total of his fame and fortune. At fifty years of age, at the climax of his distinction, announcing to her his brilliant marriage, he signs himself *Ton fils soumis*. To his old friend Madame Carraud he speaks thus of this same event: " The dénoûment of that great and beautiful drama of the heart which has lasted these sixteen years. . . . Three days ago I married the only woman I have loved, whom I love more than ever, and whom I shall love until death. I believe that this union is the recompense that God has held in reserve for me through so many adversities, years of work, difficulties suffered and surmounted. I had neither a happy youth nor a flowering spring; I shall have the most brilliant summer, the sweetest of all autumns." It had been, as Balzac says, a drama of the heart, and the dénoûment was of the heart alone. Madame Hanska, on her marriage, made over her large fortune to her children.

Balzac had at last found rest and happiness, but his enjoyment of these blessings was brief. The energy that he had expended to gain them left nothing behind it. His terrible industry had blasted the soil it passed over; he had sacrificed to his work the very things he worked for. One cannot do what Balzac did and live. He was enfeebled, exhausted, broken. He died in Paris three months after his marriage. The reader feels that premature death is the logical, the harmonious, completion of such a career. The strongest man has but a certain fixed quantity of life to expend, and we may expect that if he works habitually fifteen hours a day, he will spend it while, arithmetically speaking, he is yet young.

We have been struck in reading these letters with the strong analogy between Balzac's career and that of the great English writer whose history was some time since so expansively written by Mr. Forster. Dickens and Balzac have much in common; as individuals they strongly resemble each other; their differences are chiefly differences of race. Each was a man of affairs, an active, practical man, with a temperament of almost phenomenal vigour and a prodigious quantity of life to expend. Each had a character and a will—what is nowadays called a personality—that imposed themselves irresistibly; each had a boundless self-confidence and a magnificent egotism. Each had always a hundred irons on the fire; each was resolutely determined to make money, and made it in large quantities. In intensity of imaginative power, the power of evoking visible objects and figures, seeing them themselves with the force of hullucination and making others see them all but just as vividly, they were almost equal. Here there is little to choose between them; they have had no rivals but each other and Shakespeare. But they most of all resemble each other in the fact that they treated their extraordinary imaginative force as a matter of business; that they worked it as a goldmine, violently and brutally; overworked and ravaged it. They succumbed to the task that they had laid upon themselves and they are as similar in their deaths as in their lives. Of course, if Dickens is an English Balzac, he is a very English Balzac. His fortune was the easier of the two and his prizes were greater than the other's. His brilliant, opulent English prosperity, centered in a home and diffused through a progeny, is in strong contrast with the almost scholastic penury and obscurity of much of Balzac's career. But the analogy is still very striking.

In speaking of Balzac elsewhere in these pages we insisted upon the fact that he lacked charm; but we said that our last word upon him should be that he had incomparable power. His letters only confirm these impressions, and above all they deepen our sense of his strength. They contain little that is delicate and not a great deal that is positively agreeable; but they express an energy before which we stand lost in wonder, in an admiration that almost amounts to awe. The fact that his omnivorous observation of the great human spectacle has no echo in his letters only makes us feel how concentrated and how intense was the labour that went on in his closet. Certainly no solider intellectual work has ever been achieved by man. And in spite of the massive egotism, the personal absoluteness, to which these pages testify, they leave us with a downright kindness for the author. He was coarse, but he was tender; he was corrupt, in a way, but he was immensely natural. If he was ungracefully eager and voracious, awkwardly blind to all things that did not contribute to his personal plan, at least his egotism was exerted in a great cause. The "Comédie Humaine" has a thousand faults, but it is a monumental excuse.

GEORGE SAND.

AMONG the eulogies and dissertations called forth by the death of the great writer who shared with Victor Hugo the honour of literary pre-eminence in France, quite the most valuable was the short notice published in the "Journal des Débats," by M. Taine. In this notice the apostle of the "milieu" and the "moment" very justly remarked that George Sand is an exceptionally good case for the study of the pedigree of a genius —for ascertaining the part of prior generations in forming one of those minds which shed back upon them the light of glory. What renders Madame Sand so available an example of the operation of heredity is the fact that the process went on very publicly, as one may say; that her ancestors were people of qualities at once very strongly marked and very abundantly recorded. The record has been kept in a measure by George Sand herself. When she was fifty years old she wrote her memoirs, and in this prolix and imperfect

but extremely entertaining work a large space is devoted
to the heroine's parents and grandparents.

It was a very picturesque pedigree—quite an ideal
pedigree for a romancer. Madame Sand's great-grandfather was the Maréchal Maurice de Saxe, one of the
very few generals in the service of Louis XV. who
tasted frequently of victory. Maurice de Saxe was a
royal bastard, the son of Augustus II., surnamed the
Strong, Elector of Saxony and King of Poland, and
of a brilliant mistress, Aurore de Königsmark. The
victories of the Maréchal de Saxe were not confined to
the battlefield ; one of his conquests was an agreeable
actress much before the Parisian public. This lady
became the mother of Madame Sand's grandmother, who
was honourably brought up and married at a very early
age to the Comte de Horn. The Comte de Horn shortly
died, and his widow, after an interval, accepted the
hand of M. Dupin de Francueil, a celebrity and a very
old man. M. Dupin was one of the brilliant figures in
Paris society during the period immediately preceding
the Revolution. He had a large fortune, and he too
was a conqueror. A sufficiently elaborate portrait of
him may be found in that interesting, if disagreeable,
book, the " Mémoires " of Madame d'Epinay. This
clever lady had been one of his spoils of victory. Old
enough to be his wife's grandfather, he survived his

marriage but a few years, and died with all his illusions intact, on the eve of the Revolution, leaving to Madame Dupin an only son. His wife outweathered the tempest, which, however, swept away her fortune; though she was able to buy a small property in the country—the rustic Château de Nohant, which George Sand has so often introduced into her writings. Here she settled herself with her son, a boy of charming promise, who was in due time drawn into the ranks of Napoleon's conquering legions. Young Dupin became an ardent Bonapartist and an accomplished soldier. He won rapid promotion. In one of the so-called "glorious" Italian campaigns he met a young girl who had followed the army from Paris, from a personal interest in one of its officers; and falling very honestly in love with her he presently married her, to the extreme chagrin of his mother. This young girl, the daughter of a birdcatcher, and, as George Sand calls her, an "enfant du vieux pavé de Paris," became the mother of the great writer. She was a child of the people and a passionate democrat, and in the person of her daughter we see the confluence of a plebeian stream with a strain no less (in spite of its irregularity) than royal. On the paternal side Madame Sand was cousin (in we know not what degree) to the present Bourbon claimant of the French crown; on the other she was affiliated to the stock which, out of the "vieux pavé," makes the barricades before which Bourbons go down.

This may very properly be called a "picturesque" descent; it is in a high degree what the French term *accidenté*. Its striking feature is that each conjunction through which it proceeds is a violent or irregular one. Two are illegitimate—those of the King of Poland and his son with their respective mistresses; the other two, though they had the sanction of law, may be called in a manner irregular. It was irregular for the fresh young Comtesse de Horn to be married to a man of seventy; it was irregular in her son, young Dupin, to make a wife of another man's mistress, often as this proceeding has been reversed. If it is a fair description of Madame Sand to say that she was, during that portion of her career which established her reputation, an apostle of the rights of love *quand même*, a glance at her pedigree shows that this was a logical disposition. She was herself more sensibly the result of a series of love-affairs than most of us. In each of these cases the woman had been loved with a force that asserted itself in contradiction to propriety or to usage.

We may observe moreover, in this course of transmission, the opposition of the element of insubordination and disorder (which sufficiently translated itself in outward acts in Madame Sand's younger years) and the "official" element, the respectable, conservative, exclusive strain. Three of our author's ancestresses were light women—women at odds with society, defiant of it, and, theoretically at least, discountenanced by it. The grand-daughter of the Comtesse de Königsmark and of Mademoiselle Verrières, the daughter of Madame Dupin the younger, could hardly have been expected not to take up this hereditary quarrel. It is striking that on the feminine side of the house what is called respectability was a very relative quality. Madame Dupin the elder took it very hard when her only and passionately loved son married a *femme galante*. She did not herself belong to this category, and her opposition is easily conceivable; but the reader of "L'Histoire de ma Vie" cannot help smiling a little when he reflects that this irreconcilable mother-in-law was the offspring of two illegitimate unions, and that her mother and grandmother had each enjoyed a plurality of lovers. At the same time, if there is anything more striking in George Sand, as a literary figure, than a certain traditional Bohemianism, it is that other very different quality which we just now called official, and which is constantly interrupting and complicating her Bohemianism. "George Sand immoral?" I once heard one of her more conditional admirers exclaim. "The fault I find with her is that she is so insufferably virtuous."

The military and aristocratic side of her lineage is attested by this "virtuous" property—by her constant tendency to edification and didacticism, her love of philosophizing and preaching, of smoothing and harmonizing things, and by her great literary gift, her noble and imperturbable style, the style which, if she had been a man, would have seated her in that temple of all the proprieties, the French Academy.

It is not the purpose of these few pages to recapitulate the various items of George Sand's biography. Many of these are to be found in "L'Histoire de ma Vie," a work which, although it was thought disappointing at the time of its appearance, is very well worth reading. It was given to the world day by day, as the feuilleton of a newspaper, and, like all the author's compositions, it has the stamp of being written to meet a current engagement. It lacks plan and proportion; the book is extremely ill made. But it has a great charm, and it contains three or four of the best portraits —the only portraits, we were on the point of saying— that the author has painted. The story was begun, but was never really finished; this was the public's disappointment. It contained a great deal about Madame Sand's grandmother and her father—a large part of two volumes are given to a transcript of her father's letters (and very charming letters they are). It abounded in anecdotes of the writer's childhood, her playmates, her pet animals, her school-adventures, the nuns at the Couvent des Anglaises by whom she was educated; it related the juvenile unfolding of her mind, her fits of early piety, and her first acquaintance with Montaigne and Rousseau; it contained a superabundance of philosophy, psychology, morality and harmless gossip about people unknown to the public; but it was destitute of just that which the public desired—an explicit account of the more momentous incidents of the author's maturity. When she reaches the point at which her story becomes peculiarly interesting (up to that time it has simply been agreeable and entertaining) she throws up the game and drops the curtain. In other words, she talks no scandal—a consummation devoutly to be rejoiced in.

The reader nevertheless deems himself unfairly used, and takes his revenge in seeing something very typical of the author in the shortcomings of the work. He declares it to be a nondescript performance, which has neither the value of truth nor the illusion of fiction; and he inquires why the writer should preface her task with such solemn remarks upon the edifying properties of autobiography, and adorn it with so pompous an epigraph, if she meant simply to tell what she might tell without trouble. It may be remembered, however, that George Sand has sometimes been compared to Goethe, and that there is this ground for the comparison—that in form "L'Histoire de ma Vie" greatly resembles the "Dichtung und Wahrheit." There is the same charming, complacent expatiation upon youthful memories, the same arbitrary confidences and silences, the same digressions and general judgments, the same fading away of the narrative on the threshold of maturity. We should never look for analogies between George Sand and Goethe; but we should say that the lady's long autobiographic fragment is in fact extremely typical—the most so indeed of all her works. It shows in the highest degree her great strength and her great weakness—her unequalled faculty of improvisation, as it may be called, and her peculiar want of veracity. Every one will recognise what we mean by the first of these items. People may like George Sand or not, but they can hardly deny that she is the great *improvisatrice* of literature—the writer who best answers to Shelley's description of the skylark singing "in profuse strains of unpremeditated art." No writer has produced such great effects with an equal absence of premeditation.

On the other hand, what we have called briefly and crudely her want of veracity requires some explanation. It is doubtless a condition of her serene volubility;

but if this latter is a great literary gift, its value is impaired by our sense that it rests to a certain extent upon a weakness. There is something very liberal and universal in George Sand's genius, as well as very masculine; but our final impression of her always is that she is a woman and a Frenchwoman. Women, we are told, do not value the truth for its own sake, but only for some personal use they make of it. My present criticism involves an assent to this somewhat cynical dogma. Add to this that woman, if she happens to be French, has an extraordinary taste for investing objects with a graceful drapery of her own contrivance, and it will be found that George Sand's cast of mind includes both the generic and the specific idiosyncrasy. We have more than once heard her readers say (whether it was professed fact or admitted fiction that they had in hand), "It is all very well, but I can't believe a word of it!" There is something very peculiar in this inability to believe George Sand even in that relative sense in which we apply the term to novelists at large. We believe Balzac, we believe Gustave Flaubert, we believe Dickens and Thackeray and Miss Austen. Dickens is far more incredible than George Sand, and yet he produces much more illusion. In spite of her plausibility, the author of "Consuelo" always appears to be telling a fairy-tale. We say in spite of her plausibility, but we might rather say that her excessive plausibility is the reason of our want of faith. The narrative is too smooth, too fluent; the narrator has a virtuous independence that the Muse of history herself might envy her. The effect it produces is that of a witness who is eager to tell more than is asked him, the worth of whose testimony is impaired by its importunity. The thing is beautifully done, but you feel that rigid truth has come off as it could; the author has not a high standard of exactitude; she never allows facts to make her uncomfortable. "L'Histoire de ma Vie" is full of charming recollections and impressions of Madame Sand's early years, of delightful narrative, of generous and elevated sentiment; but we have constantly the feeling that it is what children call "made up." If the fictitious quality in our writer's reminiscences is very sensible, of course the fictitious quality in her fictions is still more so; and it must be said that in spite of its odd mixture of the didactic and the irresponsible, " L'Histoire de ma Vie " sails nearer to the shore than its professedly romantic companions.

The usual objection to the novels, and a very just one, is that they contain no living figures, no people who stand on their feet, and who, like so many of the creations of the other great novelists, have become part of the public fund of allusion and quotation. As portraits George Sand's figures are vague in outline deficient in detail. Several of those, however, which occupy the foreground of her memoirs have a remarkable vividness. In the four persons associated chiefly with her childhood and youth she really makes us believe. The first of these is the great figure which appears quite to have filled up the background of her childhood—almost to the exclusion of the child herself—that of her grandmother, Madame Dupin, the daughter of the great soldier. The second is that of her father, who was killed at Nohant by a fall from his horse, while she was still a young girl. The third is that of her mother—a particularly remarkable portrait. The fourth is the grotesque but softly-lighted image of Deschartres, the old pedagogue who served as tutor to Madame Sand and her half-brother; the latter youth being the fruit of an "amourette" between the Commandant Dupin and one of his mother's maids. Madame Dupin philosophically adopted the child; she dated from the philosophers of the preceding century. It is worth noting that George Sand's other playmate—the "Caroline" of the memoirs—was a half-sister on her mother's side, a little girl whose paternity antedated the Commandant Dupin's acquaintance with his wife.

In George Sand's account of her father there is

something extremely delightful; full of filial passion as it is, and yet of tender discrimination. She makes him a charming figure—the ideal "gallant" Frenchman of the old type; a passionate soldier and a delightful talker, leaving fragments of his heart on every bush; clever, tender, full of artistic feeling and of Gallic gaiety—having in fair weather and foul always the *mot pour rire*. His daughter's publication of his letters has been called a rather inexpensive mode of writing her own biography; but these letters—charming, natural notes to his mother during his boyish campaigns—were well worth bringing to the light. All George Sand is in the author's portrait of her mother; all her great merit and all her strange defects. We should recommend the perusal of the scattered passages of "L'Histoire de ma Vie" which treat of this lady to a person ignorant of Madame Sand and desiring to make her acquaintance; they are an excellent measure of her power. On one side an extraordinary familiarity with the things of the mind, the play of character, the psychological mystery, and a beautiful clearness and quietness, a beautiful instinct of justice in dealing with them; on the other side a startling absence of delicacy, of reticence, of the sense of certain spiritual sanctities and reservations. That a woman should deal in so free-handed a fashion with a female parent upon whom nature and time have enabled her to look down from an eminence, seems at first a considerable anomaly; and the woman who does it must to no slight extent have shaken herself free from the bonds of custom. We do not mean that George Sand talks scandal and tittle-tattle about her mother; but that Madame Dupin having been a light woman and an essentially irregular character, her daughter holds her up in the sunshine of her own luminous contemplation with all her imperfections on her head. At the same time it is very finely done—very intelligently and appreciatively; it is at the worst a remarkable exhibition of the disinterestedness of a great imagination.

It must be remembered also that the young Aurore Dupin "belonged" much more to her grandmother than to her mother, to whom in her childhood she was only lent, as it were, on certain occasions. There is nothing in all George Sand better than her history of the relations of these two women, united at once and divided (after the death of the son and husband) by a common grief and a common interest; full of mutual jealousies and defiances, and alternately quarrelling and "making up" over their little girl. Jealousy carried the day. One was a patrician and the other a jealous democrat, and no common ground was attainable. Among the reproaches addressed by her critics to the author of "Valentine" and "Valvèdre" is the charge of a very imperfect knowledge of family life and a tendency to strike false notes in the portrayal of it. It is apparent that both before and after her marriage her observation of family life was peculiarly restricted and perverted. Of what it must have been in the former case this figure of her mother may give us an impression; of what it was in the latter we may get an idea from the somewhat idealized *ménage* in "Lucrezia Floriani."

George Sand's literary fame came to her very abruptly. The history of her marriage, which is briefly related in her memoirs, is sufficiently well known. The thing was done, on her behalf, by her relatives (she had a small property) and the husband of their choice, M. Dudevant, was neither appreciative nor sympathetic. His tastes were vulgar and his manners frequently brutal; and after a short period of violent dissension and the birth of two children, the young couple separated. It is safe to say, however, that even with an "appreciative" husband Madame Sand would not have accepted matrimony once for all. She represents herself as an essentially dormant, passive and shrinking nature, upon which celebrity and productiveness were forced by circumstances, and whose unconsciousness of its own powers was dissipated only by the violent breaking of a spell. There is evidently much truth in these assertions; for of all great literary people few strike us as having had a smaller measure of the more vulgar avidities and ambitions. But for all that, it is tolerably plain that even by this profoundly slumbering genius the most brilliant matrimonial associate would have been utterly overmatched.

Madame Sand, even before she had written "Indiana," was too imperious a force, too powerful a machine, to make the limits of her activity coincide with those of wifely submissiveness. It is very possible that for her to write "Indiana" and become a woman of letters a spell had to be broken; only, the real breaking of the spell lay not in the vulgarity of a husband, but in the deepening sense, quickened by the initiations of marriage, that outside of the quiet meadows of Nohant there was a vast affair called *life*, with which she had a capacity for making acquaintance at first hand. This making acquaintance with life at first hand is, roughly speaking, the great thing that, as a woman, Madame Sand achieved; and she was predestined to achieve it. She was more masculine than any man she might have married; and what powerfully masculine person—even leaving genius apart—is content at five-and-twenty with submissiveness and renunciation ? "It was a mere accident that George Sand was a woman," a person who had known her well said to the writer of these pages; and though the statement needs an ultimate corrective, it represents a great deal of truth. What was feminine in her was the quality of her genius; the *quantity* of it—its force, and mass, and energy—was masculine, and masculine were her temperament and character. All this masculinity needed to set itself free; which it proceeded to do according to its temporary light. Her separation from her husband was judicial, and assured her the custody of her children; but as, in return for this privilege, she made financial concessions, it left her without income (though in possession of the property of Nohant) and dependent upon her labours for support. She had betaken herself to Paris in quest of labour, and it was with this that her career began.

This determination to address herself to life at first hand—this personal, moral impulse, which was not at all a literary impulse—was her great inspiration, the great pivot on which her history wheeled round into the bright light of experience and fame. It is, strictly, as we said just now, the most interesting thing about her. Such a disposition was not customary, was not what is usually called womanly, was not modest nor delicate, nor, for many other persons, in any way comfortable. But it had one great merit : it was in a high degree original and active ; and because it was this it constitutes the great service which George Sand rendered her sex—a service in which, we hasten to add, there was as much of fortune as of virtue. The disposition to cultivate an " acquaintance with life at first hand" might pass for an elegant way of describing the attitude of many young women who are never far to seek, and who render no service to their own sex—whatever they may render to the other. George Sand's superiority was that she looked at life from a high point of view, and that she had an extraordinary talent. She painted fans and glove-boxes to get money, and got very little. "Indiana," however —a mere experiment—put her on her feet, and her reputation dawned. She found that she could write, and she took up her pen never to lay it down. Her early novels, all of them brilliant, and each one at that day a literary event, followed each other with extraordinary rapidity. About this sudden entrance into literature, into philosophy, into rebellion, and into a great many other matters, there are various different things to be said. Very remarkable, indeed, was the immediate development of the literary faculty in this needy young woman who lived in cheap lodgings and looked for " employment." She wrote as a bird sings ;

but unlike most birds, she found it unnecessary to indulge, by way of prelude, in twitterings and vocal exercises; she broke out at once with her full volume of expression. From the beginning she had a great style. "Indiana," perhaps, is rather in falsetto, as the first attempts of young, sentimental writers are apt to be; but in "Valentine," which immediately followed, there is proof of the highest literary instinct —an art of composition, a propriety and harmony of diction, such as belong only to the masters.

One might certainly have asked Madame Sand, as Lord Jeffrey asked Macaulay on the appearance of his first contribution to the "Edinburgh Review," where in the world she had picked up that style. She had picked it up apparently at Nohant, among the meadows and the *traînes*—the deeply-sunken byroads among the thick, high hedges. Her language had to the end an odour of the hawthorn and the wild honeysuckle—the mark of the "climat souple et chaud," as she somewhere calls it, from which she had received "l'initiation première." How completely her great literary faculty was a matter of intuition is indicated by the fact that "L'Histoire de ma Vie" contains no allusion to it, no account of how she learned to write, no record of effort or apprenticeship. She appears to have begun at a stage of the journey at which most talents arrive only when their time is up. During the five-and-forty years of her literary career, she had something to say about most things in the universe; but the thing about which she had least to say was the writer's, the inventor's, the romancer's art. She possessed it by the gift of God, but she seems never to have felt the temptation to examine the pulse of the machine.

To the cheap edition of her novels, published in 1852-'3, she prefixed a series of short prefaces, in which she relates the origin of each tale—the state of mind and the circumstances in which it was written. These prefaces are charming; they almost justify the publisher's declaration that they form the "most beautiful examination that a great mind has ever made of itself." But they all commemorate the writer's extraordinary facility and spontaneity. One of them says that on her way home from Spain she was shut up for some days at an inn, where she had her children at play in the same room with her. She found that the sight of their play quickened her imagination, and while they tumbled about the floor near her table, she produced "Gabriel"—a work which, though inspired by the presence of infancy, cannot be said to be addressed to infants. Of another story she relates that she wrote it at Fontainebleau, where she spent all her days wandering about the forest, making entomological collections, with her son. At night she came home and took up the thread of "La Dernière Aldini," on which she had never bestowed a thought all day. Being at Venice, much depressed, in a vast dusky room in an old palace that had been turned into an inn, while the sea wind roared about her windows, and brought up the sound of the carnival as a kind of melancholy wail, she began a novel by simply looking round her and describing the room and the whistling of the mingled tumult without. She finished it in a week, and, hardly reading it over, sent it to Paris as "Léone Léoni"—a masterpiece.

In the few prefatory lines to "Isidora" I remember she says something of this kind: "It was a beautiful young woman who used to come and see me, and profess to relate her sorrows. I saw that she was attitudinizing before me, and not believing herself a word of what she said. So it is not her I described in 'Isidora.'" This is a happy way of saying how a hint—a mere starting point—was enough for her. Particularly charming is the preface to the beautiful tale of "André"; it is a capital proof of what one may call the author's limpidity of reminiscence, and want of space alone prevents me from quoting it. She was at Venice, and she used to hear her maid-servant

P

and her sempstress, as they sat at work together, chattering in the next room. She listened to their talk in order to accustom her ear to the Venetian dialect, and in so doing she came into possession of a large amount of local gossip. The effect of it was to remind her of the small social life of the little country town near Nohant. The women told each other just such stories as might have been told there, and indulged in just such reflections and "appreciations" as would have been there begotten. She was reminded that men and women are everywhere the same, and at the same time she felt homesick. "I recalled the dirty, dusky streets, the tumble-down houses, the poor moss-grown roofs, the shrill concerts of cocks, children and cats, of my own little town. I dreamed too of our beautiful meadows, of our prefumed hay, of our little running streams, and of the botany beloved of old which I could follow now only on the muddy mosses and the floating weeds that adhered to the sides of the gondolas. I don't know amid what vague memories of various types I set in motion the least complex and the laziest of fictions. These types belonged quite as much to Venice as to Berry. Change dress and language, sky, landscape and architecture, the outside aspect of people and things, and you will find that at the bottom of all this man is always the same, and woman still more, because of the tenacity of her instincts."

George Sand says that she found she could write for an extraordinary length of time without weariness, and this is as far as she goes in the way of analysis of her inspiration. From the time she made the discovery to the day of her death her life was an extremely laborious one. She had evidently an extraordinary physical robustness. It was her constant practice to write at night, beginning after the rest of the world had gone to sleep. Alexandre Dumas the younger described her somewhere, during her latter years, as an old lady who came out into the garden at midday in a broad-brimmed hat and sat down on a bench or wandered slowly about. So she remained for hours, looking about her, musing, contemplating. She was gathering impressions, says M. Dumas, absorbing the universe, steeping herself in nature; and at night she would give all this forth as a sort of emanation. Without using too vague epithets one may accept this term "emanation" as a good account of her manner.

If it is needless to go into biographical detail, this is because George Sand's real history, the more interesting one, is the history of her mind. The history of her mind is of course closely connected with her personal history; she is indeed a writer whose personal situation, at a particular moment, is supposed to be reflected with peculiar vividness in her work. But to speak of her consistently we must regard the events of her life as intellectual events, and its landmarks as opinions, convictions, theories. The only difficulty is that such landmarks are nearly as numerous as the trees in a forest. Some, however, are more salient than others. Madame Sand's account of herself is that her ideal of life was repose, obscurity and idleness — long days in the country spent in botany and entomology. She affirms that her natural indolence was extreme, and that the need of money alone induced her to take her pen into her hand. As this need was constant, her activity was constant; but it was a perversion of the genius of a kind, simple, friendly, motherly, profoundly unambitious woman, who would have been amply content to take care of her family, live in slippers, gossip with peasants, walk in the garden and listen to the piano. All this is certainly so far true as that no person of equal celebrity ever made fewer explicit pretensions. She philosophized upon a great many things that she did not understand, and toward the close of her life, in especial, was apt to talk metaphysics, in writing, with a mingled volubility and vagueness which might have been taken to denote an undue self-confidence. But in such things as these, as they come from George Sand's pen, there is an air as of not expecting any one in particular to read them. She never took herself too much *au sérieux*—she never postured at all as a woman of letters. She scribbled, she might have said—scribbled as well as she could; but when she was not scribbling she never thought of it; though she liked to think of all the great things that were worth scribbling about—love and religion and science and art, and man's political destiny. Her reader feels that she has no vanity, and all her contemporaries agree that her generosity was extreme.

She calls herself a *sphinx bon enfant*, or says at least that she looked like one. Judgments may differ as to what degree she was a sphinx; but her good nature is all-pervading. Some of her books are redolent of it —some of the more "objective" ones: "Consuelo," "Les Maîtres Sonneurs," "L'Homme de Neige," "Les beaux Messieurs de Bois-Doré." She is often passionate, but she is never rancorous; even her violent attacks upon the Church give us no impression of small acrimony. She has all a woman's loquacity, but she has never a woman's shrillness; and perhaps we can hardly indicate better the difference between great passion and small than by saying that she never is hysterical. During the last half of her career, her books went out of fashion among the new literary generation. "Realism" had been invented, or rather propagated; and in the light of "Madame Bovary" her own facile fictions began to be regarded as the work of a sort of superior Mrs. Radcliffe. She was antiquated; she belonged to the infancy of art. She accepted this destiny with a cheerfulness which it would have savoured of vanity even to make explicit. The Realists were her personal friends; she knew that they did not, and could not, read her books; for what could Gustave Flaubert make of "Monsieur Sylvestre," what could Ivan Turgénieff make of "Césarine Dietrich"? It made no difference; she contented herself with reading their productions, never mentioned her own, and continued to write charming, improbable romances for initiated persons of the optimistic class.

After the first few years she fell into this more and more; she wrote stories for the story's sake. Among the novels produced during a long period before her death I can think of but one, "Mademoiselle La Quintinie," that is of a controversial cast. All her early novels, on the other hand, were controversial—if this is not too mild a description of the passionate contempt for the institution of marriage expressed in "Indiana," "Valentine," "Lélia," and "Jacques." Her own acquaintance with matrimony had been of a painful kind, and the burden of three at least of these remarkable tales (" Lélia" stands rather apart) is the misery produced by an indissoluble matrimonial knot. "Jacques" is the story of an unhappy marriage from which there is no issue but by the suicide of one of the partners; the husband throws himself into an Alpine crevasse in order to leave his wife to an undisturbed enjoyment of her lover.

It very soon became apparent that these matters were handled in a new and superior fashion. There had been plenty of tales about husbands, wives, and "third parties," but since the "Nouvelle Héloïse" there had been none of a high value or of a philosophic tone. Madame Sand, from the first, was nothing if not philosophic; the iniquity of marriage arrangements was to her mind but one of a hundred abominations in a society which needed a complete overhauling, and to which she proceeded to propose a loftier line of conduct. The passionate eloquence of the writer in all this was only equalled by her extraordinary self-confidence. "Valentine" seems to us even now a very eloquent book, and "Jacques" is hardly less so; it is easy to imagine their having made an immense impression. The intellectual freshness, the sentimental force of "Valentine," must have had an irresistible charm; and we say this with a full sense of what there is false and fantastical in the substance of both books. Hold them up against the light of a certain sort of ripe reason, and they seem as porous as a pair of sieves; but subject them simply to the literary test, and they hold together very bravely.

The author's philosophic predilections were at once her merit and her weakness. On the one side it was a great mind, curious about all things, open to all things, nobly accessible to experience, asking only to live, expand, respond; on the other side stood a great personal volition, making large exactions of life and society and needing constantly to justify itself—stirring up rebellion and calling down revolution in order to cover up and legitimate its own agitation. George Sand's was a French mind, and as a French mind it had to theorize; but if the positive side of its criticism of most human institutions was precipitate and ill-balanced, the error was in a great measure atoned for in later years. The last half of Madame Sand's career was a period of assent and acceptance; she had decided to make the best of those social arrangements which surrounded her—remembering, as it were, the homely native proverb which declares that when one has not got what one likes one must like what one has got. Into the phase of acceptance and serenity, the disposition to admit that even as it is society *pays*, according to the vulgar locution, our author passed at about the time that the Second Empire settled down upon France. We suspect the fact we speak of was rather a coincidence than an effect. It is very true that the Second Empire may have seemed the death-knell of "philosophy"; it may very well have appeared profitless to ask questions of a world which anticipated you with such answers as that. But we take it rather that Madame Sand was simply weary of criticism; the pendulum had swung into the opposite quarter—as it is needless to remark that it always does.

We have delayed too long to say how far it had swung in the first direction; and we have delayed from the feeling that it is difficult to say it. We have seen that George Sand was by the force of heredity projected into this field with a certain violence; she took possession of a portion of it as a conqueror, and she was never compelled to retreat. The reproach brought against her by her critics is that, as regards her particular advocacy of the claims of the heart, she has for the most part portrayed vicious love, not virtuous love. But the reply to this, from her own side, would be that she has at all events portrayed something which those who disparage her activity have not portrayed. She may claim, that although she has the critics against her, the writers of her own class who represent virtuous love have not pushed her out of the field. She has the advantage that she has portrayed a *passion*, and those of the other group have the disadvantage that they have not. In English literature, which, we suppose, is more especially the region of virtuous love, we do not "go into" the matter, as the phrase is (we speak of course of English prose). We have agreed among our own confines that there is a certain point at which elucidation of it should stop short; that among the things which it is possible to say about it, the greater number had on the whole better not be said. It would be easy to make an ironical statement of the English attitude, and it would be, if not easy, at least very possible, to make a sound defence of it. The thing with us, however, is not a matter of theory; it is above all a matter of practice, and the practice has been that of the leading English novelists. Miss Austen and Sir Walter Scott, Dickens and Thackeray, Hawthorne and George Eliot, have all represented young people in love with each other; but no one of them has, to the best of our recollection, described anything that can be called a passion—put it into motion before us and shown us its various paces. To say this is to say at the same time that these writers have spared us much that we consider disagreeable, and that George Sand has not spared us; but it is to say furthermore that few persons would resort to English prose fiction for any information concerning the ardent forces of the heart—for any ideas upon them. It is George Sand's merit that she has given us ideas upon them—that she has enlarged the novel-reader's conception of them and proved herself in all that relates to them an authority. This is a great deal. From this standpoint Miss Austen, Walter Scott and Dickens will appear to have omitted the erotic sentiment altogether, and George Eliot will seem to have treated it with singular austerity. Strangely loveless, seen in this light, are those large, comprehensive fictions "Middlemarch" and "Daniel Deronda." They seem to foreign readers, probably, like vast, cold, commodious, respectable rooms, through whose window-panes one sees a snow-covered landscape, and across whose acres of sober-hued carpet one looks in vain for a fireplace or a fire.

The distinction between virtuous and vicious love is not particularly insisted upon by George Sand. In her view love is always love, is always divine in its essence and ennobling in its operation. The largest life possible is to hold one's self open to an unlimited experience of this improving passion. This, I believe, was Madame Sand's practice, as it was certainly her theory—a theory to the exposition of which one of her novels, at least, is expressly dedicated. "Lucrezia Floriani" is the history of a lady who, in the way of love, takes everything that comes along, and who sets forth her philosophy of the matter with infinite grace and felicity. It is probably fortunate for the world that ladies of Lucrezia Floriani's disposition have not as a general thing her argumentative brilliancy. About all this there would be much more to say than these few pages afford space for. Madame Sand's plan was to be open to *all* experience, all emotions, all convictions; only to keep the welfare of the human race, and especially of its humbler members, well in mind, and to trust that one's moral and intellectual life would take a form profitable to the same. One was therefore not only to extend a great hospitality to love, but to interest one's self in religion and politics. This Madame Sand did with great activity during the whole of the reign of Louis Philippe. She had broken utterly with the Church, of course, but her disposition was the reverse of sceptical. Her religious feeling, like all her feelings, was powerful and voluminous, and she had an ideal of a sort of etherealized and liberated Christianity, in which unmarried but affectionate couples might find an element friendly to their "expansion." Like all her feelings, too, her religious sentiment was militant; her ideas about love were an attack upon marriage; her faith was an attack upon the Church and the clergy; her socialistic sympathies were an attack upon all present political arrangements. These things all took hold of her by turn—shook her hard, as it were, and dropped her, leaving her to be played upon by some new inspiration; then, in some cases, returned to her, took possession of her afresh and sounded another tune. M. Renan, in writing of her at the time of her death, used a fine phrase about her; he said that she was "the Æolian harp of our time;" he spoke of her "sonorous soul." This is very just; there is nothing that belonged to her time that she had not a personal emotion about—an emotion intense enough to produce a brilliant work of art—a novel that had bloomed as rapidly and perfectly as the flower that the morning sun sees open on its stem. In her care about many things during all these years, in her expenditure of passion, reflection, and curiosity, there is something quite unprecedented. Never had philosophy and art gone so closely hand in hand. Each of them suffered a good deal; but it had appeared up to that time that their mutual concessions must be even greater. Balzac was a far superior artist; but he was incapable of a lucid reflection.

We have already said that mention has been made

of George Sand's analogy with Goethe, who claimed for his lyrical poems the merit of being each the result of a particular incident in his life. It was incident too that prompted Madame Sand to write; but what it produced in her case was not a short copy of verses, but an elaborate drama, with a plot and a dozen characters. It will help us to understand this extraordinary responsiveness of mind and fertility of imagination to remember that inspiration was often embodied in a concrete form; that Madame Sand's "incidents" were usually clever, eloquent, suggestive men. "Le style c'est l'homme"—of her, it has been epigramatically said, that is particularly true. Be this as it may, these influences were strikingly various, and they are reflected in works which may be as variously labelled: amatory tales, religious tales, political, æsthetic, pictorial, musical, theatrical, historical tales. And it is to be noticed that in whatever the author attempted, whether or no she succeeded, she appeared to lose herself. The "Lettres d'un Voyageur" read like a writer's single book. This melancholy, this desolation and weariness, might pass as the complete distillation of a soul. In the same way "Spiridion" is exclusively religious and theological. The author might, in relation to this book, have replied to such of her critics as reproach her with being too erotic, that she had performed the very rare feat of writing a novel not only containing no love save divine love, but containing not one woman's figure. We can recall but one rival to "Spiridion" in this respect—Godwin's "Caleb Williams."

But if other things come and go with George Sand, amatory disquisition is always there. It is of all kinds, sometimes very noble and sometimes very disagreeable. Numerous specimens of the two extremes might be cited. There is to our taste a great deal too much of it; the total effect is displeasing. The author illuminates and glorifies the divine passion, but she does something which may be best expressed by saying that she cheapens it. She handles it too much; she lets it too little alone. Above all she is too positive, too explicit, too business-like; she takes too technical a view of it. Its various signs and tokens and stages, its ineffable mysteries, are all catalogued and tabulated in her mind, and she whisks out her references with the nimbleness with which the doorkeeper at an exhibition hands you back your umbrella in return for a check. In this relation, to the English mind, discretion is a great point—a virtue so absolute and indispensable that it speaks for itself and cannot be analysed away; and George Sand is judged from our point of view by one's saying that for her discretion is simply non-existent. Its place is occupied by a sort of benevolent, an almost conscientious disposition to sit down, as it were, and "talk over" the whole matter. The subject fills her with a motherly loquacity; it stimulates all her wonderful and beautiful self-sufficiency of expression —the quality that we have heard a hostile critic call her "glibness."

We can hardly open a volume of George Sand without finding an example of what we mean. We glance at a venture into "Teverino," and we find Lady G., who has left her husband at the inn and gone out to spend a day with the more fascinating Léonce, "passing her beautiful hands over the eyes of Léonce, *peut-être par tendresse naïve*, perhaps to convince herself that it was really tears she saw shining in them." The *peut-être* here, the *tendresse naïve*, the alternatives, the impartial way in which you are given your choice, are extremely characteristic of Madame Sand. They remind us of the heroine of "Isidora," who alludes in conversation to "une de mes premières fautes." In the list of Madame Sand's more technically amatory novels, however, there is a distinction to be made; the earlier strike us as superior to the later. The fault of the earlier—the fact that passion is too intellectual, too pedantic, too sophistical, too much bent upon proving itself abnegation and humility, maternity, fraternity, humanity, or some fine thing that it really is not and that it is much simpler and better for not pretending to be—this fault is infinitely exaggerated in the tales written after "Lucrezia Floriani." "Indiana," "Valentine," "Jacques," and "Mauprat" are, comparatively speaking, frankly and honestly passionate; they do not represent the love that declines to compromise with circumstances as a sort of eating of one's cake and having it too—an eating it as pleasure and a having it as virtue. But the stories of the type of "Lucrezia Floriani," which indeed is the most argumentative,[1] have an indefinable falsity of tone. Madame Sand had here begun to play with her topic intellectually; the first freshness of her interest in it had gone, and invention had taken the place of conviction. To acquit one's self happily of such experiments, one must certainly have all the gifts that George Sand possessed. But one must also have two or three that she lacked. Her sense of purity was certainly defective. This is a brief statement, but it means a great deal, and of what it means there are few of her novels that do not contain a number of illustrations.

There is something very fine, for instance, about "Valentine," in spite of its contemptible hero; there is something very sweet and generous in the figure of

[1] "Constance Verrier," "Isidora," "Pauline," "Le dernier Amour," "La Daniella," "Francia," "Mademoiselle Merquem."

the young girl. But why, desiring to give us an impression of great purity in her heroine, should the author provide her with a half-sister who is at once an illegitimate daughter and the mother of a child born out of wedlock, and who, in addition, is half in love with Valentine's lover? though George Sand thinks to better the matter by representing this love as partly maternal. After Valentine's marriage, a compulsory and most unhappy one, this half-sister plots with the doctor to place the young wife and the lover whom she has had to dismiss once more *en rapport*. She hesitates, it is true, and inquires of the physician if their scheme will not appear unlawful in the eyes of the world. But the old man reassures her, and asks, with a "sourire malin et affectueux," why she should care for the judgment of a world which has viewed so harshly her own irregularity of conduct. Madame Sand constantly strikes these false notes; we meet in her pages the most startling confusions. In "Jacques" there is the oddest table of relations between the characters. Jacques is possibly the brother of Silvia, who is probably, on another side, sister of his wife, who is the mistress of Octave, Silvia's dismissed *amant!* Add to this that if Jacques be *not* the brother of Silvia, who is an illegitimate child, he is convertible into her lover. *On s'y perd.* Silvia, a clever woman,

is the guide, philosopher, and friend of this melancholy
Jacques; and when his wife, who desires to become
the mistress of Octave (*her* discarded lover), and yet,
not finding it quite plain sailing to do so, weeps over
the crookedness of her situation, she writes to the
injured husband that she has been obliged to urge
Fernande not to take things so hard: "je suis forcée
de la consoler et de la relever à ses propres yeux."
Very characteristic of Madame Sand is this fear lest
the unfaithful wife should take too low a view of herself. One wonders what had become of her sense of
humour. Fernande is to be "relevée" before her fall,
and the operation is somehow to cover her fall prospectively.

Take another example from "Léone Léoni." The
subject of the story is the sufferings of an infatuated
young girl, who follows over Europe the most faithless,
unscrupulous and ignoble, but also the most irresistible
of charmers. It is "Manon Lescaut," with the incurable fickleness of Manon attributed to a man; and as
in the Abbé Prévost's story the touching element is
the devotion and constancy of the injured and deluded
Desgrieux, so in "Léone Léoni" we are invited to
feel for the too closely-clinging Juliette, who is dragged
through the mire of a passion which she curses and yet
which survives unnameable outrage. She tells the tale

herself and yet it might have been expected that, to deepen its effect, the author would have represented her as withdrawn from the world and cured of her excessive susceptibility. But we find her living with another charmer, jewelled and perfumed; in her own words, she is a *fille entretenue*, and it is to her new lover that she relates the story of the stormy life she ed with the old. The situation requires no comment beyond our saying that the author had morally no taste. Of this want of moral taste we remember another striking instance. Mademoiselle Merquem, who gives her name to one of the later novels, is a young girl of the most elevated character, beloved by a young man, the intensity of whose affection she desires to test. To do this she contrives the graceful plan of introducing into her house a mysterious infant, of whose parentage she offers an explanation so obtrusively vague, that the young man is driven regretfully to the induction that its female parent is none other than herself. We forget to what extent he is staggered, but, if we rightly remember, he withstands the test. We do not judge him, but it is permitted to judge the young lady.

We have called George Sand an *improvisatrice*, and in this character, where she deals with matters of a more "objective" cast, she is always delightful; nothing could be more charming than her tales of mystery, intrigue, and adventure. "Consuelo," "L'Homme de Neige," "Le Piccinino," "Teverino," "Le Beau Laurence" and its sequel, "Pierre qui Roule," "Antonia," "Tamaris," "La Famille de Germandre," "La Filleule," "La dernière Aldini," "Cadio," "Flamarande"—these things have all the spontaneous inventiveness of the romances of Alexandre Dumas, his open-air quality, his pleasure in a story for a story's sake, together with an intellectual refinement, a philosophic savour, a reference to spiritual things, in which he was grotesquely deficient.

We have given, however, no full enumeration of the author's romances, and it seems needless to do so. We have lately been trying to read them over, and we frankly confess that we have found it impossible. They are excellent reading for once, but they lack that quality which makes things classical—makes them impose themselves. It has been said that what makes a book a classic is its style. We should modify this, and instead of style say *form*. Madame Sand's novels have plenty of style, but they have no form. Balzac's have not a shred of style, but they have a great deal of form. Posterity doubtless will make a selection from each list, but the few volumes of Balzac it preserves will remain with it much longer, we suspect, than those which it borrows from his great contemporary. We cannot easily imagine posterity travelling with "Valentine" or "Mauprat," "Consuelo" or the "Marquis de Villemer" in its trunk. At the same time we can imagine that if these admirable tales fall out of fashion, such of our descendants as stray upon them in the dusty corners of old libraries will sit down on the bookcase ladder with the open volume and turn it over with surprise and enchantment. What a beautiful mind! they will say; what an extraordinary style! Why have we not known more about these things? And as, when that time comes, we suppose the world will be given over to a "realism" that we have not as yet begun faintly to foreshadow, George Sand's novels will have, for the children of the twenty-first century, something of the same charm which Spenser's "Fairy Queen" has for those of the nineteenth. For a critic of to-day to pick and choose among them seems almost pedantic; they all belong quite to the same intellectual family. They are the easy writing which makes hard reading.

In saying this we must immediately limit our meaning. All the world can read George Sand once and not find it in the least hard. But it is not easy to return to her; putting aside a number of fine descriptive pages, the reader will not be likely to resort to any volume that he has once laid down for a particular chapter, a brilliant passage, an entertaining conversation. George Sand invites reperusal less than any mind of equal eminence. Is this because after all she was a woman, and the laxity of the feminine intellect could not fail to claim its part in her ? We will not attempt to say ; especially as, though it may be pedantic to pick and choose among her works, we immediately think of two or three that have as little as possible of intellectual laxity. "Mauprat" is a solid, masterly, manly book; "André" and "La Mare au Diable" have an extreme perfection of form. M. Taine, whom we quoted at the beginning of these remarks, speaks of our author's rustic tales (the group to which the "Mare au Diable" belongs [1]) as a signal proof of her activity and versatility of mind. Besides being charming stories, they are in fact a real study in philology—such a study as Balzac made in the "Contes Drôlatiques," and as Thackeray made in "Henry Esmond." George Sand's attempt to return to a more artless and archaic stage of the language which she usually handled in so modern and voluminous a fashion was quite as successful as that of her fellows. In "Les Maîtres Sonneurs" it is extremely felicitous, and the success could only have been achieved by an extraordinarily sympathetic and flexible talent. This is one of the impressions George Sand's reader—even if he have read her but once—brings away with him. His

[1] "François le Champi," "La Petite Fadette."

other prevailing impression will bear upon that quality which, if it must be expressed in a single word, may best be called the generosity of her genius. It is true that there are one or two things which limit this generosity. We think, for example, of Madame Sand's peculiar power of self-defence, her constant need to justify, to glorify, to place in a becoming light, to "arrange," as we said at the outset, those errors and weaknesses in which her own personal credit may be at stake. She never accepts a weakness as a weakness; she always dresses it out as a virtue; and if her heroines abandon their lovers and lie to their husbands, you may be sure it is from motives of the highest morality. Such productions as "Lucrezia Floriani" and "Elle et Lui" may be attributed to an ungenerous disposition—both of them being stories in which Madame Sand is supposed to have described her relations with distinguished men who were dead, and whose death enabled her without contradiction to portray them as monsters of selfishness, while the female protagonist appeared as the noblest of her sex. But without taking up the discussion provoked by these works, we may say that, on the face of the matter, there is a good deal of justification for their author. She poured her material into the crucible of art, and the artist's material is of necessity in a large measure his experience. Madame

Sand never described the actual; this was often her artistic weakness, and as she has the reproach she should also have the credit. "Lucrezia Floriani" and "Elle et Lui" were doubtless to her imagination simply tales of what might have been.

It is hard not to feel that there is a certain high good conscience and passionate sincerity in the words in which, in one of her prefaces, she alludes to the poor novel which Alfred de Musset's brother put forth as an incriminative retort to "Elle et Lui." Some of her friends had advised her not to notice the book; "but after reflection she judged it to be her duty to attend to it at the proper time and place. She was, however, by no means in haste. She was in Auvergne following the imaginary traces of the figures of her new novel along the scented byways, among the sweetest scenes of spring. She had brought the pamphlet with her to read it; but she did not read it. She had forgotten her herbarium, and the pages of the infamous book, used as a substitute, were purified by the contact of the wild flowers of Puy-de-Dôme and Sancy. Sweet perfumes of the things of God, who to you could prefer the memory of the foulnesses of civilization?"

It must, however, to be just all round, be farther remembered that those persons and causes which Madame Sand has been charged first and last with misrepresenting belonged to the silent, inarticulate, even defunct class. She was always the talker, the survivor, the adversary armed with a gift of expression so magical as almost to place a premium upon sophistry. To weigh everything, we imagine she really *outlived* experience, morally, to a degree which made her feel, in retrospect, as if she were dealing with the history of another person. " Où sont-ils, où sont-ils, nos amours passés ? " she exclaims in one of her later novels. (What has become of the passions we have shuffled off?—into what dusky limbo are they flung away?) And she goes on to say that it is a great mistake to suppose that we die only once and at last. We die piecemeal; some part of us is always dying; it is only what is left that dies at last. As for our "amours passés," where are they indeed? Jacques Laurent and the Prince Karol may be fancied, in echo, to exclaim.

In saying that George Sand lacks truth the critic more particularly means that she lacks exactitude— lacks the method of truth. Of a certain general truthfulness she is full to overflowing; we feel that to her mind nothing human is alien. We should say of her, not that she *knew* human nature, but that she felt it. At all events she loved it and enjoyed it. She was contemplative; but she was not, in the deepest sense, observant. She was a very high order of sentimentalist, but she was not a moralist. She perceived a thousand things, but she rarely in strictness judged; so that although her books have a great deal of wisdom, they have not what is called weight. With the physical world she was as familiar as with the human, and she knew it perhaps better. She would probably at any time have said that she cared much more for botany, mineralogy and astronomy, than for sociology. "Nature," as we call it—landscape, trees and flowers, rocks and streams and clouds—plays a larger part in her novels than in any others, and in none are they described with such a grand general felicity. If Turner had written his landscapes rather than painted them he might have written as George Sand has done. If she was less truthful in dealing with men and women, says M. Taine, it is because she had too high an ideal for them; she could not bear not to represent them as better than they are. She delights in the representation of virtue, and if we sometimes feel that she has not really measured the heights on which she places her characters, that so to place them has cost little to her understanding, we are nevertheless struck with the nobleness of her imagination. M. Taine calls her an idealist; we should say, somewhat more narrowly, that she was an optimist. An optimist "lined," as the French say, with a romancer, is not the making of a moralist. George Sand's optimism, her idealism, are very beautiful, and the source of that impression of largeness, luminosity and liberality which she makes upon us. But we suspect that something even better in a novelist is that tender appreciation of actuality which makes even the application of a single coat of rose-colour seem an act of violence.

CHARLES DE BERNARD AND GUSTAVE FLAUBERT.

I.

SAINTE-BEUVE, whose literary judgments are always worth noting, whether they strike us as correct or not, has somewhere a happy sentence about Charles de Bernard—about "that ease and irresponsible grace which was the gift of this first of Balzac's pupils—of him who might have been superior to the master if a pupil ever were so, and especially if he had done more—if, in short, he had lived." We call these words happy in spite of their slight fundamental unsoundness. Charles de Bernard was only in a very imperfect sense a pupil of Balzac. His style has as little as possible in common with that of his great contemporary, and he is guilty of no visible attempt to tread in the latter's footsteps. The two writers belong to two very distinct categories—Balzac to the type of mind that takes things hard, and Charles de Bernard to the type of mind that takes things easily. The author of

"Gerfaut" was Balzac's protégé rather than his pupil, and though we have Sainte-Beuve's affirmation that Balzac's literary vanity was the "most gross and rapacious" he had ever known, it does not appear that he took umbrage at his "pupil's" ripening talent. How many budding reputations Balzac may have endeavoured to drive to the wall, we are of course unable to say; but there are at least two recorded cases of his extending to unfriended genius an open hand. When Stendhal, who for a long time was at once the most powerful and the most obscure of romancers, published his "Chartreuse de Parme," Balzac greeted the book in a long, florid, redundant review, with a series of the handsomest compliments that one literary man ever paid to another. And his admiration was perfectly sincere; the artist was captivated by the artist. In like manner, in 1834, when Charles de Bernard, after coming up to Paris from his native Besançon to seek his literary fortune and quite failing to find it, had returned to his provincial nest in some discouragement, Balzac, struck with the promise of a volume of verse which had been the principal result of his excursion, sought him out, urged him to try again, and gave him some fraternal literary advice. He "started" him, as the phrase is. It is true that he started him left foot foremost, and his advice has a singular sound. He recommended him to try his hand at historical novels—something in the line of Walter Scott. Fortunately Charles de Bernard had taken his own measure. He began to write tales, but they were anything but historical. They were short stories of the day, in the lightest style of improvisation. "Gerfaut," his first regular novel, and on the whole his best, alone reveals some traces of Balzac's advice. There is an old castle, and a good deal of killing, a secret closet in the wall, and a very good portrait of a feudal nobleman born too late.

Charles de Bernard has at the present day hardly more than an historical value, and his novels are not to be recommended to people who have anything of especial importance at hand to read. But in speaking of the secondary French novelists it is but fair to allow him a comfortable niche, for if he be not especially worth studying he at least leaves you a very friendly feeling for him if he comes in your way. He is old-fashioned, faded, ineffectively realistic; his cleverness is not the cleverness of the present hour; his art and his artifice seem a trifle primitive and meagre; and yet for all that he is more enjoyable than many of his highly perfected modern successors. If the prime purpose of a novel is to give us pleasure, Charles de Bernard is a better novelist than Gustave

Flaubert. "Gerfaut" and "Les Ailes d'Icare" proceed doubtless from a very much less powerful and original mind than "Madame Bovary"; but they are at any rate works of entertainment, of amenity. "Realism," as we understand it now, has been invented since this writer's day, and however much we may admire and applaud it, we cannot but feel that it was a good fortune for a charming story-teller to have come a little before it. And since Balzac has been mentioned, it may really be said that when it comes to being agreeable Charles de Bernard need not shrink from comparison with even so imposing a name. He is slight and loose in tissue, pale in colouring; in a word, a second-rate genius. Balzac is a genius of all time; he towers and overshadows; and yet if half a dozen volumes of each writer were standing on your shelf, and you should feel an impulse to taste of the sweets of fiction, you were wiser to take down Charles de Bernard than Balzac. The writer of these lines feels for the author of "Gerfaut" that particular kindness which many people who relish the beautiful qualities of the French mind in their purity entertain for the talents that flourished and fell before the second Empire set its seal upon things. It is not taking the matter too tragically to say that Charles de Bernard just escaped. Certainly, many of the brilliant writers of the same generation have lived through the Empire and held their own against it. To George Sand and Victor Hugo the Empire could give nothing, and it could take nothing away from them. But Charles de Bernard was not of their calibre; he ranks, in the degree of his talent, with the Feydeaus, the Octave Feuillets, the Edmond Abouts of literature. Readers who appreciate shades of difference, and who, while they admire the extreme cleverness of these writers, find something in their tone that fails to attract personal sympathy, will discover a great deal to relish in Charles de Bernard. Whether he too would have been corrupted, whether his easy, natural manner would have learned the perversities and sophistries of the Decadence, is more than I can say. At any rate, fortune was kind to him; she never gave him a chance. She broke him smoothly off, and in compensation for the brevity of his career, she made him a type of some of the agreeable things that were about to pass away. He may represent, to an imaginative critic, the old French cleverness as distinguished from the new. Of the lightness, the ease, the gaiety, the urbanity, the good taste, the good spirits, the discretion —of all those charming things that have traditionally marked the cultivated French character at its best Charles de Bernard is an excellent illustration. He seems to me the last of the light writers in whom these gifts are fresh and free. In the later generation the quality of wit undergoes an indefinable transformation. The cleverness is greater than ever, but the charm is gone; the music is elaborate, but the instrument is cracked. The gaiety becomes forced and hard and the urbanity ironical; the lightness turns to levity. Charles de Bernard answers to our notion of the Frenchman of an earlier date, who was before all things good company—who had in a supreme degree the sociable virtues. Thackeray, in his "Paris Sketch-Book," devotes a chapter to him (he was then a contemporary) and gives an abstract of one of his novels. He evidently relished this urbane quality in him, and we remember even to have seen it somewhere affirmed that he had taken him for his model and declared that it was the height of his own ambition to do for English society what Charles de Bernard had done for French. This last strikes us as a rather apocryphal tale; Charles de Bernard was a satirist, but his satire is to that of "Vanity Fair" what lemonade is to prime Burgundy. In Thackeray there are, morally, many Charles de Bernards. It is as against Eugène Sue and George Sand (whom he seems rather unphilosophically to lump together) that he praises the author of "Les Ailes d'Icare," and he especially commends his gentlemanly tone. The "gentlemanly tone," with its merits and limitations, is an incontestable characteristic of our author. It may be said that in a thoroughly agreeable style good-breeding is never an aggressive quality, and that a gentleman who keeps reminding you that he is a gentleman is a very ambiguous personage. But Charles de Bernard is gentlemanly by juxtaposition, as it were. He quietly goes his way, and it is only when you compare his gait with that of his neighbours that you see how very well he holds himself. The truth is, that many of his companions in this matter swagger deplorably; and here again, curiously (to return to Balzac) is another point at which the small man is superior to the great. The tone of good-breeding Balzac never in any degree possessed; the greatest genius in his line conceivable, he was absolutely and positively not a gentleman. He sweats blood and water to appear one, but his efforts only serve to betray more vividly his magnificently middle-class temperament. M. Armand de Pontmartin, the author of the biographical sketch prefixed to the collected edition of Charles de Bernard's novels, has some rather felicitous remarks upon the difference, in this respect, between his hero and the latter's rivals. "Eugène Sue and Alexandre Dumas, who have had their phase of rubbing shoulders (or of trying to) with the aristocracy, their repeated attempts at flattery and advances to what the hairdressers and the milliners call the *monde élégant*, have never been able to produce anything but caricatures when they endeavoured to represent it. Its doors were open to them; they found a passport in the irresistible although imprudent curiosity of its members; the models were there in position, before their eyes; they were dying with the desire to persuade their readers that they lived the same life and breathed the same air; that they were not naturalized, but indigenous. No expenditure of dazzling description, bespangled with armorial mottoes and shields; no female portraits à *la* Lawrence, smothered in silk, and lace, and velvet; no inventories of coachmakers and architects, tailors and jewellers—nothing of all this was spared. But, alas, it might have been; the struggle was vain! The false note sounded in the finest place—the long ear peeped out of the thickest of the lion's skin." This is very well—though it is painful to have to record that M. de Pontmartin too, who understands the matter so well, has been accused of snobbery by no less acute a literary detective than Sainte-Beuve. But Charles de Bernard, though he often wrote of the *monde élégant*, was emphatically not a snob. The point of view of the man who is conscious of good blood in his veins was the one he instinctively took; but in dealing with the people and things that usually excite the snobbish passion, he is always perfectly simple. He is never pretentious; he is easy, natural, and impartially civil.

His literary career was very short; his novels were all published between 1838 and 1847—a period of nine years. His life was uneventful; it was altogether in his works. The author of the short memoir I have mentioned notes the singular fact that although his novels are essentially what are called novels of manners, he led a secluded life and went very little into the world. Gaiety and hilarity abound in his tales, and yet M. de Pontmartin intimates that the man himself was rather sombre. "He had long had the good taste to prefer domestic life to the *vie de salon*, and in the evening he liked much better to remain with his wife and children than to go into the world in pursuit of models and originals. And nevertheless, muffled in from the outer world, inaccessible or deaf to its sounds, solitary, almost misanthropic, he seems to have listened at doors, to have painted from nature. He guessed what he did not see; he heard what he did not listen to." He had this mark of a man of genius —he divined. His literary personality was apparently quite distinct from his private one, and this, taken in connection with the extreme facility and neatness of his style, entitles him in a measure to be called a man of genius. His inspiration was his own, and he was an excellent writer. If his inspiration was his own, however, it must be added that it was never of a very high order. The most general praise we can give his novels is that they are extremely diverting. The humour is neither broad nor coarse; it is always discriminating, and it is often delicate; but it is humour of the second-rate sort. It is not rich nor suggestive; your entertainment begins and ends with your laugh. Many of his tales are very short, so that half a dozen go into a volume. These are always highly readable, and if you begin one you will be sure to finish it. The best of his novels, "Les Ailes d'Icare," "Un Homme Sérieux," "Le Gentilhomme Campagnard," are no less clever; and yet it may be that here and there even a well-disposed reader will lay the book down at the end of a hundred pages. For a serious writer, he will say, you are really too light; it is all too smooth and shallow, too artificial. Once at least, however, in "Gerfaut," Charles de Bernard seems to have felt the impulse to grasp a subject nearer its roots. In spite of a number of signs of immaturity, this is his solidest and most effective work. His tales are usually comedies; this is a tragedy. The reader cares little for his hero, who is a gentleman of a type excessively familiar in French literature—a distinguished man of letters, of restless imagination, who comes down to the Château de Bergenheim for the express purpose of seducing its pretty mistress, and who, when installed among its comforts, and smothered in hospitality by the husband, proceeds in the most scientific manner to bombard the affections of the wife. Nor are we much more interested in Madame de Bergenheim herself, who surrenders after a barely nominal siege and without having at all convinced us that her affections are worth possessing. But the book, in spite of a diffuseness of which afterward the author was rarely guilty, is written with infinite spirit and point, and some of the subordinate figures are forcibly and wittily sketched. Nothing could be lighter and more picturesquely humorous than the portrait of Marillac, the irrepressible Bohemian and the *fidus Achates* of the hero. "Talent apart, Marillac was an artist tooth and nail—an artist from the point, or rather from the plateau, of his great crop of hair to the tips of his boots, which he would have liked to pull out to the mediæval longitude; for he excelled especially in dressing for his profession, and possessed the longest moustaches in literature. If he had no great amount of art in his brain, he had at least its name perpetually in his mouth. Art!—to pronounce the word he rounded his lips like M. Jourdain saying O! Farces or pictures, poetry or music, he did a bit of everything, like a horse who is warranted good either for the shafts or the saddle. When he came out of the musical shafts he bravely got into the literary harness, which he considered his veritable vocation and his principal glory. He signed his name 'Marillac, man of letters.' Nevertheless, in spite of a profound disdain for the bourgeois, whom he spoke of as a grocer, and for the French Academy, to which he had taken an oath never to belong, one could accuse him of no serious defects. One could forgive him being an artist before everything, in spite of everything, an artist—damnation!" A still better image is that of Christian de Bergenheim, the husband of the decidedly inexpensive heroine. It reads, for definiteness and vigour, like a page torn from Balzac. "He was one of those men whom Napoleon had in some sort brought to life again—the type which had been gradually dying out since the feudal ages; a man of action exclusively, spending nothing superfluous in imagination or sensibility, and, on momentous occasions, never letting his soul travel farther than the swing of his sabre. The complete absence of that sense which most people call morbid irritability and others poetry had caused the springs of his character to retain their native hardness and stiffness. His soul lacked wings to leave the world of the real; but this incapacity had its compensation. It was impossible to apply a more vigorous arm than his to anything that came under the head of material resistance. He lived neither yesterday nor to-morrow; he lived to-day. Of small account before or after, he displayed at the critical moment an energy the more powerful that no waste, no leakage of untimely emotion, had diminished its force. The few ideas contained in his brain had become clear, hard, and impenetrable, like diamonds. By the inner light of these fixed stars he walked in all things, as one walks in the sunshine, his head erect, straight before him, ready to crush with his foot all obstacles and interruptions." A few passages of that sort, scattered through his novels, mark Charles de Bernard's maximum as an analyst. But if this is the maximum, the average is very high. He has described all sorts of social types, narrated all kinds of intrigues, always ingeniously, vividly, and with a natural, epicurean irony. Considering that we do not recommend the reader who is unacquainted with him to make any great point of retracing his steps along the crowded highway of what we nowadays call culture, to bend over our author where his own march stopped and left him, it may seem that we are lingering too long upon Charles de Bernard. But there is another word to say, and it is an interesting one. Charles de Bernard's talent is great—very great, greater than the impression it leaves; and the reason why this clever man remains so persistently second-rate is, to our sense, because he had no morality. By this we of course do not mean that he did not choose to write didactic tales, winding up with a goody lecture and a distribution of prizes and punishments. We mean that he had no moral emotion, no preferences, no instincts—no moral imagination, in a word. His morality was altogether traditional, and, such as it was, it seems to have held him in a very loose grasp. It was not the current social notion of right and wrong, of honour and dishonour, that he represented, but something even less consistent. What we find in him is not the average morality, but a morality decidedly below the average. He does not care, he does not feel, and yet his indifference is not philosophic. He has no heat of his own, save that of the *raconteur*; his laugh is always good-natured, but always cold. He describes all sorts of mean and ignoble things without in the least gauging their quality. He belongs to the intellectual family—and very large it is in France— of the amusing author of "Gil Blas." All its members know how to write, and how, up to a certain point, to observe; but their observation has no reflex action, as it were, and they remain as dry as they are brilliant. Yet for all this the author of these lines is conscious of a tender regard for Charles de Bernard, which he would be sorry not to confess to in conclusion. He remembers turning over, as a child, an old back-parlour volume of the "keepsake" genus, bound in tarnished watered silk, as such volumes are apt to be. It was called, if memory serves him, the "Idler in France," and it was written—if written is the word—by the Countess of Blessington. With the text he was too timorous to grapple; but the volume was embellished with beautiful steel plates, depicting the delights of the French capital. There was the good old crooked, dirty, picturesque Paris of Charles X. and Louis Philippe—the Paris ignorant of Louis Napoleon and Baron Haussmann, the new Boulevards and the "American quarter." There were pictures of the old Boulevards and the Palais Royal, the staircase at the Opera, the table d'hôte at the Hôtel des Princes, a salon in the Chaussée d'Antin. The gentlemen all wore high rolling coat-collars and straps to their trousers; the ladies wore large-brimmed bonnets and cross-laced slippers. The Paris of these antediluvian Parisians seemed to his fancy a paradise; and he supposes that a part of his lurking tenderness for Charles de Bernard rests upon the fact that it appears to live again in his pages.

II.

Since those days the novel has flourished more and more, and if all that is needful to make us like a certain order of things is to see it vividly and picturesquely portrayed, we should assuredly long since have been won over to an æsthetic *tendresse* for the Empire. The Empire has had its novelists by the dozen ; emulation, competition, and the extraordinary favour which this branch of literature has come to enjoy, have rendered them remarkably skilful and audacious. For entertainment of a high flavour we have only to choose at hazard. If at the same time, however, we are modestly inclined to edification, there must be a certain logic in our choice. The array is somewhat embarrassing; to the roll-call of novelists of the second Empire a formidable host responds. Octave Feuillet, Gustave Flaubert, Ernest Feydeau, Edmond About, the brothers De Goncourt, Gustave Droz, the younger Dumas, Victor Cherbuliez, Erckmann-Chatrian—these are some of the names that immediately present themselves. All these names, with one exception (that of Alexandre Dumas), represent a constellation of romances more or less brilliant; and in their intervals glitters here and there a single star—a very clever tale by an author who has tried, or succeeded, but once.

A couple of examples of this latter class are the exquisite "Dominique" of Eugène Frometin, and the crude and vulgar, but powerful and touching, "Divorce" of Mme. André Leo. When we cannot look at everything, we must look at what is most characteristic. The most characteristic work in this line, in France, of the last five-and-twenty years, is the realistic, descriptive novel which sprang out of Balzac, began in its effort at intensity of illusion where Balzac halted, and which, whether or no it has surpassed him, has at least exceeded him. Everything in France, proceeds by "schools," and there is no artist so bungling that he will not find another to call him "dear master." Gustave Flaubert is of the school of Balzac; the brothers De Goncourt and Emile Zola are of the school of Flaubert. This last writer is altogether the most characteristic and powerful representative of what has lately been most original in the evolution of the French imagination, and he has for ourselves the farther merit that he must always be strange and curious. English literature has certainly been doing some very odd things of late, and striving hard to prove she is able to be anything that individual writers choose to make her. But at the best we are all flies in amber, and however furiously we may buzz and rattle, the amber sticks to our wings. It is not in the temper of English vision to see things as M. Flaubert sees them, and it is not in the genius of the English language to present them as he presents them. With all respect to "Madame Bovary," "Madame Bovary" is fortunately an inimitable work.

"Madame Bovary" was M. Flaubert's first novel, and it has remained altogether his best. He has produced little and his works bear the marks of the most careful preparation. His second work of fiction was "Salammbô," an archæological novel of the highest pretensions. Salammbô is a Carthaginian princess, the elder sister of Hannibal. After this came, at a long interval, "L'Education Sentimentale," a tale of the present day, and lastly appeared "La Tentation de St. Antoine" —archæology, but in the shape of something that was neither novel nor drama; a sort of free imitation of the mediæval "mystery." "Madame Bovary" was a great success—a success of merit, and, as they say in France, a success of scandal; but the public verdict has not been flattering to its companions. The mass of the public finds them dull, and wonders how a writer can expend such an immensity of talent in making himself unreadable. To a discriminating taste, however, M. Flaubert can write nothing that does not repay attention.

The "scandal" in relation to "Madame Bovary" was that the book was judicially impeached and prosecuted for immorality. The defence was eloquent, and the writer was aquitted; the later editions of the book contain, in an appendix, a full report of the trial. It is a work upon which it is possible to be very paradoxical, or rather in relation to which sincere opinion may easily have the air of paradox. It is a book adapted for the reverse of what is called family reading, and yet we remember thinking, the first time we read it, in the heat of our admiration for its power, that it would make the most useful of Sunday-school tracts. In M. Taine's elaborate satire, "The Opinions of M. Graindorge," there is a report of a conversation at a dinner party between an English spinster of didactic habits and a decidedly audacious Frenchman. He begs to recommend to her a work which he has lately been reading and which cannot fail to win the approval of all persons interested in the propagation of virtue. The lady lends a sympathetic ear, and he gives a rapid sketch of the tale—the history of a wicked woman who goes from one abomination to another, until at last the judgment of Heaven descends upon her, and, blighted and blasted, she perishes miserably. The lady grasps her pencil and note-book and begs for the name of the edifying volume, and the gentleman leans across the dinner table and answers with a smile—"'Madame Bovary; or, The Consequences of Misconduct.'" This is a very pretty epigram and it is more than an epigram. It may be very seriously maintained that M. Flaubert's masterpiece is the pearl of "Sunday reading." Practically M. Flaubert is a potent moralist; whether, when he wrote his book, he was so theoretically is a matter best known to himself. Every out-and-out realist who provokes serious meditation may claim that he is a moralist for that, after all, is the most that the moralists can do for us. They sow the seeds of virtue; they can hardly pretend to raise the crop. Excellence in this matter consists in the tale and the moral hanging well together, and this they are certainly more likely to do when there has been a definite intention—that intention of which artists who cultivate "art for art" are usually so extremely mistrustful; exhibiting thereby, surely, a most injurious disbelief in the illimitable alchemy of art. We may say on the whole, doubtless, that the highly didactic character of "Madame Bovary" is an accident, inasmuch as the works that have followed it, both from its author's and from other hands, have been things to read much less for meditation's than for sensation's sake. M. Flaubert's theory as a novelist, briefly expressed, is to begin on the outside. Human life, we may imagine him saying, is before all things a spectacle, an occupation and entertainment for the eyes. What our eyes show us is all that we are sure of; so with this we will, at any rate, begin. As this is infinitely curious and entertaining, if we know how to look at it, and as such looking consumes a great deal of time and space, it is very possible that with this also we may end. We admit nevertheless that there is something else, beneath and behind, that belongs to the realm of vagueness and uncertainty, and into this we must occasionally dip. It crops up sometimes irrepressibly, and of course we do not positively count it out. On the whole, we will leave it to take care of itself and let it come off as it may. If we propose to represent the pictorial side of life, of course we must do it thoroughly well—we must be complete. There must be no botching, no bungling, no scamping; it must be a very serious matter. We will "render" things—anything, everything, from a chimney-pot to the shoulders of a duchess—as painters render them. We believe there is a certain particular phrase, better than any other, for everything in the world, and the thoroughly accomplished writer ends by finding it. We care only for what *is*— we know nothing about what ought to be. Human life is interesting, because we are in it and of it; all kinds of curious things are taking place in it (we do not analyse the curious—for artists it is an ultimate fact); we select as many of them as possible. Some of the most curious are the most disagreeable, but the chance for "rendering" in the disagreeable is as great as anywhere else (some people think even greater), and moreover the disagreeable is extremely characteristic. The real is the most satisfactory thing in the world, and if we once fairly advance on this line nothing shall frighten us back.

Some such words as those may stand as a rough sketch of the sort of intellectual conviction under which "Madame Bovary" was written. The theory in this case at least was applied with brilliant success; it produced a masterpiece. Realism seems to us with "Madame Bovary" to have said its last word. We doubt whether the same process will ever produce anything better. In M. Flaubert's own hands it has distinctly failed to do so. "L'Education Sentimentale" is in comparison mechanical and inanimate. The great good fortune of "Madame Bovary" is that here the theory seems to have been invented after the fact. The author began to describe because he had laid up a great fund of disinterested observations; he had been looking at things for years, for his own edification, in that particular way. The imitative talents in the same line, those whose highest ambition is to "do" their Balzac or their Flaubert, give us the sense of looking at the world only with the most mercenary motives—of going about to stare at things only for the sake of their forthcoming novel. M. Flaubert knew what he was describing —knew it extraordinarily well. One can hardly congratulate him on his knowledge; anything drearier, more sordid, more vulgar and desolate than the greater part of the subject-matter of this romance it would be impossible to conceive. "Mœurs de Province," the sub-title runs, and the work is the most striking possible example of the singular passion, so common among Frenchmen of talent, for disparaging their provincial life. Emma Bovary is the daughter of a small farmer, who has been able to send her to boarding-school, and to give her something of an "elegant" education. She is pretty and graceful, and she marries a small country doctor—the kindest, simplest, stupidest of husbands. He takes her to live in a squalid little country town, called Yonville-l'Abbaye, near Rouen; she is luxurious and sentimental : she wastes away with ennui, loneliness, and hatred of her narrow lot and absent opportunities, and on the very first chance she takes a lover. With him she is happy for a few months, and then he deserts her brutally and cynically. She falls violently ill, and comes near dying; then she gets well, and takes another lover of a different kind. All the world—the very little world of Yonville-l'Abbaye—sees and knows and gossips; her husband alone neither sees nor suspects. Meanwhile she has been spending money remorselessly and insanely; she has made promissory notes, and she is smothered in debt. She has undermined the ground beneath her husband's feet; her second lover leaves her; she is ruined, dishonoured, utterly at bay. She goes back as a beggar to her first lover, and he refuses to give her a sou. She tries to sell herself and fails; then, in impotence and desperation, she collapses. She takes poison, and dies horribly, and the bailiffs come down on her husband, who is still heroically ignorant. At last he learns the truth, and it is too much for him; he loses all courage, and dies one day on his garden-bench, leaving twelve francs fifty centimes to his little girl, who is sent to get her living in a cotton-mill. The tale is a tragedy, unillumined and unredeemed, and it might seem, on this rapid and imperfect showing, to be rather a vulgar tragedy. Women who get into trouble with the extreme facility of Emma Bovary, and by the same method, are unfortunately not rare, and the better opinion seems to be that they deserve but a limited degree of sympathy. The history of M. Flaubert's heroine is nevertheless full of substance and meaning. In spite of the elaborate system of portraiture to which she is subjected, in spite of being minutely described in all her attitudes and all her moods, from the hem of her garment to the texture of her finger-nails, she remains a living creature, and as a living creature she interests us. The only thing that poor Charles Bovary, after her death, can find to say to her lovers is, "It's the fault of fatality." And in fact, as we enter into the situation, it is. M. Flaubert gives his readers the impression of having known few kinds of women, but he has evidently known intimately this particular kind. We see the process of her history; we see how it marches from step to step to its horrible termination, and we see that it could not have been otherwise. It is a case of the passion for luxury, for elegance, for the world's most agreeable and comfortable things, of an intense and complex imagination, corrupt almost in the germ, and finding corruption, and feeding on it, in the most unlikely and unfavouring places—it is a case of all this being pressed back upon itself with a force which makes an explosion inevitable. Madame Bovary has an insatiable hunger for pleasure, and she lives in the midst of dreariness; she is ignorant, vain, naturally depraved; of the things she dreams about not an intimation ever reaches her; so she makes her *trouée*, as the French say, bores her opening, scrapes and scratches her way out into the light, where she can. The reader may protest against a heroine who is "naturally depraved." You are welcome, he may say, to make of a heroine what you please, to carry her where you please; but in mercy do not set us down to a young lady of whom, on the first page, there is nothing better to be said than that. But all this is a question of degree. Madame Bovary is typical, like all powerfully-conceived figures in fiction. There are a great many potential Madame Bovarys, a great many young women, vain, ignorant, leading ugly, vulgar, intolerable lives, and possessed of irritable nerves and of a high natural appreciation of luxury, of admiration, of agreeable sensations, of what they consider the natural rights of pretty women, who are more or less launched upon the rapid slope which she descended to the bottom. The gentleman who recommended her history to the English lady at M. Taine's dinner-party would say that her history was in intention a solemn warning to such young women not to allow themselves to think too much about the things they cannot have. Does M. Flaubert in this case complete his intention? does he suggest an alternative—a remedy? plenty of plain sewing, serious reading, general house-work? M. Flaubert keeps well out of the province of remedies; he simply relates his facts in all their elaborate horror. The accumulation of detail is so immense, the vividness of portraiture of people, of places, of times and hours, is so poignant and convincing, that one is dragged into the very current and tissue of the story; the reader himself seems to have lived in it all, more than in any novel we can recall. At the end the intensity of illusion becomes horrible; overwhelmed with disgust and pity he closes the book.

Besides being the history of the most miserable of women, "Madame Bovary" is also an elaborate picture of small bourgeois rural life. Anything in this direction more remorseless and complete it would be hard to conceive. Into all that makes life ignoble and vulgar and sterile M. Flaubert has entered with an extraordinary penetration. The dullness and flatness of it all suffocate us; the pettiness and ugliness sicken us. Every one in the book is either stupid or mean, but against the shabby-coloured background two figures stand out in salient relief. One is Charles Bovary, the husband of the heroine; the other is M. Homais, the village apothecary. Bovary is introduced to us in his childhood, at school, and we see him afterwards at college and during his first marriage—a union with a widow of meagre charms, twenty years older than himself. He is the only good person of the book, but he is stupidly, helplessly good. At school "he had for correspondent a wholesale hardware merchant of the Rue Ganterie, who used to fetch him away once a month, on a Sunday, send him to walk in the harbour and look at the boats, and then bring him back to college, by seven o'clock, before supper. Every Thursday evening he wrote a long letter to his mother, with red ink and three wafers; then he went over his copy books, or else read an old volume of 'Anacharsis' which was knocking about the class-room. In our walks he used to talk with the servant, who was from the country like himself." In Homais, the apothecary, M. Flaubert has really added to our knowledge of human nature—at least as human nature is modified by French social conditions. To American readers, fortunately, this figure represents nothing familiar; we do not as yet possess any such mellow perfection of charlatanism. The apothecary is that unwholesome compound, a Philistine radical—a *père de famille*, a freethinker, a rapacious shopkeeper, a stern moralist, an ardent democrat and an abject snob. He is a complete creation; he is taken, as the French say, *sur le vif*, and his talk, his accent, his pompous vocabulary, his attitudes, his vanities, his windy vacuity, are superbly rendered. Except her two lovers, M. Homais is Mme. Bovary's sole male acquaintance, and her only social relaxation is to spend the evening with his wife and her own husband in his back shop. Her life has known, in the way of recreation, but two other events. Once she has been at a ball at the house of a neighbouring nobleman, for whom her husband had lanced an abscess in the cheek, and who sends the invitation as part payment—a fatal ball, which has opened her eyes to her own deprivations and intolerably quickened her desires; and once she has been to the theatre at Rouen. Both of these episodes are admirably put before us, and they play a substantial part in the tale. The book is full of expressive episodes; the most successful in its hideous relief and reality is the long account of the operation performed by Charles Bovary upon the club-foot of the ostler at the inn—an operation superfluous, ridiculous, abjectly unskilful and clumsy, and which results in the amputation of the poor fellow's whole leg after he has lain groaning under the reader's eyes and nose for a dozen pages, amid the flies and dirt, the brooms and pails, the comings and goings of his squalid corner of the tavern. The reader asks himself the meaning of this elaborate presentation of the most repulsive of incidents, and feels inclined at first to charge it to a sort of artistic bravado on the author's part—a desire to complete his theory of Realism by applying his resources to the simply disgusting. But he presently sees that the whole episode has a kind of metaphysical value. It completes the general picture; it characterizes the daily life of a community in which such incidents assume the importance of leading events, and it gives the final touch to our sense of poor Charles Bovary's bungling mediocrity. Everything in the book is ugly;

turning over its pages, our eyes fall upon only this one little passage in which an agreeable "effect" is rendered. It treats of Bovary's visits to Emma, at her father's farm, before their marriage, and it is a happy instance of the way in which this author's style arrests itself at every step in a picture. "Once, when it was thawing, the bark of the trees was reeking in the yard, the snow was melting on the roofs of the outbuildings. She was upon the threshold; she went in and fetched her umbrella and opened it. The umbrella, of dove-coloured silk, with the sun coming through it, lighted up her white complexion with changing reflections. Beneath it she smiled in the soft warmth, and he heard the water-drops fall one by one upon the tense silk." To many people "Madame Bovary" will always be a hard book to read and an impossible one to enjoy. They will complain of the abuse of description, of the want of spontaneity, of the hideousness of the subject, of the dryness and coldness and cynicism of the tone. Others will continue to think it a great performance. They will admit that it is not a sentimental novel, but they will claim that it may be regarded as a philosophical one; they will insist that the descriptions are extraordinary, and that beneath them there is always an idea that holds them up and carries them along. We cannot but think, however, that he is a very resolute partisan who would venture to make this same plea on behalf of "L'Education Sentimentale." Here the form and method are the same as in "Madame Bovary"; the studied skill, the science, the accumulation of material, are even more striking; but the book is in a single word a *dead* one. "Madame Bovary" was spontaneous and sincere; but to read its successor is, to the finer sense, like masticating ashes and sawdust. "L'Education Sentimentale" is elaborately and massively dreary. That a novel should have a certain charm seems to us the most rudimentary of principles, and there is no more charm in this laborious monument to a treacherous ideal than there is perfume in a gravel heap. To nothing that such a writer as Gustave Flaubert accomplishes—a writer so armed at all points, so informed, so ingenious, so serious,—can we be positively indifferent; but to think of the talent, the knowledge, the experience, the observation that lie buried, without hope of resurrection, in the pages of "L'Education Sentimentale," is to pass a comfortless half hour. That imagination, invention, taste and science should concentrate themselves, for human entertainment, upon such a result, strikes us as the most unfathomable of anomalies. The reader feels behind all M. Flaubert's writing a large intellectual machinery. He is a scholar, a man of erudition. Of all this "Salammbô" is a most accomplished example. "Salammbô" is not easy reading, nor is the book in the least agreeable; but it displays in the highest degree what is called the historical imagination. There are passages in it in which the literary expression of that refined, subtilized and erudite sense of the picturesque which recent years have brought to so high a development, seems to have reached its highest level. The "Tentation de Saint Antoine" is, to our sense, to "Salammbô" what "L'Education Sentimentale" is to "Madame Bovary" —what the shadow is to the substance. M. Flaubert seems to have had in him the material of but two spontaneous works. The successor, in each case, has been an echo, a reverberation.

IVAN TURGÉNIEFF.

WE know of several excellent critics who to the question, Who is the first novelist of the day? would reply, without hesitation, Ivan Turgénieff. Comparisons are odious, and we propose to make none that shall seem merely invidious. We quote our friends' verdict as a motive for this brief record of our own impressions. These, too, are in the highest degree favourable; and yet we wish not to impose a conclusion, but to help well-disposed readers to a larger enjoyment. To many such Turgénieff is already vaguely known as an eminent Russian novelist. Twelve years ago he was little more than a name, even in France, where he perhaps now finds his most sympathetic readers. But all his tales, we believe without exception, have now been translated into French—several by the author himself; an excellent German version of the best is being published under his own supervision, and several very fair English versions have appeared in England and America. He enjoys what is called a European reputation, and it is constantly spreading. The Russians, among whom fiction flourishes vigorously, deem him their greatest artist. His tales are not numerous, and many of them are very short. He gives us the impression of writing much more for love than for lucre. He is particularly a favourite with people of cultivated taste ; and nothing, in our opinion, cultivates the taste more than to read him.

I.

He belongs to the limited class of very careful writers. It is to be admitted at the outset that he is a zealous genius, rather than an abundant one. His line is narrow observation. He has not the faculty of rapid, passionate, almost reckless improvisation—that of Walter Scott, of Dickens, of George Sand. This is an immense charm in a story-teller; on the whole, to our sense, the greatest. Turgénieff lacks it; he charms us in other ways. To describe him in the fewest terms, he is a story-teller who has taken notes. This must have been a life-long habit. His tales are a magazine of small facts, of anecdotes, of discriptive traits, taken, as the phrase is, *sur le vif.* If we are not mistaken, he notes down an idiosyncracy of character, a fragment of talk, an attitude, a feature, a gesture, and keeps it, if need be, for twenty years, till just the moment for using it comes, just the spot for placing it. "Stachoff spoke

French tolerably, and as he led a quiet sort of life, passed for a philosopher. Even as an ensign, he was fond of disputing warmly whether, for instance, a man in his life might visit every point of the globe, or whether he might learn what goes on at the bottom of the sea, and was always of the opinion that it was impossible." The writer of this description may sometimes be erratic, but he is never vague. He has a passion for distinctness, for bringing his characterization to a point, for giving you an example of his meaning. He often, indeed, strikes us as loving details for their own sake, as a bibliomaniac loves the books he never reads. His figures are all portraits; they have each something special, something peculiar, something that none of their neighbours have, and that rescues them from the limbo of the gracefully general. We remember, in one of his stories, a gentleman who makes a momentary appearance as host at a dinner-party, and after being described as having such and such a face, clothes, and manners, has our impression of his personality completed by the statement that the soup at his table was filled with little paste figures, representing hearts, triangles, and trumpets. In the author's conception, there is a secret affinity between the character of this worthy man and the contortions of his vermicelli. This habit of specializing people by vivid oddities was the gulf over which Dickens danced the tight-rope with such agility. But Dickens, as we say, was an improvisatore; the practice, for him, was a lawless revel of the imagination. Turgénieff, on the other hand, always proceeds by book. What could be more minutely appreciative, and at the same time less like Dickens, than the following portrait?

"People in St. Petersburg still remember the Princess R——. She appeared there from time to time at the period of which we speak. Her husband was a well-bred man, but rather stupid, and she had no children. The Princess used to start suddenly on long journeys, and then return suddenly to Russia. Her conduct in all things was very strange. She was called light, and a coquette. She used to give herself up with ardour to all the pleasures of society: dance till she dropped with exhaustion, joke and laugh with the young men she received before dinner in her darkening drawing-room, and pass her nights praying and weeping, without finding a moment's rest. She often remained till morning in her room stretching her arms in anguish; or else she remained bowed, pale and cold, over the leaves of a hymn-book. Day came, and she was transformed again into an elegant creature, paid visits, laughed, chattered, rushed to meet everything that could give her the smallest diversion. She was admirably shaped. Her hair, the colour of gold, and as heavy as gold, formed a tress that fell below her knees. And yet she was not spoken of as a beauty: she had nothing fine in her face except her eyes. This even, perhaps, is saying too much, for her eyes were grey and rather small; but their deep keen gaze, careless to audacity, and dreamy to desolation, was equally enigmatical and charming. Something extraordinary was reflected in them, even when the most futile speeches were passing from her lips. Her toilets were always too striking."

These lines seem to carry a kind of historical weight. It is the Princess R—— and no one else. We feel as if the author could show us documents and relics; as if he had her portrait, a dozen letters, some of her old trinkets. Or take the following few lines from the admirable tale called "The Wayside Inn": "He belonged to the burgher class, and his name was Nahum Ivanoff. He had a thick short body, broad shoulders, a big round head, long waving hair already grizzled, though he was not yet forty. His face was full and fresh-coloured; his forehead low and white. His little eyes, of a clear blue, had a strange look, at once oblique and impudent. He kept his head always bent, his neck being too short; he walked fast, and never let his hands swing, keeping them always closed. When he smiled, and he smiled often, but without laughing and as if by stealth, his red lips parted disagreeably, showing a row of very white, very close teeth. He spoke quickly, with a snarling tone." When fiction is written in this fashion, we believe as we read. The same vividly definite element is found in the author's treatment of landscape: "The weather continued to stand at set-fair; little rounded white clouds moved through the air at a great height, and looked at themselves in the water; the reeds were stirred by movements and murmurs produced by no wind; the pond, looking in certain places like polished steel, absorbed the splendid sunshine." There is an even greater reality, because it is touched with the fantastic, without being perverted by it, in this brief sketch of the Pontine Marshes, from the beautiful little story of "Visions" :—

"The cloud before my eyes divided itself. I became aware of a limitless plain beneath me. Already, from the warm soft air which fanned my cheeks, I had observed that I was no longer in Russia. This plain, moreover, was not like our Russian plains. It was an immense dusky level, overgrown, apparently, with no grass, and perfectly desolate. Here and there, over the whole expanse, glittered pools of standing water, like little fragments of looking-glass. In the distance, the silent, motionless sea was vaguely visible. In the intervals of the broad beautiful clouds glittered great stars. A murmur, thousand-voiced, unceasing, and yet not loud, resounded from every spot; and strangely rang this penetrating, drowsy murmur, this nightly voice of the desert. . . . 'The Pontine Marshes,' said Ellis. 'Do you hear the frogs? Do you recognise the smell of sulphur?'"

This is a cold manner, many readers will say, and certainly it has a cold side; but when the character is one over which the author's imagination really kindles, it is an admirable vehicle for touching effects. Few stories leave on the mind a more richly poetic impression than "Hélène"; all the tenderness of our credulity goes forth to the heroine. Yet this exquisite image of idealized devotion swims before the author's vision in no misty moonlight of romance; she is as solidly fair as a Greek statue; his dominant desire has been to understand her, and he retails small facts about her appearance and habits with the impartiality of a judicial, or even a medical, summing up. The same may be said of his treatment of all his heroines, and said in evidence of the refinement of his art; for if there are no heroines we see more distinctly, there are none we love more ardently. It would be difficult to point, in the blooming fields of fiction, to a group of young girls more radiant with maidenly charm than M. Turgénieff's Hélène, his Lisa, his Katia, his Tatiana and his Gemma. For the truth is that, taken as a whole, he regains on another side what he loses by his apparent want of joyous invention. If his manner is that of a searching realist, his temper is that of a devoutly attentive observer, and the result of this temper is to make him take a view of the great spectacle of human life more general, more impartial, more unreservedly intelligent, than that of any novelist we know. Even on this line he proceeds with his characteristic precision of method; one thinks of him as having divided his subject-matter into categories, and as moving from one to the other—with none of the magniloquent pretensions of Balzac, indeed, to be the great showman of the human comedy—but with a deeply intellectual impulse toward universal appreciation. He seems to us to care for more things in life, to be solicited on more sides, than any novelist save George Eliot. Walter Scott cares for adventure and bravery and honour and ballad-figures and the humour of Scotch peasants; Dickens cares, on an immense, far-reaching scale, for picturesqueness; George Sand cares for love and mineralogy. But these writers care also, greatly, and indeed almost supremely, for their fable, for its twists and turns and surprises, for the work they have in hand of amusing the reader. Even George Eliot, who cares for so many other things besides, has a weakness for making a rounded plot, and often swells out her tales with mechanical episodes, in the midst of which their moral unity quite evaporates. The Bulstrode-Raffles episode in "Middlemarch," and the whole fable of "Felix Holt," are striking cases in point. M. Turgénieff lacks, as regards form, as we have said, this immense charm of absorbed inventiveness; but in the way of substance there is literally almost nothing he does not care for. Every class of society, every type of character, every degree of fortune, every phase of manners, passes through his hands; his imagination claims its property equally, in town and country, among rich and poor, among wise people and idiots, *dilettanti* and peasants, the tragic and the joyous, the probable and the grotesque. He has an eye for all our passions, and a deeply sympathetic sense of the wonderful complexity of our souls. He relates in "Mumu" the history of a deaf-and-dumb serf and a lap-dog, and he portrays in "A Strange Story" an extraordinary case of religious fanaticism. He has a passion for shifting his point of view, but his object is constantly the same—that of finding an incident, a person, a situation, *morally* interesting. This is his great merit, and the underlying harmony of his apparently excessive attention to detail. He believes in the intrinsic value of "subject" in art; he holds that there are trivial subjects and serious ones, that the latter are much the best, and that their superiority resides in their giving us absolutely a greater amount of information about the human mind. Deep into the mind he is always attempting to look, though he often applies his eye to very dusky apertures. There is perhaps no better evidence of his minutely psychological attitude than the considerable part played in his tales by simpletons and weak-minded persons. There are few novelists who have not been charmed by the quaintness and picturesqueness of mental invalids; but M. Turgénieff is attracted by something more—by the opportunity of watching the machinery of character, as it were, through a broken window-pane. One might collect from his various tales a perfect regiment of incapables, of the stragglers on life's march. Almost always, in the background of his groups of well-to-do persons there lurks some grotesque, under-witted poor relation, who seems to hover about as a vague memento, in his scheme, of the instability both of fortune and of human cleverness. Such, for instance, is Uvar Ivanovitsch, who figures as a kind of inarticulate chorus in the tragedy of "Hélène." He sits about, looking very wise and opening and closing his fingers, and in his person, in this attitude, the drama capriciously takes leave of us. Perhaps the most moving of all the author's tales—moving, not in the sense that it makes us shed easy tears, but as reminding us vividly of the solidarity, as we may say, of all human weakness—has for its hero a person made imbecile by suffering. The admirable little story of "The Brigadier" can only be spoilt by an attempt to retail it; we warmly recommend it to the reader, in the French version. Never did Romance stoop over a lowlier case of moral decomposition, but never did she gather more of the perfume of human truth. To a person able to read but one of M. Turgénieff's tales, we should perhaps offer this one as a supreme example of his peculiar power; for here the artist, as well as the analyst, is at his best. All rigid critical formulas are more or less unjust, and it is not a complete description of our author—it would be a complete description of no real master of fiction—to say that he is simply a searching observer. M. Turgénieff's imagination is always lending a hand and doing work on its own account. Some of this work is exquisite; nothing could have more of the simple magic of picturesqueness than such tales as "The Dog," "The Jew," "Visions," "The Adventure of Lieutenant Jergounoff," "Three Meetings," a dozen episodes in the "Memoirs of a Sportsman." Imagination guides his hand and modulates his touch, and makes the artist worthy of the observer. In a word, he is universally sensitive. In susceptibility to the sensuous impressions of life—to colours and odours and forms, and the myriad ineffable refinements and enticements of beauty—he equals, and even surpasses, the most accomplished representatives of the French school of story-telling; and yet he has, on the other hand, an apprehension of man's religious impulses, of the *ascetic* passion, the capacity of becoming dead to colours and odours and beauty, never dreamed of in the philosophy of Balzac and Flaubert, Octave Feuillet and Gustave Droz. He gives us Lisa in "A Nest of Noblemen," and Madame Polosoff in "Spring Torrents." This marks his range. Let us add, in conclusion, that his merit of form is of the first order. He is remarkable for concision; few of his novels occupy the whole of a moderate volume, and some of his best performances are tales of thirty pages.

II.

M. Turgénieff's themes are all Russian; here and there the scene of a tale is laid in another country, but the actors are genuine Muscovites. It is the Russian type of human nature that he depicts; this perplexes, fascinates, inspires him. His works savour strongly of his native soil, like those of all great novelists, and give one who has read them all a strange sense of having had a prolonged experience of Russia. We seem to have travelled there in dreams, to have dwelt there in another state of being. M. Turgénieff gives us a peculiar sense of being out of harmony with his native land—of his having what one may call a poet's quarrel with it. He loves the old, and he is unable to see where the new is drifting. American readers will peculiarly appreciate this state of mind; if they had a native novelist of a large pattern, it would probably be, in a degree, his own. Our author *feels* the Russian character intensely, and cherishes, in fancy, all its old manifestations—the unemancipated peasants, the ignorant, absolute, half-barbarous proprietors, the quaint provincial society, the local types and customs of every kind. But Russian society, like our own, is in process of formation, the Russian character is in solution, in a sea of change, and the modified, modernized Russian, with his old limitations and his new pretensions, is not, to an imagination fond of caressing the old, fixed contours, an especially grateful phenomenon. A satirist at all points, as we shall have occasion to say, M. Turgénieff is particularly unsparing of the new intellectual fashions prevailing among his countrymen. The express purpose of one of his novels, "Fathers and Sons," is to contrast them with the old; and in most of his recent works, notably "Smoke," they have been embodied in various grotesque figures.

It was not, however, in satire, but in thoroughly genial, poetical portraiture, that our author first made his mark. "The Memoirs of a Sportsman" were published in 1852, and were regarded, says one of the two French translators of the work, as much the same sort of contribution to the question of Russian serfdom as Mrs. Stowe's famous novel to that of American slavery. This, perhaps, is forcing a point, for M. Turgénieff's group of tales strikes us much less as a passionate *pièce de circonstance* than as a disinterested work of art. But circumstances helped it, of course, and it made a great impression—an impression that testifies to no small culture on the part of Russian readers. For never, surely, was a work with a polemic bearing more consistently low in tone, as painters say. The author treats us to such a scanty dose of flagrant horrors that the moral of the book is obvious only to attentive readers. No single episode pleads conclusively against the "peculiar institution" of Russia; the lesson is in the cumulative testimony of a multitude of fine touches—in an after-sense of sadness that sets wise readers thinking. It would be difficult to name a work that contains better instruction for those heated spirits who are fond of taking sides on the question of "art for art." It offers a capital example of moral meaning giving a sense to form and form giving relief to moral meaning. Indeed, all the author's characteristic merits are to be found in the "Memoirs," with a certain amateurish looseness of texture which will charm many persons who find his later works too frugal, as it were, in shape. Of all his productions, this is indeed the most purely delightful. We especially recommend the little history of Foma, the forest keeper, who, one rainy night, when the narrator has taken refuge in his hut, hears a peasant stealing faggots in the dark, dripping woods; rushes forth and falls upon him, drags the poor wretch home, flings him

into a corner, and sits on in the smoky hovel (with
the author, whom we perceive there, noting, feeling,
measuring it all), while the rain batters the roof and
the drenched starveling howls and whines and im-
precates. Anything more dismally real in a narrower
compass we have never read—anything more pathetic,
with less of the machinery of pathos. In this case,
as at every turn with M. Turgénieff, "It is life itself,"
we murmur as we read, "and not this or that or the
other story-teller's more or less clever 'arrangement'
of life." M. Turgénieff deserves this praise in its
largest application; for "life" in his pages is very far
from meaning a dreary liability to sordid accidents, as
it seems to mean with those writers of the grimly
pathetic school who cultivate sympathy to the detri-
ment of comprehension. He does equal justice—
joyous justice—to all brighter accidents—to everything
in experience that helps to keep it within the pale of
legend. Two of the Sportsman's reminiscences are
inexpressibly charming—the chapter in which he spends
a warm summer night lying on the grass listening to
the small boys who are sent out to watch the horses at
pasture, as they sit chattering to each other of hob-
goblins and fairies; and the truly beautiful description
of a singing-match in a village ale-house, between two
ragged serfs. The latter is simply a perfect poem.

Very different, but in its way as characteristic, is the story of "A Russian Hamlet"—a poor gentleman whom the Sportsman, staying overnight at a fine house where he has been dining, finds assigned to him as room-mate, and who, lying in bed and staring at him grotesquely over the sheets, relates his lugubrious history. This sketch, more than its companions, strikes the deep moral note that was to reverberate through the author's novels.

The story of "Rudin," which followed soon after, is perhaps the most striking example of his preference for a theme which takes its starting-point in character —if need be, in morbid character. We have had no recent opportunity to refresh our memory of the tale, but we have not forgotten the fine quality of its interest—its air of psychological truth, unencumbered with the usual psychological apparatus. The theme is one which would mean little enough to a coarse imagination—the exhibition of a character peculiarly unrounded, unmoulded, unfinished, inapt for the regular romantic attitudes. Dmitri Rudin is a moral failure, like many of the author's heroes—one of those fatally complex natures who cost their friends so many pleasures and pains; who might, and yet, evidently, might not, do great things; natures strong in impulse, in talk, in responsive emotion, but weak in will, in

action, in the power to feel and do singly. Madame
Sand's "Horace" is a broad, free study of this type
of person, always so interesting to imaginative and so
intolerable to rational people; M. Turgénieff's hero is
an elaborate miniature-portrait. Without reading
Rudin we should not know just how fine a point he
can give to his pencil. But M. Turgénieff, with his
incisive psychology, like Madame Sand, with her expansive synthesis, might often be a vain demonstrator
and a very dull novelist if he were not so constantly
careful to be a dramatist. Everything, with him, takes
the dramatic form; he is apparently unable to conceive
anything independently of it, he has no recognition of
unembodied ideas; an idea, with him, is such and such
an individual, with such and such a nose and chin,
such and such a hat and waistcoat, bearing the same
relation to it as the look of a printed word does to
its meaning. Abstract possibilities immediately become, to his vision, concrete situations, as elaborately
defined and localized as an interior by Meissonier. In
this way, as we read, we are always looking and
listening; and we seem, indeed, at moments, for want
of a running thread of explanation, to see rather more
than we understand.

It is, however, in "Hélène" that the author's closely
commingled realism and idealism have obtained their

greatest triumph. The tale is at once a homely chronicle and a miniature epic. The scene, the figures, are as present to us as if we saw them ordered and moving on a lamp-lit stage; and yet, as we recall it, the drama seems all pervaded and coloured by the light of the moral world. There are many things in "Hélenè," and it is difficult to speak of them in order. It is both so simple and so various, it proceeds with such an earnest tread to its dark termination, and yet it entertains and beguiles us so unceasingly as it goes, that we lose sight of its simple beauty in its confounding, entrancing reality. But we prize it, as we prize all the very best things, according to our meditative after-sense of it. Then we see its lovely unity melting its brilliant parts into a single harmonious tone. The story is all in the portrait of the heroine, who is a heroine in the literal sense of the word; a young girl of a will so calmly ardent and intense that she needs nothing but opportunity to become one of the figures about whom admiring legend clusters. She is a really elevated conception; and if, as we shall complain, there is bitterness in M. Turgénieff's imagination, there is certainly sweetness as well. It is striking that most of his flights of fancy are in his conceptions of women. With them only, occasionally, does he wholly forswear his irony and become frankly sympathetic. We hope it is not false ethnology to suppose that this is a sign of something, potentially at least, very fine in the character of his country-women. As fine a poet as you will would hardly have devised a Maria Alexandrovna (in "A Correspondence,"), an Hélène, a Lisa, a Tatiana, an Irene even, without having known some very admirable women. These ladies have a marked family likeness, an exquisite something in common which we may perhaps best designate as an absence of frivolous passion. They are addicted to none of those *chatteries* which French romancers consider the "adorable" thing in women. The baleful beauty, in "Smoke," who robs Tatiana of her lover, acts in obedience to an impulse deeper than vulgar coquetry. And yet these fair Muscovites have a spontaneity, an independence, quite akin to the English ideal of maiden loveliness. Directly, superficially, they only half please. They puzzle us almost too much to charm, and we fully measure their beauty only when they are called upon to act. Then the author imagines them doing the most touching, the most inspiring things.

Hélène's loveliness is all in unswerving action. She passes before us toward her mysterious end with the swift, keen movement of a feathered arrow. She finds her opportunity, as we have called it, in her sympathy with a young Bulgarian patriot who dreams of rescuing his country from Turkish tyranny; and she surrenders herself to his love and his project with a tranquil passion which loses none of its poetry in M. Turgénieff's treatment. She is a supreme example of his taste for " original " young ladies. She would certainly be pronounced *queer* in most quiet circles. She has, indeed, a fascinating oddity of outline; and we never lose a vague sense that the author is presenting her to us with a charmed expectancy of his own, as a travelled friend would show us some quaintly-feathered bird brought from beyond the seas, but whose note he had not yet heard. To appreciate Hélène's oddity, you must read of the orthodoxy of the people who surround her. All about the central episode the story fades away into illimitable irony, as if the author wished to prove that, compared with the deadly seriousness of Hélène and Inssaroff, everything else is indeed a mere playing at life. We move among the minor episodes in a kind of atmosphere of sarcasm: now kindly, as where Bersenieff and Schubin are dealt with; now unsparingly comical, as in the case of her foolish parents and their tardy bewilderment—that of loquacious domestic fowls who find themselves responsible for the hatching of an eagle. The whole story is charged with lurking meanings, and to retail them would be as elaborate a task as picking threads out of a piece of fine tapestry. What is Mademoiselle Zoe, for instance, the little German *dame de compagnie*, but a humorous sidelight upon Hélène's intensity—Mademoiselle Zoe, with the pretty shoulders, and her presence in the universe a sort of mere general rustle of muslin, accompanied, perhaps, by a faint toilet-perfume? There is nothing finer in all Turgénieff than the whole matter of Bersenieff's and Schubin's relation to Hélène. They, too, in their vivid reality, have a symbolic value, as they stand watching the woman they equally love whirled away from them in a current swifter than any force of their own. Schubin, the young sculptor, with his moods and his theories, his exaltations and depressions, his endless talk and his disjointed action, is a deeply ingenious image of the artistic temperament. Yet, after all, he strikes the practical middle key, and solves the problem of life by the definite application of what he *can*. Bersenieff, though a less fanciful, is perhaps, at bottom, a still more poetical figure. He is condemned to inaction, not by his intellectual fastidiousness, but by a conscious, intelligent, intellectual mediocrity, by the dogged loyalty of his judgment. There is something in his history more touching than even in that of Hélène and Inssaroff. These two, and Schubin as well, have their consolations. If they are born to suffering, they are born also to rapture. They stand at the open door of passion, and they can sometimes forget. But poor Bersenieff, wherever he turns, meets conscience with uplifted finger, saying to him that though Homer may sometimes nod, the sane man never misreasons and the wise man assents to no mood that is not a working mood. He has not even the satisfaction of lodging a complaint against fate. He is by no means sure that he has one; and when he finds that his love is vain he translates it into friendship with a patient zeal capable almost of convincing his own soul that it is not a renunciation, but a consummation. Berseniff, Schubin, Zoe, Uvar Ivanovitsch, the indigent house-friend, with his placid depths of unuttered commentary, the pompous egotist of a father, the feeble egotist of a mother—these people thoroughly animate the little world that surrounds the central couple; and if we wonder how it is that from half a dozen figures we get such a sense of the world's presence and complexity, we perceive the great sagacity of the choice of the types.

We should premise, in speaking of "A Nest of Noblemen" (the English translation bears, we believe, the simple title of "Lisa"), that of the two novels it was the earlier published. It dates from 1858;

"Hélène" from 1859. The theme is an unhappy marriage and an unhappy love. Fedor Ivanovitsch Lavretzky marries a pretty young woman, and after three years of confident bliss finds himself grossly deceived. He separates from his wife, returns from Paris, where his eyes have been unsealed, to Russia, and, in the course of time, retires to his patrimonial estates. Here, after the pain of his wound has ached itself away and the health and strength of life's prime have reaffirmed themselves, he encounters a young girl whom he comes at last to love with the double force of a tender heart that longs to redeem itself from bitterness. He receives news of his wife's death, and immediately presumes upon his freedom to express his passion. The young girl listens, responds, and for a few brief days they are happy. But the report of Madame Lavretzky's death has been, as the newspapers say, premature; she suddenly reappears, to remind her husband of his bondage and to convict Lisa almost of guilt. The pathetic force of the story lies, naturally, in its taking place in a country unfurnished with the modern facilities for divorce. Lisa and Lavretzky of course must part. Madame Lavretzky lives and blooms. Lisa goes into a convent, and her lover, defrauded of happiness, determines at least to try and be useful. He ploughs his fields and instructs his serfs. After the lapse of years he obtains entrance into her convent and catches a glimpse of her as she passes behind a grating, on her way across the chapel. She knows of his presence, but she does not even look at him; the trembling of her downcast lids alone betrays her sense of it. "What must they both have thought, have felt?" asks the author. "Who can know? who can say? There are moments in life, there are feelings, on which we can only cast a glance without stopping." With an unanswered question his story characteristically closes. The husband, the wife, and the lover—the wife, the husband, and the woman loved —these are combinations in which modern fiction has been prolific; but M. Turgénieff's treatment renews the youth of the well-worn fable. He has found its moral interest, if we may make the distinction, deeper than its sentimental one; a pair of lovers accepting adversity seem to him more eloquent than a pair of lovers grasping at happiness. The moral of his tale, as we are free to gather it, is that there is no effective plotting for happiness, that we must take what we can get, that adversity is a capable mill-stream, and that our ingenuity must go toward making it grind our corn. Certain it is that there is something very exquisite in Lavretzky's history, and that M. Turgénieff has drawn from a theme associated with all manner of uncleanness a story embalmed in a lovely aroma of purity. This purity, indeed, is but a pervasive emanation from the character of Lisaveta Michailovna. American readers of Turgénieff have been struck with certain points of resemblance between American and Russian life. The resemblance is generally superficial; but it does not seem to us altogether fanciful to say that Russian young girls, as represented by Lisa, Tatiana, Maria Alexandrovna, have to our sense a touch of the faintly acrid perfume of the New England temperament—a hint of Puritan angularity. It is the women and young girls in our author's tales who mainly represent strength of will—the power to resist, to wait, to attain. Lisa represents it in all that heroic intensity which says so much more to M. Turgénieff's imagination than feline grace. The character conspicuous in the same tale for feline grace—Varvara Pavlovna, Lavretzky's heartless wife—is conspicuous also for her moral flimsiness. In the integrity of Lisa, of Hélène, even of the more dimly shadowed Maria Alexandrovna —a sort of finer distillation, as it seems, of masculine honour—there is something almost formidable: the strongest men are less positive in their strength. In the keenly pathetic scene in which Marfa Timofievna (the most delightful of the elderly maiden aunts of fiction) comes to Lisa in her room and implores her to renounce her project of entering a convent, we feel that there are depths of purpose in the young girl's deferential sweetness that nothing in the world can overcome. She is intensely religious, as she ought to be for psychological truth, and nothing could more effectually disconnect her from the usual *ingénue* of romance than our sense of the naturalness of her religious life. Her love for Lavretzky is a passion in its essence half renunciation. The first use she makes of the influence with him which his own love gives her is to try and reconcile him with his wife; and her foremost feeling, on learning that the latter is not dead, as they had believed, is an irremissible sense of pollution. The dusky, antique consciousness of sin in this tender, virginal soul is a combination which we seem somehow to praise amiss in calling it picturesque, but which it would be still more inexact to call didactic. Lisa is altogether a most remarkable portrait, and one that readers of the heroine's own sex ought to contemplate with some complacency. They have been known to complain on the one hand that romancers abuse them, and on the other that they insufferably patronise them. Here is a picture drawn with all the tenderness of a lover, and yet with an indefinable — an almost unprecedented — respect. In this tale, as always with our author, the drama is quite uncommented; the poet never plays chorus; situations speak for themselves. When Lavretzky reads in the *chronique* of a French newspaper that his wife is dead, there is no description of his feelings, no portrayal of his mental attitude. The living, moving narrative has so effectually put us in the way of feeling with him that we can be depended upon. He had been reading in bed before going to sleep, had taken up the paper and discovered the momentous paragraph. He "threw himself into his clothes," the author simply says, "went out into the garden, and walked up and down till morning in the same alley." We close the book for a moment and pause, with a sense of personal excitement. But of M. Turgénieff's genius for infusing a rich suggestiveness into common forms, the character of Gottlieb Lemm, the melancholy German music-master, is a perhaps surpassing example. Never was homely truth more poetical; never was poetry more minutely veracious.

Lavretzky, sorely tried as he is, is perhaps the happiest of our author's heroes. He suffers great pain, but he has not the intolerable sense of having inflicted it on others. This is the lot, both of the hero of "Smoke" and of the fatally passive youth whose adventures we follow in the author's latest work. On "Smoke" we are unable to linger, as its theme is almost identical with that of "Spring-Torrents," and the latter will be a novelty to a greater number of our readers. "Smoke," with its powerful and painful interest, lacks, to our mind, the underlying sweetness of most of its companions. It has all their talent, but it has less of their spirit. It treats of a dangerous beauty who robs the loveliest girl in Russia of her plighted lover, and the story duly absorbs us; but we find that, for our own part, there is always a certain langour in our intellectual acceptance of the grand coquettes of fiction. It is obviously a hard picture to paint; we always seem to see the lady pushing about her train before the foot-lights, or glancing at the orchestra-stalls during her victim's agony. In the portrait of Irene, however, there are very fine intentions, and the reader is charmed forward very much as poor Litvinof was. The figure of Tatiana, however, is full of the wholesome perfume of nature. "Smoke" was preceded by "Fathers and Sons," which dates from ten years ago, and was the first of M. Turgénieff's tales to be translated in America. In none of them is the subject of wider scope or capable of having more of the author's insidious melancholy expressed from it; for the figures with which he has filled his foreground are, with their personal interests and adventures, but the symbols of the shadowy forces that are fighting for ever a larger battle—the battle of the old and the new, the past and the future, of the ideas that arrive with the ideas that linger. Half the tragedies in human history are born of this conflict; and in all that poets and philosophers tell us of it the clearest fact is still its perpetual necessity. The opposing forces in M. Turgénieff's novel are an elder and a younger generation; the drama can indeed never have a more poignant interest than when we see the young world, as it grows to a sense of its strength and its desires, turning to smite the old world which has brought it forth with a mother's tears and a mother's hopes. The young world, in "Fathers and Sons," is the fiercer combatant; and the old world in fact is simply for ever the *victa causa* that even stoics pity. And yet with M. Turgénieff, characteristically, the gaining cause itself is purely relative, and victors and vanquished are commingled in a common assent to fate. Here, as always, his rare discretion serves him, and rescues him from the danger of exaggerating his representative types. Few figures in his pages are more intelligibly human than Pavel Petrovitsch and Eugene Bazaroff—human each of them in his indefeasible weakness; the one in spite of his small allowances, the other in spite of his brutal claims. In the elder Kirsanoff the author has imaged certain things he instinctively values—the hundred fading traditions of which the now vulgarized idea of the "gentleman" is the epitome. He loves him, of course, as a romancer must, but he has done the most impartial justice to the ridiculous aspect of his position. Bazaroff is a so-called "nihilist"—a red-handed radical, fresh from the shambles of criticism, with Büchner's *Stoff und Kraft* as a text-book, and everything in nature and history for his prey. He is young, strong, and clever, and strides about, rejoicing in his scepticism, sparing nothing, human or divine, and proposing to have demolished the universe before he runs his course. But he finds there is something stronger, cleverer, longer-lived than himself, and that death is a fiercer nihilist than even Dr. Büchner. The tale traces the course of the summer vacation that he comes to spend in the country with a college friend, and is chiefly occupied with the record of the various trials to which, in this short period, experience subjects his philosophy. They all foreshadow, of course, the supreme dramatic test. He falls in love, and tries to deny his love as he denies everything else, but the best he can do is only to express it in a coarse formula. M. Turgénieff is always fond of contrasts, and he has not failed to give Bazaroff a foil in his young comrade, Arcadi Kirsanoff, who represents the merely impermanent and imitative element that clings to the skirts of every great movement. Bazaroff is silenced by death, but it takes a very small dose of life to silence Arcadi. The latter belongs to the nobility, and Bazaroff's exploits in his tranquil, conventional home are those of a lusty young bull in a cabinet of rococo china. Exquisitely imagined is the whole attitude and demeanour of Pavel Petrovitsch, Arcadi's uncle, and a peculiarly happy invention the duel which this perfumed conservative considers it his manifest duty to fight in behalf of gentlemanly opinions. The deeper interest of the tale, however, begins when the young Büchnerite repairs to his own provincial home and turns to a pinch of dust the tender superstitions of the poor old parental couple who live only in their pride in their great learned son and have not even a genteel prejudice, of any consequence, to oppose to his terrible positivism. M. Turgénieff has written nothing finer than this last half of his story; every touch is masterly, every detail is eloquent. In Vassili Ivanovitsch and Arina Vlassievna he has shown us the sentient heart that still may throb in disused forms and not be too proud to subsist a while yet by the charity of science. Their timid devotion to their son, their roundabout caresses, their longings and hopes and fears, and their deeply pathetic stupefaction when it begins to be plain that the world can spare him, all form a picture which, in spite of its dealing with small things in a small style, carries us to the uttermost limits of the tragical. A very noticeable stroke of art, also, is Bazaroff's ever-growing discontentment—a chronic moral irritation, provoked not by the pangs of an old-fashioned conscience, but, naturally enough, by the absence of the agreeable in a world that he has subjected to such exhaustive disintegration. We especially recommend to the reader his long talk with Arcadi as they lie on the grass in the midsummer shade, and Bazaroff kicks out viciously at everything propounded by his ingenuous companion. Toward him too he feels vicious, and we quite understand the impulse, identical with that which in a nervous woman would find expression in a fit of hysterics, through which the overwrought young rationalist, turning to Arcadi with an alarming appearance of real gusto, proposes to fight with him, "to the extinction of animal heat." We must find room for the portrait of Arina Vlassievna :—

She "was a real type of the small Russian gentry of the old *régime ;* she ought to have come into the world two hundred years sooner, in the time of the grand-dukes of Moscow. Easily impressed, deeply pious, she believed in all signs and tokens, divinations, sorceries, dreams ; she believed in the *Iourodivi* [half-witted persons, popularly held sacred], in familiar spirits, in those of the woods, in evil meetings, in the evil eye, in popular cures, in the virtue of salt placed upon the altar on Good Friday, in the impending end of the world ; she believed that if the tapers at the midnight mass in Lent do not go out, the crop of buckwheat will be good, and that mushrooms cease to grow as soon as human eye has rested on them ; she believed that the Devil likes places where there is water, and that all Jews have a blood-spot on their chests ; she was afraid of mice, snakes, toads, sparrows, leeches, thunder, cold water, draughts of air, horses, goats, red-haired men and black cats, and considered crickets and dogs as impure creatures ; she ate neither veal, nor pigeons, nor lobsters, nor cheese, nor asparagus, nor hare, nor watermelon (because a melon opened resembled the dissevered head of John the Baptist), and the mere idea of oysters, which she did not know even by sight, caused her to shudder ; she liked to eat well, and fasted rigorously ; she slept ten hours a day, and never went to bed at all if Vassili Ivanovitsch complained of a headache. The only book that she had read was called 'Alexis, or The Cottage in the Forest' ; she wrote at most one or two letters a year, and was an excellent judge of sweatmeats and preserves, though she put her own hand to nothing, and, as a general thing, preferred not to move. . . . . She was anxious, was perpetually expecting some great misfortune, and began to cry as soon as she remembered anything sad. Women of this kind are beginning to be rare ; God knows whether we should be glad of it."

The novel which we have chosen as the text of these remarks was published some six years since. It strikes us at first as a reproduction of old material, the subject being identical with that of "Smoke" and very similar to that of the short masterpiece called "A Correspondence." The subject is one of the saddest in the world, and we shall have to reproach M. Turgénieff with delighting in sadness. But "Spring-Torrents" has a narrative charm that sweetens its bitter waters, and we may add that, from the writer's point of view, the theme does differ by several shades from that of the tales we have mentioned. These treat of the fatal weakness of will that M. Turgénieff apparently considers the peculiar vice of the new generation in Russia; "Spring-Torrents" illustrates, more generally, the element of folly which mingles, in a certain measure, in all youthful spontaneity, and makes us grow to wisdom by the infliction of suffering. The youthful folly of Dmitri Sanin has been great, the memory of it haunts him for years and lays on him at last such an icy grip that his heart will break unless he can repair it. The opening sentences of the story indicate the key in which it is pitched. We may quote them as an example of the way in which M. Turgénieff almost invariably appeals at the outset to our distinctively *moral* curiosity, our sympathy with character. Something tells us, in this opening strain, that we are not invited to lend ear to the mere dead rattle that rises for ever from the surface of life:—

". . . . Towards two o'clock at night, he came back into his sitting-room. The servant who had lighted the candles he sent away, threw himself into a chair by the chimney-piece, and covered his face with his hands. Never had he felt such a weariness of body and soul. He had been spending the whole evening with graceful women, with cultivated men; some of the women were pretty, almost all the men were distinguished for wit and talent; he himself had talked with good effect, even brilliantly; and yet with all this, never had that *tædium vitæ*, of which the Romans already speak, that sense of disgust with life, pressed upon him and taken possession of him in such an irresistible fashion. Had he been somewhat younger, he would have wept for sadness, for ennui and overwrought nerves : a corroding, burning bitterness, like the bitterness of wormwood, filled his whole soul. Something inexpugnable—cold, sickening, oppressive—crowded in upon him from all sides like autumn dusk, and he knew not how he could free himself from this duskiness and bitterness. He could not count upon sleep ; he knew he should not sleep. . . . . He began to muse — slowly, sadly, bitterly. . . . . He thought of the vanity, the uselessness, the common falsity of the whole human race. . . . . He shook his head, sprang up from his seat, walked several times up and down the room, sat down at his writing-table, pulled out one drawer after the other, and began to fumble among old papers, mostly letters in a woman's hand. He knew not why he did it—he was looking for nothing, he simply wished to seek refuge in an outward occupation from the thoughts that tormented him. . . . . He got up, went back to the fireplace, sank into his chair again, and covered his face with his hands. . . . . 'Why to-day, just to-day?' he thought ; and many a memory from the long-vanished past rose up in him. He remembered—this is what he remembered."

On his way back to Russia from a foreign tour he meets, at Frankfort, a young girl of modest origin but extraordinary beauty—the daughter of an Italian confectioner. Accident brings them together, he falls in love with her, holds himself ardently ready to marry her, obtains her mother's consent, and has only, to make the marriage possible, to raise money on his Russian property, which is of moderate value. While he is revolving schemes he encounters an old schoolfellow,

an odd personage, now married to an heiress who, as
fortune has it, possesses an estate in the neighbour-
hood of Sanin's own. It occurs to the latter that
Madame Polosoff may be induced to buy his land, and,
as she understands "business" and manages her own
affairs, he repairs to Wiesbaden, with leave obtained
from his betrothed, to make his proposal. The reader
of course foresees the sequel—the reader, especially,
who is versed in Turgénieff. Madame Polosoff understands business and much else besides. She is young,
lovely, unscrupulous, dangerous, fatal. Sanin succumbs
to the spell, forgets honour, duty, tenderness, prudence,
everything, and after three days of bewildered resistance
finds himself packed into the lady's travelling-carriage
with her other belongings and rolling toward Paris.
But we foresee that he comes speedily to his senses; the
spring-torrent is spent. The years that follow are
as arid as brooding penitence can make them.
Penitence, after that night of bitter memories, takes an
active shape. He makes a pilgrimage to Frankfort
and seeks out some trace of the poor girl he had
deserted. With much trouble he obtains tidings, and
learns that she is married in America, that she is
happy, and that she serenely forgives him. He returns
to St. Petersburg, spends there a short, restless interval, and suddenly disappears. People say he has gone to

America. The spring torrents exhale themselves in autumn mists. Sanin, in the Frankfort episode, is not only very young, but very Russian; how young, how Russian, this charming description tells :—

"He was, to begin with, a really very good-looking fellow. He had a tall, slender figure, agreeable, rather vague features, kindly blue eyes, a fair complexion suffused with a fresh red, and, above all, that genial, joyous, confiding, upright expression, which at the first glance, perhaps, seems to give an air of limitation, but by which, in former times, you recognised the son of a tranquil aristocratic family—a son of the 'fathers,' a good country gentleman, born and grown up, stoutly, in those fruitful provinces of ours which border on the steppe ; then a somewhat shuffling gait, a slightly lisping way of speaking, a childlike laugh as soon as any one looked at him, ... health, in short, freshness and a softness,—a softness ! . . . . there you have all Sanin. Along with this he was by no means dull, and had learnt a good many things. He had remained fresh in spite of his journey abroad ; those tumultuous impulses that imposed themselves upon the best part of the young men of that day were little known to him."

If we place beside this vivid portrait the sketch, hardly less expressive, of Madame Polosoff, we find in the mere apposition the germ of a novel :—

"Not that she was a perfect beauty ; the traces of her plebeian origin were perceptible enough. Her forehead was low, her nose rather thick and inclining to an upward inflection ; she could boast neither of a fine skin nor of pretty hands and feet. But what did all this signify ? Not before the 'sanctity of beauty'—to use Puschkin's words—would he who met her have stood lingering, but before the charm of the powerful half-Russian, half-Bohemian, blooming, womanly body—and he would not have lingered without a purpose."

Madame Polosoff, though her exploits are related in a short sixty-five pages, is unfolded in the large dramatic manner. We seem to be in her presence, to listen to her provoking, bewildering talk, to feel the danger of her audacious, conscious frankness. Her quite peculiar cruelty and depravity make a large demand on our credulity; she is perhaps a trifle too picturesquely vicious. But she is strangely, vividly natural, and our imagination goes with her in the same charmed mood as with M. Turgénieff's other evil-doers. Not without an effort, too, do we accept the possibility of Sanin's immediate infidelity to the object of the pure still passion with which his heart even yet overflows. But these are wonderful mysteries; its immediacy, perhaps, best accounts for it; spring torrents, the author would seem to intimate, *must* flow, and ravage their blooming channels. To give a picture of the immeasurable blindness of youth, of its eagerness of desire, its freshness of impression, its mingled rawness and ripeness, the swarming, shifting possibilities of its springtime, and to interfuse his picture with something of the softening poetizing harmony of retrospect—this has been but half the author's purpose. He has designed beside to paint the natural conflict between soul and sense, and to make the struggle less complex than the one he has described in "Smoke," and less brutal, as it were, than the fatal victory of sense in "A Correspondence." "When will it all come to an end?" Sanin asks, as he stares helpless at Maria Nikolaievna, and feels himself ignobly paralysed. "Weak men," says the author, "never themselves make an end,—they always wait for the end." Sanin's history is weighted with the moral that salvation lies in being able, at a given moment, to bring one's will down like a hammer. If M. Turgénieff pays his tribute to the magic of sense he leaves us also eloquently reminded that soul in the long run claims her own. He has given us no sweeter image of uncorrupting passion than this figure of Gemma, the frank young Italian nature blooming in northern air from its own mere wealth of joyousness. Yet, charming as Gemma is, she is but a half-sister to Lisa and Tatiana. Neither Lisa or Tatiana, we suspect, would have read popular comedy with her enchanting mimicry; but, on the other hand, they would have been withheld by a delicate, indefinable conscientiousness from caricaturing the dismissed lover of the day before for the entertainment of the accepted lover of the present. But Gemma is a charming piece of colouring, and all this only proves how many different ways there are of being the loveliest girl in the world. The accessories of her portrait are as happily rendered; the whole picture of the little Italian household, with its narrow backshop life in the

German town, has a mellow enclosed light in which the reader gratefully lingers. It touches the figure of the usual half-fantastic house-friend, the poor old ex-barytone Pantaleone Cippatola, into the most vivacious relief.

III.

We always desire more information about the writers who greatly interest us than we find in their works, and many American readers have probably a friendly curiosity as to the private personality of M. Turgénieff. We are reduced, however, to regretting our own meagre knowledge. We gather from his writings that our author is much of a cosmopolitan, a dweller in many cities and a frequenter of many societies, and, along with this, an indefinable sense of his being of a so-called "aristocratic" temperament; so that if a man's genius were visible to the eye, like his fleshly integument, that of M. Turgénieff would be observed to have, say, very shapely hands and feet, and a nose expressive of the patrician graces. A friend of ours, indeed, who has rather an irresponsible fancy, assures us that the author of "Smoke" (which he deems his masterpiece) is, personally, simply his own Pavel Kirsanoff. Twenty to one our friend is quite wrong; but we may nevertheless say that, to readers disposed now and then to risk a conjecture, much of the charm of M. Turgénieff's manner resides in this impalpable union of an aristocratic temperament with a democratic intellect. To his inquisitive intellect we owe the various, abundant, human substance of his tales, and to his fastidious temperament their exquisite form. But we must not meddle too freely with causes when results themselves are so suggestive. The great question as to a poet or a novelist is, How does he feel about life? what, in the last analysis, is his philosophy? When vigorous writers have reached maturity we are at liberty to look in their works for some expression of a total view of the world they have been so actively observing. This is the most interesting thing their works offer us. Details are interesting in proportion as they contribute to make it clear.

The foremost impression of M. Turgénieff's reader is that he is morbidly serious, that he takes life terribly hard. We move in an atmosphere of unrelieved sadness. We go from one tale to the other in the hope of finding something cheerful, but we only wander into fresh agglomerations of gloom. We try the shorter stories with a hope of chancing upon something pitched in the traditional key of "light reading," but they strike us alike as so many ingenious condensations of melancholy. "A Village Lear" is worse than "The Antchar"; "The Forsaken" is hardly an improvement on "A Correspondence"; "The Journal of a Superfluous Man" does little to lay the haunting ghost of "Three Portraits." The author has written several short dramas. Appealing to them to beguile us of our dusky vapours, we find the concentrated tragedy of "The Bread of Charity," and, by way of an after-piece, the lugubrious humour of " The Division." Sad beginnings, worse endings, good people ineffably wretched, happy ones hugely ridiculous; disappointment, despair, madness, suicide, degrading passions, and blighted hopes —these seem, on first acquaintance, the chief ingredients of M. Turgénieff's version of the human drama; and to deepen our sense of its bitterness we discover the author in the background winding up his dismal demonstration with a chuckle. We set him down forthwith as a cold-blooded pessimist, caring for nothing in life but its misery, and for nothing in misery but its picturesqueness—its capacity for furnishing cynical epigrams. What is each of the short tales we have mentioned, we ask, but a ruthless epigram, in the dramatic form, upon human happiness? Evlampia Charloff, in "A Village Lear," drives her father to madness and death by her stony depravity, and then joins a set of religious fanatics, among whom she plays a great part as the "Holy Mother of God." In "The Bread of Charity," a young heiress brings home to her estates her newly-wedded husband, and introduces him to her old neighbours. They dine with him, and one of them, an officious coxcomb, conceives the brilliant idea of entertaining him by an exhibition of a poor old gentleman who has long been hanging about the place as a pensioner of the late parents of the young wife, and is remarkable for a dumb canine attachment to herself. The heartless guest plies the modest old man with wine, winds him up and makes him play the fool. But suddenly Kusofkin, through the fumes of his potations, perceives that he is being laughed at, and breaks out into a passionate assurance that, baited and buffeted as he is, he is nothing less than the father of the mistress of the house. She overhears his cry, and though he, horrified at his indiscretion, attempts to retract it, she wins from him a confession of the fact that he had been her mother's lover. The husband, however, makes him swallow his words, and do public penance. He turns him out of the house with a small pension, and the curtain falls on the compliment offered this fine fellow by the meddlesome neighbour on his generosity: "You are a true Russian gentleman!" The most perfectly epigrammatic of our author's stories, however, is perhaps that polished little piece of misery, "A Correspondence."

A young man, idle, discontented, and longing for better things, writes, for a pastime, to a young girl whom he has formerly slightly known and greatly esteemed, who has entertained an unsuspected and unrequited passion for him, and who lives obscurely in the country, among very common people. A correspondence comes of it, in the course of which they exchange confidences and unburden their hearts. The young girl is most pitiable, most amiable, in her sadness, and her friend begins to suspect that she, at last, may give a meaning to his aimless life. She, on her side, is compassionately interested, and we see curiosity and hope throbbing timidly beneath the austere resignation to which she has schooled herself, and the expression of which, mingled with our sense of her blooming beauty of character, makes of Maria Alexandrovna the most nobly fascinating, perhaps, of our author's heroines. Alexis Petrovitsch writes at last that he must see her, that he will come to her, that she is to expect him at such a date, and we imagine tenderly, in the unhastening current of her days, the gentle eddy of her expectation. Her next letter, after an interval, expresses surprise at his non-appearance; her next, several months later, is a last attempt to obtain news of him. The correspondence closes with his confession, written as he lies dying at Dresden. Just as he was starting to join her, he had encountered another woman, a dancing-girl at the opera, with whom he had fallen madly in love. She was low, stupid, heartless; she had nothing to recommend her to anything but his senses. It was ignoble, but so it was. His passion has led him such a life that his health is gone. He has brought on disease of the lungs, by waiting for the young lady at the opera-door in the winter nights. Now his hours are numbered, and this is the end of all! And on this lugubrious note the story closes. We read with intent curiosity, for the tale is a masterpiece of narration; but we wonder, in some vexation, what it all means. Is it a piece of irony for irony's sake, or is it a disinterested picture of the struggle between base passion and pure passion? Why, in that case, should it seem a matter of course for the author that base passion should carry the day? Why, as for Rudin, for Sanin, for the distracted hero of "Smoke," should circumstances also have been too many, as the phrase is, for poor Alexis Petrovitsch? If we pursue our researches, in the hope of finding some method in this promiscuous misery, examples continue to seem more numerous than principles. The author continues everywhere to imply that there is something essentially ridiculous in human nature, something indefeasibly vain in human effort. We are amazed, as we go, at the portentous number of his patent fools; no novelist has drawn a tenth as many. The large majority of his people are the people we laugh at, and a large fraction of the remainder the people we half disgustedly pity. There is little room left, therefore, for the people we esteem, and yet room enough perhaps, considering that our very benevolence is tempered with scepticism. What with the vicious fools and the well-meaning fools, the prosperous charlatans and the grotesque nonentities, the dead failures and the sadder failures that regret and protest and rebel, the demoralized lovers and the jilted maidens, the dusky pall of fatality, in a word, suspended over all human things, it may be inferred that we are not invited to a particularly exhilarating spectacle. Not a single person in the novel of "Fathers and Sons" but has, in some degree, a lurking ironical meaning. Every one is a more or less ludicrous parody on what he ought to have been, or an ineffectual regret at what he might have been. The only person who compasses a reasonable share of happiness is Arcadi, and even his happiness is a thing for strenuous minds to smile at—a happiness based on the *pot au feu*, the prospect of innumerable babies and the sacrifice of "views." Arcadi's father is a vulgar failure; Pavel Petrovitsch is a poetic failure; Bazaroff is a tragic failure; Anna Sergheievna misses happiness from an ungenerous fear of sacrificing her luxurious quietude; the elder Bazaroff and his wife seem a couple of ingeniously grotesque manikins, prepared by a melancholy *fantoccinista* to illustrate the mocking vanity of parental hopes. We lay down the book, and we repeat that, with all the charity in the world, it is impossible to pronounce M. Turgénieff anything better than a pessimist.

The judgment is just, but it needs qualifications, and it finds them in a larger look at the author's position. M. Turgénieff strikes us, as we have said, as a man disappointed, for good reasons or for poor ones, in the land that is dear to him. Harsh critics will say for poor ones, reflecting that a fastidious imagination has not been unconcerned in his discontentment. To the old Muscovite virtues, and especially the old Muscovite *naïveté*, his imagination filially clings, but he finds these things, especially in the fact that his country turns to the outer world, melting more and more every day into the dimness of tradition. The Russians are clever, and clever people are ambitious. Those with whom M. Turgénieff has seen himself surrounded are consumed with the desire to pass for intellectual cosmopolites, to know, or seem to know, everything that can be known, to be astoundingly modern and progressive and European. Madame Kukshin, the poor little literary lady with a red nose, in "Fathers and Sons," gives up George Sand as "nowhere" for her want of knowledge of embryology, and, when asked why she proposes to remove to Heidelberg, replies with "Bunsen, you know." The fermentation of social change has thrown to the surface in Russia a deluge of hollow pretensions and vicious presumptions, amid which the love either of old virtues or of new achievements finds very little gratification. It is not simply that people flounder laughably in deeper waters than they can breast, but that in this discord of crude ambitions the integrity of character itself is compromised and men and women make, morally, a very ugly appearance. The Russian colony at Baden-Baden, depicted in "Smoke," is a collection of more or less inflated profligates. Panschin, in "A Nest of Noblemen," is another example; Sitnikoff, in "Fathers and Sons," a still more contemptible one. Driven back, depressed and embittered, into his imagination for the edification which the social spectacle immediately before him refuses him, and shaped by nature to take life hard and linger among its shadows, our observer surrenders himself with a certain reactionary, irresponsible gusto to a sombre portrayal of things. An imaginative preference for dusky subjects is a perfectly legitimate element of the artistic temperament; our own Hawthorne is a signal case of its being innocently exercised; innocently, because with that delightfully unconscious genius it remained ima-

ginative, sportive, inconclusive, to the end. When
external circumstances, however, contribute to confirm
it, and reality lays her groaning stores of misery at its
feet, it will take a rarely elastic genius altogether to
elude the charge of being morbid. M. Turgénieff's
pessimism seems to us of two sorts—a spontaneous
melancholy and a wanton melancholy. Sometimes in
a sad story it is the problem, the question, the idea,
that strikes him; sometimes it is simply the picture.
Under the former influence he has produced his masterpieces; we admit that they are intensely sad, but we
consent to be moved, as we consent to sit silent in a
death-chamber. In the other case he has done but his
second best; we strike a bargain over our tears, and
insist that when it comes to being simply entertained,
wooing and wedding are better than death and burial.
"The Antchar," "The Forsaken," "A Superfluous
Man," "A Village Lear," "Toc . . . toc . . . toc," all
seem to us to be gloomier by several shades than they
need have been; for we hold to the good old belief that
the presumption, in life, is in favour of the brighter side,
and we deem it, in art, an indispensable condition of
our interest in a depressed observer that he should have
at least tried his best to be cheerful. The truth, we
take it, lies for the pathetic in poetry and romance very
much where it lies for the "immoral." Morbid pathos

is reflective pathos; ingenious pathos, pathos not freshly born of the occasion; noxious immorality is superficial immorality, immorality without natural roots in the subject. We value most the "realists" who have an ideal of delicacy and the elegiasts who have an ideal of joy.

"Picturesque gloom, possibly," a thick and thin admirer of M. Turgénieff's may say to us, "at least you will admit that it *is* picturesque." This we heartily concede, and, recalled to a sense of our author's brilliant diversity and ingenuity, we bring our restrictions to a close. To the broadly generous side of his imagination it is impossible to pay exaggerated homage, or, indeed, for that matter, to its simple intensity and fecundity. No romancer has created a greater number of the figures that breathe and move and speak, in their habits as they might have lived; none, on the whole, seems to us to have had such a masterly touch in portraiture, none has mingled so much ideal beauty with so much unsparing reality. His sadness has its element of error, but it has also its larger element of wisdom. Life *is*, in fact, a battle. On this point optimists and pessimists agree. Evil is insolent and strong; beauty enchanting but rare; goodness very apt to be weak; folly very apt to be defiant; wickedness to carry the day; imbeciles to be in great places, people of sense in small, and mankind generally, unhappy. But the world as it stands is no illusion, no phantasm, no evil dream of a night; we wake up to it again for ever and ever; we can neither forget it nor deny it nor dispense with it. We can welcome experience as it comes, and give it what it demands, in exchange for something which it is idle to pause to call much or little so long as it contributes to swell the volume of consciousness. In this there is mingled pain and delight, but over the mysterious mixture there hovers a visible rule, that bids us learn to will and seek to understand. So much as this we seem to decipher between the lines of M. Turgénieff's minutely written chronicle. He himself has sought to understand as zealously as his most eminent competitors. He gives, at least, no meagre account of life, and he has done liberal justice to its infinite variety. This is his great merit; his great defect, roughly stated, is a tendency to the abuse of irony. He remains, nevertheless, to our sense, a very welcome mediator between the world and our curiosity. If we had space, we should like to set forth that he is by no means our ideal story-teller—this honourable genius possessing, attributively, a rarer skill than the finest required for producing an artful *réchauffé* of the actual. But even for better romancers we must wait for a better world. Whether the world in its higher state of perfection will occasionally offer colour to scandal, we hesitate to pronounce; but we are prone to conceive of the ultimate novelist as a personage altogether purged of sarcasm. The imaginative force now expended in this direction he will devote to describing cities of gold and heavens of sapphire. But, for the present, we gratefully accept M. Turgénieff, and reflect that his manner suits the most frequent mood of the greater number of readers. If he were a dogmatic optimist we suspect that, as things go, we should long ago have ceased to miss him from our library. The personal optimism of most of us no romancer can confirm or dissipate, and our personal troubles, generally, place fictions of all kinds in an impertinent light. To our usual working mood the world is apt to seem M. Turgénieff's hard world, and when, at moments, the strain and the pressure deepen, the ironical element figures not a little in our form of address to those short-sighted friends who have whispered that it is an easy one.

THE TWO AMPÈRES.

WE have before us three volumes[1] which we have read with extraordinary pleasure. They are the records of the lives of a father and a son; they contain a complete family history. In 1831 Alexis de Tocqueville made in this country that tour which was to be the prelude to the publication of his "Democracy," the most serious book written on America up to that moment by a foreigner. De Tocqueville and Jean-Jacques Ampère were united by a passionate friendship (an *amitié-passion* Sainte-Beuve calls it), and the latter, twenty years afterward, in 1851, followed in the footsteps of the author of the "Democracy," and made a rapid journey from Canada to Mexico. He, too, of course wrote a book, and his "Promenade en Amérique" is a very genial and kindly

[1] "Journal et Correspondance de André-Marie Ampère." Publiés par Mme. H. C. Paris, Hetzel, 1873.

"André-Marie Ampère et Jean-Jacques Ampère. Souvenirs et Correspondance." Recueillis par Mme. H. C. Paris, Hetzel, 1875.

composition. We bestow at present a very much less irritable attention upon the impressions of the foreign promenader than at the very distant date of M. Ampère's tour. We ourselves should say, indeed, that the European optimist on our shores would at present find it convenient, as a general thing, to keep watch upon his enthusiasm. But M. Ampère's amiable book was certainly disinterested; it was the expression of an eminently appreciative and sociable mind, and we make no exaggerated claim for it in saying that it introduces the author agreeably to American readers. They may be advised, after a glance at it, to pass on to the volumes whose titles are here transcribed and which embody a mass of literary matter now more entertaining to people in general than the author's formal compositions. Jean-Jacques Ampère was an accomplished scholar and a very clever man; but he seems to us a rather striking illustration of the common axiom that between two stools one falls to the ground. He was at once a man of books and a man of the world; an ardent savant and an indefatigable traveller. "He could read," says Sainte-Beuve, "a hieroglyphic phrase on the sarcophagus of a Pharaoh; it befell him one evening before going to sleep to read a Chinese book among the ruins of Ephesus. We must agree that these are high dilettantisms of the mind, such as are within the reach of a very select few." He wrote so much, on questions of learning, that you wonder he should ever have found a moment to leave his study; and he travelled so much, moved so much in the world, formed so many personal and social ties, had such a genius for conversation, for society, and for friendship, that you wonder he found time to open a book or mend his pen. The verdict of competent criticism has been that Jean-Jacques Ampère sacrificed erudition to observation and observation to erudition; that he lacked exactness as a savant and that he lacked vividness as a tourist. Scholars find his "Histoire Romaine à Rome" superficial, and, for what it attempts to be, the profane find it dry. "In the middle of June," he writes in 1862, "I went with Hébert to Subiaco, a wild spot to which the artist-poet loved to go in search of models. It was during this little journey, on the road to Tivoli, while the horses were resting, that I read to Hébert the first lines of 'L'Histoire Romaine à Rome,' and he then told me frankly that my picture of the Roman Campagna left him cold." Ampère endeavoured to infuse a little more colour into his sketch; but the opinion of the artist-poet Hébert has, we imagine, remained that of the general reader, while it is probable, on the other hand, that the author's lighter touches have done little to mitigate the severity of such an authority as Professor Mommsen when, for instance, he finds his *confrère* exclaiming with emotion, "I believe in Romulus!" Sainte-Beuve applies to Ampère's style a judgment which he had heard passed upon another writer whose literary manner was too undemonstrative. "He is like a man who has made a drawing in black-lead. When he has done he thinks it still too sharp, and he passes his coat-cuff over it." But if Ampère as a historian falls short of being a first-rate authority (as a philologist we believe he is considered much sounder), and if, as a describer, he is less brilliant and incisive than some men of greater genius and (possibly) scantier conscience, he recovers his advantages in his letters, in the things that reveal the man himself. Then we see how intelligent, how accomplished, how sympathetic, how indefatigable he was. His letters are always entertaining and in the highest degree natural. But what completes their charm here is their graceful and harmonious setting—the fact that they are offered us in alternation with a hundred other memorials of a singularly pleasing and interesting circle. We gather from the whole collection the complete picture of a society—a society which by this time has pretty well passed away and can know no more changes. It is motionless in its place; it is sitting for its likeness. Best of all, the picture has one episode as charming as any that was ever imagined by an idyllic poet. André-Marie Ampère, the father of Jean-Jacques, was an eminent man of science; he was the first French mathematician of his time and the inventor of the electric telegraph in so far as the following statement, made in the presence of the French Academy of Sciences, entitled him to the name. "As many magnetized needles as letters of the alphabet, put into movement by conductors communicating with the electric battery by means of a key-board which might be lowered at will, would make possible a telegraphic correspondence that would traverse all distances and be more prompt to transmit thought than either writing or speech." Why this idea was merely enunciated, and never applied, we are unable to say; if it had been at that early day put into practice, André-Marie Ampère would now enjoy a renown that would render these few words of introduction quite superfluous. Invented in time to be used at the battle of Waterloo, the electric telegraph might have given a very different turn to the affairs of mankind. But this contingency having failed, we are reduced to considering the elder Ampère in the comparatively humble light of the extremely diffident lover of Mademoiselle Julie Carron. He was the most candid and artless of men, and the history of his courtship is one of the prettiest love-stories we know.

Jean-Jacques Ampère, as has been said, had a genius for friendship. He never married, but in the course of his life he had two extremely characteristic affections for women. The object of one was Madame Récamier, whose acquaintance he made in his twentieth year (in 1820) and to whom he remained devoted until her death, in 1849. The object of the second was a certain Madame L——, with whom he became intimate in 1853, in Rome. This lady was a young widow, in feeble health, obliged to spend her winters in the South, where she was accompanied by her parents and her little girl. Ampère had spent much of his life in Rome, and it was about this time that he entered upon that long sojourn of which the principal aim was the composition of a history of the Latin State in relation to the present local aspects, and which terminated only with his death. Madame L—— died in Rome in 1859, in a temper of mind which, as Ampère said, made him "touch with his finger the immortality of the soul." His friendship with her parents was intimate, and his affection for her little girl almost paternal. Ampère died at Pau, in March, 1864, leaving a will by which he bequeathed all his literary remains to M. and Madame Cheuvreux, and his private papers (those especially relating to his father) to their young granddaughter. It is in this way that the volumes before us have come to be put forth by Madame Cheuvreux, for the benefit at once of Mademoiselle L—— and of the public at large. We do not know what this young lady has thought of this mass of literature, but the public has given it a very cordial welcome. Madame Cheuvreux is a most graceful and intelligent commentator, and her publication has rapidly passed through several editions.

It is unjust to say that we have here simply the history of a father and a son. The Ampère stock was apparently an excellent one, and the reader is interested in taking it a degree farther back. The father of André-Marie Ampère was a retired merchant at Lyons when the French revolution broke out. Lyons in 1793 revolted from its Terrorist government and was besieged by the National Convention. The victory of the Convention was of course a harvest for the guillotine, and Jean-Jacques Ampère the elder was one of the most admirable of its victims. In prison, before his death, he wrote his wife a letter, which we regret not having space to quote; it gives one a better opinion of human nature. "Do not speak to Josephine," he says at the end, "of her father's misfortune; take good care that she does not know it; as for my son, there is nothing I do not expect from him. So long as you possess them and they possess you, embrace each other in memory of me. I leave my heart to all of you."

For so pure an old stoic as this to say on the edge of the scaffold that there was nothing he did not expect from his only son, left the sole support of two desolate women—this was a great deal. André was at first stupefied with sorrow, but in time he justified his father's confidence. It seems most singular that in this blood-drenched soil an episode so tender, so redolent of youthful freshness, as the story embodied in the earliest of these letters should so speedily have bloomed—that, with the hideous shadow of the scaffold still upon him, André Ampère should make so artless, so ingenuous, so innocently awkward a figure. His "adorable *bonhomie*"—that is the quality the editor chiefly insists upon, and it certainly must have been of the purest strain not to have been embittered by the contact of wholesale massacre. It was indeed most genuine, and the young man's notes and letters are full of it. The story is a very simple one: he encountered Julie Carron, he fell in love with her, he was put upon probation, he married her, she bore him a child, she died. The charm is in the way the tale is told—by himself, by the young girl, and by her sister (the latter an admirably graphic letter-writer).

At twenty-three André Ampère, stuffed with algebra and trigonometry, felt in his own small way the lassitude, the nameless yearnings of Faust. He had given the measure of his scientific genius and his universal curiosity. We have his own word for it that by the time he was eighteen he knew as much mathematics as he ever knew; he had also pushed far into chemistry and he had cultivated the muse. He had begun various tragedies and he had placed upon the stocks an epic poem with Columbus for hero and the "Americid" for title. Many years afterwards his son found among his papers an ancient yellow scrap, on which the following lines were written: "Having reached the age at which the laws rendered me my own master, my heart sighed in secret at my still being so. Free and insensible up to that time, it wearied of its idleness. Brought up in almost complete solitude, study and reading, which had long been my dearest delights, suffered me to fall into an apathy that I had never felt, and the cry of nature diffused through my soul a vague, insupportable unrest. One day as I was walking after sunset beside a lonely brook . . . . ." And here the fragment ends. What did he see beside the brook? Julie Carron, perhaps. If this is so, it was on a Sunday in April, 1796, that he took that momentous stroll. He kept a record of his meetings with the young girl, and either then or later he superscribed it in large letters—AMORUM. It is filled with small entries like this, which mean little to us now, but which meant much to the poor trembling, hoping, fearing young mathematician: —"26*th September*. I found her in the garden, without daring to speak to her.—3*d October*. I went there. I slipped in a few words more to the mother.—6*th October*. I found myself alone with her, without daring to speak to her; they gave me the first *bouts-rimés*.—10*th October*. I filled them out, and slipped them adroitly into her hand.—13*th October*. I had carried back the seventh volume of Sévigné; I forgot the eighth and my umbrella.—2*d November*. I went to get my umbrella.—7*th November*. I didn't speak that day, on account of the death of M. Montpetit.—9*th November*. I spoke again; Julie told me not to come so often.—12*th November*. Mme. Carron was out; I said a few words to Julie, who regularly blew me up and went off. Elise told me to spend the winter without speaking again.—16*th November*. . . . Julie brought me with grace the 'Lettres Provinciales.'— 9*th December*. She opened the door for me in her nightcap and spoke to me a moment, *tête-à-tête*, in the kitchen." He stands there before us like an effigy of bashfulness, tongue-tied, with his heart in his throat, a book under his arm and the simple good faith of unspotted youth upon his brow. Mademoiselle Julie was a trifle difficult, as the phrase is; she had already had an excellent offer of marriage, but she had declined it because she thought nothing could make up to her for leaving her parents and her sister. These were plain people, with little money, but what one may call an excellent family tone. They lived in the country, close to Lyons. They thought well of Jean-Jacques, but they thought also that there was no hurry, especially as he had as yet no avocation, and it was their idea to keep him at arm's length, though certainly not to let him go. Elise Carron was Julie's elder, and a girl who seems to have combined an excellent heart with the keenest, frankest wit, and with a singular homely felicity of style. She is shrewd, impulsive, positive, humorous, and we should like to quote all her letters. During a part of the winter which followed the entries we have just transcribed Julie Carron was absent from home, and Elise makes it her duty to entertain poor Ampère and to report his condition to his mistress. She has a great kindness for him and, though she wishes to amuse her sister, she stops short of tempting her to laugh cruelly. "Poor A—— is certainly frozen in some corner, or else he is thawing near you, for I have seen him neither through hole nor through window. . . . Will he come to-morrow? I look always from my place and I see nothing. If he comes and mamma goes out, he will call me to an account; I have prepared a thousand little answers—always the same; I wish I knew some

that would content him without bringing things on too
fast, for he interests me by his frankness and his softness, and especially by his tears, which come out
without his meaning it. Not the slightest affectation,
none of those high-strung phrases which are the language of so many others. Arrange it as you will, but
let *me* love him a little before you love him; he is so
good! . . . Mamma insists that Providence will
arrange everything; but I say that we must help Providence." Elise's next letter is in its natural vividness
almost a little genre picture. "At last he came yesterday, trembling with cold, and still more with the fear
that mamma would be displeased at his having been to
see you, or rather to get letters for us. But this is
how the thing happened: I see that you want details.
You must know that mamma now sits in your place,
because she has closed up the door, which used to freeze
the room, and in consequence we don't see a bit too well,
especially when the snow has been piled up. In short,
he comes in and doesn't see the little Pelagot who was
behind the nose of the stove. As soon as Claudine
went out he said: ' Madame, I saw mademoiselle your
daughter.' I stopped him short off, making more and
more signs; and he, thinking to plaster it up, replied,
' Claudine is gone out; no one can hear us, I will speak
lower.' The child opened her eyes as wide as she was

able; when I saw that signs didn't help me I spoke to the wench about her work, about her stocking that was not coming on. He was petrified and wanted to patch it up again, but the piece wouldn't fit the hole." At last the little Pelagot goes out with her dilatory stocking, and Elise has a long talk with Ampère, which she relates, *verbatim*, to her sister:—" He perceived the first that it was beginning to be late—which he forgets so easily when you are here. He went off and left me quite amazed at his hat in lacquered cloth, at his fashionable breeches and his little air, which, I assure you, will change again." "Guess, dear Julie," she writes later, "at what we pass our time. We make verses, we scratch them out, and then begin again." And she goes on to narrate that M. Ampère has been with them and has filled them with the sacred fire. She must close, for she has to help her mamma to begin a play, a drama, perhaps a tragedy! It sounds very odd, hearing of those two little rustic bourgeoises sitting down among their pots and pans, at their snow-darkened windows, to literary compositions of this heroic magnitude, and there certainly can be no better illustration of the literary passion of the last century, or of the universal culture of what was called sensibility.

But the spring came, Julie was at home again, and

in André's diary the idyllic strain is more emphasized:
—" 24*th March*. Mlle. Bœuf came while I was reading
the tragedy of Louis XVI.; we went into the orchard.
Elise sat upon the bench; Julie upon a chair which I
brought to her, and I at her feet; *she* chose my purse
to her own taste.—26*th April*. I went to carry back
La Rochefoucauld; I found no one but Mme. Carron,
and asked her leave to bring mamma. I received only
a vague answer, but it was satisfactory enough. Julie,
Elise, my aunt, and my cousin came to lunch; I served
the white wine and drank in a glass which *she* had
rinsed." A couple of months later he prefixes to an
entry a date in large capitals. The record deserved the
honour, for it has a charming quaintness.—" MONDAY,
3D JULY. They came at last to see us, at three-quarters
past three. [His poor mother had called, and the
Carron ladies were returning her visit.] We went
into the alley, where I climbed into the great cherry-
trees and threw cherries to Julie. Elise, my sister,
all of them, came afterward. I gave up my place
to François, who lowered branches to us, from which
we picked ourselves, to Julie's great entertainment.
She sat on a plank on the ground with my sister and
Elise, and I sat on the grass beside her. I ate some
cherries which had been on her knees. We all four
went into the great garden, where she accepted a lily

from my hand, and then we went to see the brook. I gave her my hand to climb the little wall, and both hands to get over it again; I remained by her side on the edge of the brook, far from Elise and my sister. We went with them in the evening as far as the windmill, where I sat down near her again, while we all four observed the sunset, which gilded her clothes with a charming light. She carried away a second lily which I gave her in passing." André Ampère was a man of genius and destined to be recognised as one; but he was a profoundly simple soul, and his *naïveté* seems to have been unfathomable. It would be impossible to enumerate with a homelier verity the enormous trifles on which young love feeds. André wrote verses; we know not what they were; certainly there is as little attempt here as possible at elegance of form; the poetry is all in the spirit. There, however, it is deep. The little narrative we have just quoted might have been scratched with a clasp-knife on the windmill tower; but the passion it commemorates is of classic purity. Extremes meet; the whole man is in it; it is the passion of Petrarch for Laura, of Dante for Beatrice, of Romeo for Juliet. Extremes meet, we say; and so it seems to us that this artless fragment is, by a happy chance, as graphic, as pictorial, as if a consummate artist had retouched it.

By the time the autumn had come round again Julie knew her mind. When a certain M. Vial comes in and urges André, if his family does nothing for him, to go and seek his fortune in Paris, she pushes him out by the shoulders, and tells him they have no need of his advice. The day apparently has come for Julie to feel the flutters of the heart; we have had no intimation until now that her pretty person (the editor is happily able to establish that it was pretty) was not even a trifle impertinently self-possessed.—" 26th October. I carried there a little basket of chestnuts. . . . Mme. Carron told me to go into the orchard where *they* were. I found only Julie, who seemed as much embarrassed as I; she called Périsse, but I slipped in some words which had relation to my sentiments. . . . I wanted to go back a moment to the orchard, where she had gone to dry some linen, but she avoided me with even more earnestness than the first time. In the evening she told me to read 'Adéle,' and this led to our talking again upon the passions." He adds a few days later: "We went into the orchard, where I helped to take up the washing; in sport, after some jest of Elise, Julie gave me a charming blow, with her fist, on the arm. We supped on chestnuts and we came home very late." Upon this the editor comments very happily: "The orchard, the linen-drying, the reading of 'Adèle,' which provokes a conversation on the passions, André's basket of chestnuts, the charming blow with the fist that he gets in play, the frugal supper—is not the picture quite of another age? Only sixty-and-something years separate us from the moment when André wrote his journal, and yet we are far from that innocent idyll. Ah, messieurs the realists, you have made us grow old fast!"

At last, in the spring of 1799, poor André's probation terminates and Julie bestows her hand upon him. We have some of his letters after the betrothal, in which he addresses his affianced ceremoniously as "Mademoiselle." There is something very agreeable in this observance of high courtesy in circumstances amid which it might have been expected to be a trifle relaxed. Mademoiselle Carron was a poor girl; she helped in the family washing. But she conversed upon the passions and she was familiar with a superior standard of manners. The young couple were married in the month of August of the same year, and André's friend M. Ballanche read a long prose rhapsody, by way of an epithalamium, at the simple wedding-feast. André Ampère obtained some pupils in mathematics at Lyons, and his wife spent much of the first year of her marriage with her mother in the country. She was at times, however, with her mother-in-law Madame Ampère, at the latter's modest dwelling at Polémieux, near Lyons. While she is away her sister Elise writes to her with inimitable vigour. Elise really makes the dead things of the past live again. The Carron ladies were hesitating as to where they should spend the winter. In their actual quarters, the elder daughter writes, "Mamma finds a great many diversions, and her health is better. Our good neighbours tell us that if we were to remain they wouldn't think of carting themselves over to Charelet, where nevertheless they have already hired lodgings and laid in a stock of wood, which they would quickly sell again. In short, they press us, offer us so heartily all the little distractions that they might share with us. Mme. Darsay makes much of her books and newspapers; her daughter puts forward all the people whom she would catch up in one way or another. She says to me: 'We will amuse our mothers, we will both make little caps for the poor, and fritters and tarts; we will pray God, we will write, and then time passes so fast, so fast.' She makes a hotch-potch of all this, and then kisses me with such friendliness, and shows as much enthusiasm as if I were a being capable of inspiring it. Formerly I shouldn't have been surprised at such greetings; I used with these ladies to put in my little word in the talk; I was gay; we were something for them, because they didn't see many people. But at present it is the reverse." I continue to quote Elise Carron for her extreme reality: "There are moments when we must not think of calculating—very true. But there is a time for everything. *A propos* of calculations, I have reason to thank myself for the one which made me decide not to buy a grey dress. What should I have done with it? I should have spoiled it nicely if I had wished to put it on on Sundays on our pretty roads and among the peasant-women at mass, who mount atop of you and surround you with goloshes and muddy sabots. Mme. Mayeuvre herself wouldn't have been so fine as I, and yet she always comes to church in a carriage, but in such simple gowns that I shouldn't have dared to wear mine. I never saw her so much dressed as last evening at the Darsay ladies'. She had been making visits in the afternoon, and had exchanged her little dyed morning dress for a very pretty blue calico, with white sleeves and a hood like ours. Mme. Courageau is also very simple, and if on Sundays I only put on a muslin apron over my old petticoat in green cloth (I wear it with my black spencer) they already cry out that I am dressed up. Yet, since the cold weather, it is only what I wear every day. All this, my sister, may very well not interest you. So much the worse! I *must* write to you and talk to you as if you were here. Haven't I told you that my scribblings don't oblige you to write a line? I send them to you for nothing, and out of it all you can take your choice; you can fish out some things you may be glad to know, as, for example, about our health." In December, 1801, André Ampère obtained the post of Professor of Mathematics at the central school of the department of the Ain, the seat of which was at Bourg. Julie, who had a baby several months old and whose health had begun visibly to decline, remained, for economy and comfort, with her mother. The most charming part of this volume is perhaps the series of letters that passed, during this separation, between the ailing, caressing, chiding, solicitous, practical young wife, and the tender, adoring young husband, whose inadvertences and small extravagances and want of worldly wisdom are the themes of many a conjugal admonition. Poor Ampère was for ever staining his clothes with chemicals; he had his coats and breeches doled out to him like a boy at school. He begins his career at Bourg by deciding not to lodge at the inn, on account of the bad company that frequents it, and then makes himself the joke of the town by going to live with a certain M. Beauregard, whose wife was notoriously disreputable.

"I think you very pastoral," Julie writes, "to go reading my letters in the fields; I'm afraid that you scatter them along the road, and that the first people who pass pick them up. If I knew you were more careful, how many pretty things I would confide to you! You would know that I love you, that I have a great desire to see you again, that every evening I have a thousand things to say to you that don't come out, save in sighs; you would know, in short, that when one has gone so far as to take a husband one loves him too much to be separated from him, and that your absence vexes me." Her injunctions about his taking care of her letters seem to have little effect; for shortly after this André writes to her gleefully of another "pastoral" day: "How sweet your letters are to read! One must have your soul to write things which go so straight to the heart—without trying to, it would seem. I remained till two o'clock sitting under a tree, a pretty meadow on the right, the river, with some amiable ducks floating on it, on the left and in front of me; behind was the hospital building. You will understand that I had taken the precaution of saying to Mme. Beauregard, when I left my letter to go on this tramp, that I shouldn't dine at home. She thinks I am dining in town; but as I had made a good breakfast, I only feel the better for dining upon love. At two o'clock I felt so calm, and my mind so at ease, in place of the weariness that oppressed me this morning, that I wanted to walk about and botanize. I went up along the river in the meadows, and arrived within twenty steps of a charming wood that I had seen in the distance at a half hour from the town, and had desired to go through. When I reached it the river, by suddenly coming between us, destroyed every hope of going further, so I had to give it up, and I came home by the road from Bourg to Cezeyriat—a superb avenue of Lombardy poplars."

This gentle strain is intermingled with sadder notes —allusions to the extreme scarcity of money with the young couple and to Julie's constantly failing health. She had an incurable malady and her days were numbered. But in the midst of her troubles she is tenderly vigilant and practical. "Be careful to close your bureau, your room, and my letters, or I shall not dare to write to you. I know nothing of M. Roux. Don't you open yourself too much to M. Clerc? He's a very new acquaintance; suppose he were to take your ideas for himself. Send me your cloth trousers, so that the rats don't eat them." "I don't burn my things," he answers, "and do my chemistry only in my breeches, my grey coat, and my green velvet waistcoat. . . .

I beg you to send my new trousers, so that I may appear before MM. Delambre and Villars. I don't know what I shall do; my nice breeches smell still of turpentine. . . . You'll be afraid of my spoiling my nice trousers, but I promise you to return them as clean as I get them." Julie too visibly declines, and the downright Elise, writing to André, breaks out into an almost passionate appeal. "What a happiness if among all the plants whose properties you know there were one that could put all in order again in her nature! What is the use of science if there is none that can restore health to Julie? Make inquiries, talk to the learned, to the ignorant! Simple people often have remedies as simple as themselves—light which God gives them for their preservation. . . . . Ah, why, why did I push self-sacrifice so far as to advise Julie to marry? I admired myself then as I shed my tears; they were for me the triumph of reason; whereas it was to feeling alone that I ought to have listened!" Julie sank rapidly, and died in the summer of 1803.

We have many of André Ampère's letters after the death of his wife, but as he grows older, they naturally lose much of their quaintness and freshness. He becomes absorbed in scientific research and embarks upon metaphysics, and it is with a certain sadness we learn that the image of Julie Carron fades from his mind sufficiently to enable him, in 1807, to marry a second time. There is a note from his sister-in-law Elise upon this occasion, in which, beneath the expression of an affectionate sympathy with his desire to make himself happy again, we detect a certain proud disappointment in his not finding the memory of her sister a sufficient source of happiness. There is some poetic justice in his second marriage proving a miserable delusion; he was obliged to separate from his wife after a few months. He had gone up to Paris after Julie's death and become instructor in the Polytechnic School, and from this time opportunity, prosperity, and fame began to wait upon him. He was a signal example of the almost infantile simplicity, the incorruptible moral purity, that so often are associated with great attainments in science, and the history of his courtship was worth sketching because it shows this temperament in its flower.

After the death of Jean-Jacques Ampère's young mother, the interest of these volumes is transferred to her son. The boy grew up among all-favouring influences, surrounded by doting grandmothers and aunts, in an atmosphere of learning and morality. As he is revealed in his own early letters and those of his friends (there are many of these) he is quite the type of the ingenuous and intelligent youth who feels, in an easy, general way, that he is heir of all the ages. More than anything else Jean-Jacques Ampère is sympathetic; he is versatile, spontaneous, emotional; in 1820 the days of "sensibility" were hardly yet over and the accomplished young man possessed this treasure. The world was all before him where to choose. His father, when he had resigned himself to his not being a mathematician, wished him of all things to write a tragedy; for, next after algebra and chemistry, verses were what the elder Ampère most prized. Jean-Jacques, nothing loth, looked about for a subject, and meanwhile he fell in love with Madame Récamier. His devotion to this illustrious lady was the great fact of thirty years of his life, and it is possible, in the letters before us and in those of the lady herself, published with a commentary by her niece, who was so many years at her side, to trace even in detail the history of the affair. It is difficult at this time of day to know just how to speak of Madame Récamier, and it is a tolerably plausible view of the case to say that there is no need of speaking at all. History has rendered her enthusiastic justice, and in her present reputation there is perhaps something a trifle forced and factitious. She was very beautiful, very charming, and very much at the service of her friends—these are her claims to renown. To people of taste and fancy at the present day, however much they may regret not having known her, she can be little more than a rose-coloured shadow. To hear her surviving friends say to each other with a glance of intelligence, "Ah, *there* was a woman!" simply makes us uncomfortably jealous; we feel like exclaiming, with a certain asperity, that there are as good fish in the sea as ever were caught. To know her by literature is, moreover, not really to know her. We cannot see her beauty, we cannot hear the gracious inflections of her voice, we cannot appeal to her for sympathy; we can only read her letters, and her letters are not remarkable. They have no especial wit or grace; they have only great good sense and, in certain express directions, an immense friendliness. Her history certainly is a remarkable one. Born in the middle class, she married into the middle class and lost early in life the wealth that her marriage conferred upon her. She was never perceived to push or strive; no effort, no eagerness, were ever observable in her career, and yet for fifty years she was literally a social sovereign. She distributed bliss and bale; she made and unmade felicity. She might have unmade it, that is, but fortunately she was incorruptibly kind; her instincts were constructive, not destructive. In 1829, for instance, Prosper Mérimée, then a young man upon the threshold of life, had a fancy to adopt a diplomatic career, and, as a first step, to be appointed secretary of legation in London. The simplest way to compass his desire seems to him to be to apply through a friend to Madame Récamier. Madame Récamier can apply to the ambassador with the certainty of not meeting a refusal. The striking thing is that it is a question not at all of her doing what she can and taking what comes, but of her simply uttering her gentle fiat. Of course her remarkable influence was not simply an accident; she had exquisite gifts, and circumstances favoured her; but it seems rather a mistake to attempt to make a woman whose action in the world was altogether personal and destined to expire with her person an object of lasting interest. None of the various ministers of her renown—not even the possessor of the infallible memory of Sainte-Beuve—has to our knowledge repeated any definite utterance of the " incomparable Juliette " which seems at all noticeable. To write about her is like attempting to describe a perfume, and her clever niece, Madame Lenormant, in the volumes she has devoted to her memory, has perhaps run the risk of making her the least bit of a bore.

But of course she appeals to our imagination, and if we are well-disposed that way she may live yet a while by her picturesqueness. Seated every evening in her

little economical secular cell at the convent of the
Abbaye-au-Bois, or, of a summer morning, under the
trees at the Vallée-aux-Loups, the natural accessories in
her portrait are the figures of the people who formed
the best society in Continental Europe. In her relations
with Jean-Jacques Ampère she is perhaps especially
picturesque, for they contain just that element of potential oddity which is considered essential to picturesqueness. Madame Récamier was forty-three years of age
when young Ampère was presented to her, he himself
being just twenty; she was exactly of the age which,
had she lived, his mother would have reached. Jean-Jacques then and there fell in love with her. It was
one evening in her little drawing-room, which was full
of great people. She was, as Madame Cheuvreux says
(seeming in feminine fashion to have exactly divined it)
"sitting, almost reclining, half hidden in a cloud of
muslin, on a sofa of sky-blue damask of the old 'Empire' form, with the neck of a gilt swan for its arm."
It is not necessary to accuse Madame Récamier of inordinate coquetry—a charge which, although we are bound
to believe that she enjoyed her sway there is no other
evidence to support—to explain the fact that two years
later, when she was forty-five, his passion was still
burning. Might she have quenched it? These are of
course mysteries; but it is our duty to suppose that

what she did was wisely done. The event, in fact, proved it. She was an expert in these matters and she had learned the prudence of sacrificing a part to save the whole. Ampère's flame flickered down in time to the steady glow of friendship; and if Madame Récamier knew when the golden age ended and the silver began it is very likely that, under her exquisite direction, the young man himself never did. But there was certainly a prepossessing boldness in a young fellow of two-and-twenty writing in this fashion to an extremely distinguished woman of middle age: "Oh, tell me with truth that there *are* moments in which it seems that your soul is touched by my fate and takes an interest in my future? sometimes I have even thought that the sentiment so pure and tender with which you inspire me was not without a certain charm for yourself. But I am so afraid of being in error! Day by day my life centres itself in this affection. How cruel would it be to take the expression of your compassion for that of your interest! It is now especially, while I am away from you, that I am agitated by these fears. A few words, I entreat you, by way of consolation; but in heaven's name take care that in order to calm me you don't let yourself go beyond that which you really feel. What have I done, indeed, that you should love me? Ah, I have loved you with all my soul, without deceiving myself about our situation, without entertaining for an instant the thought of disturbing the tranquillity of your existence. I have given myself up to a hopeless sentiment, which has filled all my heart. I cannot live either without you or for you; I see all that is impossible in my fate, and yet how can I renounce that which is my only joy?" Madame Récamier quietly devised a *modus vivendi* for her ardent young friend, and he adopted it so successfully that three years later, she being at Rome and in the first glow of a friendship with Madame Swetchine, the famous ultramontane pietist, he found it natural to write to her, in allusion to this lady: "In good faith, madame, is it not true that my place is taken in your heart? I have no right to complain of it; it is not your fault if I have not that sort of religious and romantic imagination which it would be so natural to have. But I have it less than ever; the desire to please you made me force my nature; solitude and the law that punishes sacrilege have sent me back to it. . . . Madame Swetchine is worth much more to your imagination than I. Bring me back some friendship; it is all that I deserve and all that I exact of you." It seems an anomaly that five months after this Ampère, taking fire at a few words uttered on a certain evening by Madame Récamier, should be writing to her to ask almost passionately whether their union is after all impossible. M. Récamier is still living, but there had apparently been some allusion to a divorce. Ampère demands an assurance that if, on being at liberty, she should decide to marry, she will bear him in mind. He wishes to feel that there is no one else between them. The thing seems to be less a serious proposal than a sudden, rather fantastic desire on his part to fill out a certain intellectual ideal of the situation. In the way of ideals that of the reader, at this point, is that there should be a record that Madame Récamier, forty-eight years old, and with a husband in excellent health, was annoyed at having this marrying mood attributed to her.

In the autumn of 1823 she had gone to Italy with a little retinue of friends, of whom Ampère was not the least assiduous. She passed the winter in Rome, and the young man, remaining near her, formed, with the stimulus of her sympathy, that attachment for the Eternal City which was to increase from year to year and be the motive of his principal literary work. To be with Madame Récamier was to be socially on a very agreeable footing, for wherever she established herself she was speedily surrounded by brilliant people. This winter and the following summer, which the party spent at Naples, must have been for young Ampère a supremely happy season. To enjoy in Rome the society of the woman whom one considers the embodiment of everything admirable, to have that delightful city offer at every turn its happy opportunities and suggestions—this is to an appreciative spirit a particular refinement of bliss. Madame Récamier remained a second winter in Italy, and Ampère came home at the summons of his father, who appears at this time to have "worried" greatly, in vulgar phrase, about the young man's future, and who was especially impatient to see his tragedies coming forward at the Théâtre Français. During his son's absence in Rome the elder Ampère constantly writes to him on this question, and reports upon the MS. readings that have been given in his own circle—one, for instance, of all places in the world, at the Veterinary School—and upon the corrections and alterations that have been proposed. André Ampère, as he grew older, developed some rather uncomfortable eccentricities; he was in his private life and conversation the most unpractical and ill-regulated of men; and this persistent desire to make a third-rate playwright of a young man really gifted in other directions seems to indicate no little inconsequence of mind. Jean-Jacques's pieces were accepted, or half accepted, at the great theatre, but they were never played, and they are sleeping at this day in its dustiest pigeon-holes. He had indeed a passion for writing verses, and produced, first and last, a prodigious quantity of indifferent rhyme. Often, after having hammered all day at recondite philology, he would sit up half the night scribbling at the dictation of a rather drowsy muse. He wrote in general, thanks to his roving habits, which made odd scraps and snatches of time of value, at all sorts of hours and in all sorts of places. He would begin a chapter of his "Histoire Romaine" on the edge of a table at a café in the Corso; in one of his later letters he speaks of having written a comedy in a railway carriage.

The editor of these volumes gives a great number of his letters to Mme. Récamier, both during the year that followed his separation from her at Naples and at later periods. "It rains," he writes to her from Rome on his way northward; "I am writing this in a dark room, looking out on a dismal little street. At Naples, at least, when it rains, you have before your eyes a great expanse. Instead of the sea and the island of Capri I see an ugly white wall, four feet off. I should have found a certain consolation in going to sit in the Villa Pamfili, on that rock on the edge of the lake where we read about the gardens of Armida and found them again, or on the grass, near Santa Croce in Gerusalemme, where we went on Easter day, or in wandering in Saint Peter's, in the Coliseum, or on the edge of the Tiber."

There is little we could quote from these letters, however, even if we had space; they are charming, they speak equally well for the writer and for the sweet sagacity of the woman who inspired them, they denote a delightful relation, but they lack salient points, and in their quality of love-letters they are liable sometimes to weary the cold-hearted third person. Here, nevertheless, is a noteworthy paragraph: "You like me to tell you of my work—to describe my studies as a school-boy does to his mamma. Well, then, this is what seems to me at this moment the most delightful thing in the world, and an infallible means of arriving at almost universal knowledge. It's very simple. It is to note in every book I read the very important points, to concentrate all my attention upon these and to try to completely forget all the rest—and to join to this another observance, namely, that of reading on every subject and in every language only the best that there is. In this way, it seems to me, without uselessly overloading one's mind, one can acquire a deal of very positive and very various knowledge." This was written in 1825, and it may at that moment have been true; it doubtless, indeed, will always have a certain measure of truth. But the march of mind has been so rapid these last fifty years that it is to be feared that no particular method of study, however ingenious, will carry one very far on the way to "universal knowledge." To read even the best only, nowadays, is a task beyond the compass of individuals. But in one way on another Ampère was bent upon superior science, and in pursuit of it he went in the autumn of 1826 to Germany, and spent the winter at Bonn, under the inspiration of Niebuhr and Wilhelm von Schlegel. Madame de Staël had discovered Germany, earlier in the century, for the French at large— Ampère discovered it afresh for the younger generation. Schlegel was an old adorer of Madame Récamier, and a word from her ensured her young friend a prompt and impressive greeting. "At our first interview," Ampère writes, "I admit I was rather disconcerted by his affectation of fine manners and of the French tone; he seemed to avoid speaking of literature, as if it were pedantry. This was not in my account, but I was not discouraged; I let him play the fine gentleman, and now that he has fairly set himself up before me as a man of the world, that I have seen his yellow livery and his order of Sweden, he begins to talk of Sanscrit and the Middle Ages. By a happy chance he is going to begin a course on the German language and literature. What a master of German! This attraction, and that of a magnificent country, will keep me here some time. The mountains which edge the Rhine before reaching this place," he adds—and the writer of these lines has made the same observation—" recall in a striking manner the horizon of Rome." From Niebuhr he got what he could. "I have done very well," he says, "to take no great trouble to learn the old history of Rome ; I should have to begin it afresh." For the rest of Ampère's life, it was always a feather in his cap that on leaving Bonn he paid a visit to Weimar and spent three weeks with Goethe. He must himself have recalled this episode complacently, for the great man had made much of him and of the intelligent articles which Ampère had written about his works in the "Globe" newspaper, the organ of serious young France at that time. Wherever he went Madame Récamier's recommendation was of service to him; she had *ci-devant* admirers stationed here and there on purpose, as it were. In Berlin it was the Prince Augustus of Prussia—he who in 1811 had very seriously wished to marry her. Here, in conclusion, are Ampère's impressions of the German mind: "Up to this time Germany inspires me with the greatest respect for its superior men, but with little interest in the common life. Their true superiority resides in imagination and learning; the men who are without these two gifts, who make neither systems nor poems, appear to me plain good people, with little cleverness or sensibility; you need to make an effort of will to talk with them. But a German in whom learning has not extinguished imagination, in whom imagination does not lead learning astray, if good luck wills it that he have lived in Italy to thaw out his senses, and that he have gained experience of practical life by affairs—that man is a man such as one can find only in Germany. There is such a one here—Niebuhr, of whom you must not speak in your letter to Schlegel."

On leaving Germany Ampère went to Sweden and Norway, and for the rest of his life he usually spent half the year in foreign lands. To travel was a passion with him, and though he had little money and was famous for his awkward management of his personal affairs, he appears to have been able to satisfy every impulse of his restlessness. His father's house was not a comfortable home, not because André Ampère was not an extremely affectionate parent, but because extreme naïveté, when the character has taken a melancholy turn, is not always identical with geniality. Jean-Jacques once posted back to Paris from a distance in response to an urgent summons from his sire. The two sat down to dinner, and in a moment—"It's very odd," cried the elder, "but I should have thought that it would give me more pleasure to see you!"

This was the lover of Julie Carron at fifty. From the third of these volumes we have left ourselves space to quote nothing. We can only recommend the whole work to curious readers. The letters contained in the third volume are more and more the record of a busy life. Ampère was professor at the Collége de France, member of the Academy of Inscriptions and the Académie Française, and a frequent contributor to the "Revue des Deux Mondes." He was no politician, but he was a consistent anti-imperialist. The letters which Madame Cheuvreux has gathered together throw light here and there on many agreeable and interesting figures—the most pleasing, perhaps, being that very superior man and, in temperament and turn of mind, half Anglican Frenchman, Alexis de Tocqueville. But the whole society represented here—the cultivated liberal France of before the Empire—of outside the Empire—makes, intellectually and morally, a very honourable show. We said just now that it seemed to be sitting for its likeness; we only meant that the portrait was not blurred. We see it at all its hours and in all its moods, and we may believe that, taken by surprise, observed unawares, no group of people could on the whole have supported publicity more gracefully than the two Ampères and their many friends.

MADAME DE SABRAN.

THE present century in France has been the golden age of editors. It might have been supposed that the mine of literary wealth bequeathed to that country by the eighteenth century had been exhausted, and that the occupation of the exhibitory fraternity was gone. The mine has been worked with extraordinary industry and with the most perfect appliances of erudition and criticism, and its contents have been brought to light in particles of all dimensions—in massive boulders, such as only the more skilled engineers might safely transport, in fragments convenient for immediate use, and in barely ponderable powder and dust. More even than our own time the eighteenth century was an age of scribbling. This indeed is untrue if taken in the sense that the amount of published writing, in proportion to the size of society, was larger than in our own day; but it is true if we speak with an eye to the quality of production. In proportion to the size of society, we suspect that there were more things written in private between 1720 and 1790 which might go to press without professional revision (save in the matter of orthography) than between 1800 and 1875. There was in other words, so far as form was concerned, less merely wasted and squandered literary effort than we witness nowadays. The distinction between padding and substance had not then been invented; and it is not only more charitable but more accurate to say that all the writing (so far as it went) was substance rather than padding. There are vast quantities of it that we cannot read—that we should not be able to read even if our own age made no appeal to us; but this is in a great measure because the whole body of civilisation has taken a jump, and we are wofully out of relation with our ancestors. We are a thousand times more clever; but it may be questioned whether, just as the Venetians in the sixteenth century knew something about the art of painting that all our cleverness will not put us into possession of, the ladies and gentlemen who sowed the ultimate seeds of the French Revolution had not a natural sense of agreeable literary expression which is quite irrecoverable by our straining modern wit. Comparisons, however, are odious, and it is certain that our ancestors had their bores and that we have our charmers. What we may say is that people of the eighteenth century wrote much and wrote well—so much that some lost or unsuspected yellow manuscript is still constantly drawn from hiding, and so well that the presumption is always in favour of its being very readable.

The best society at least wrote in those days more than it does now, and the obvious reason is that it had vastly more time on its hands. It had nothing to do with trade; the men who composed it had no daily duties in "stores" and counting rooms. The gentlemen of the eighteenth century were either in the Army, the Church, the diplomatic service, or the civil service; and these are all eminently sociable professions. The occupations of women were proportionately less exacting, for women's lives have always been fashioned in that portion of the piece, as one may say, which remains after men's have been cut out. Ladies, therefore, wrote a great deal, and at a first glance at the field it seems as if every woman of good fashion had produced certain volumes of letters, of reminiscences, of memoirs, of maxims, or of madrigals. Since Madame de Sévigné French gentlewomen have been excellent letter writers, and those lessons in easy style to which allusion was made above may often be culled from their ill-spelled gossip with their absent friends. (They all spelled very much at random. Even Madame du Châtelet, the learned coquette with whom Voltaire lived so many years, and who edited Newton and competed for the prizes of the Academy of Sciences, gained appreciably as a correspondent by being charitably read aloud.) French society in the eighteenth century was indeed very small, and we know it nowadays with surprising minuteness; we know it almost as well as if a brilliant Balzac of that age had laboriously constructed it and, with all the pains in the world, had not been able to make his people seem really more multitudinous than a pre-Raphaelite painter does the leaves of his trees. It is a multitude, but it is a multitude that we can count. For an historic group its outlying edges have very little nebulosity or mystery—very little of the look of continuity with the invisible. The fierce light that beats upon the subject-matter of French *études critiques* has illumined every corner and crevice of it. The people who are fond of remarking that, after all, the world is very small, must make their assertion with emphasis after a course of French memoirs, with an eye to the notes, or simply after reading Sainte-Beuve's "Causeries." The same names, the same figures, the same anecdotes, the same allusions, constantly recur; it is a dense cross web of relations, distinctly circumscribed. It is hardly too much to say that for all purposes save those of specialists the time is all contained in Sainte-Beuve's forty volumes. A collection of newspaper articles fairly comprehends it, even to many of its *minutiæ*.

The situation has a certain resemblance to those portions of modern Rome and Athens in which there are still chances of disinterring Greek statues. Excavation has been so systematically pursued that we may reasonably suppose there are now many more maimed divinities above ground than beneath it; and yet the explorer's spade still rings against a masterpiece often enough to maintain us in hopeful attention. It was but the other day—compared to the duration of its mouldy concealment—that the beautiful mailed Augustus of the Vatican was restored to the light, and it was but yesterday that MM. de Magnieu and Prat put forward, in a beautiful and substantial volume, the letters of Madame de Sabran.[1] This excellent publication belongs to a class to which there is good reason for expecting more recruits. Madame de Sabran's letters are love-letters, and in such missives the female hand has at all times been prolific. The author was not in her day a woman of eminent distinction; she moved in the best society, she was known to be clever, and those who corresponded with her had a high

[1] "Correspondance Inédite de la Comtesse de Sabran et du Chevalier de Boufflers." Paris, Plon. 1875.

appreciation of her epistolary talent. But she never published anything (although she alludes to a work on the Conduct of Life which she has in hand), and you will not find her name in the "Biographie Universelle." She was one of the multitudinous minor satellites of the French court; she represents the average clever woman of quality of her time. Many other women were presumably esteemed equally clever, and many others must have left letters as voluminous and, on some grounds, as valuable as hers. Many such, as we know, have already seen the light. This is not said to depreciate the merit of Madame de Sabran's epistles, but simply to note the fact that, charming as they are, they belong to a numerous family. Madame de Sabran's letters were piously preserved by her son, recently deceased (of whose childhood they contain much mention), and are published in execution of his testamentary injunctions. For him at least his mother had claims to renown. Few readers of the volume before us will fail to agree with him. In France it has been highly relished, and the relations of Madame de Sabran and the Chevalier de Boufflers have taken their place as one of the most touching episodes in the history of the old French society. The writer of these lines has read the book with extreme pleasure, and he cannot resist the temptation to prolong his pleasure and share it with such readers as have a taste for delicate things.

Madame de Sabran, who was born in 1750, married with the usual docility of the young women of her country. M. de Sabran was an officer in the navy, fifty years his wife's senior, and possessed of a meagre fortune, though also of what we call nowadays a handsome "record." She speaks of her marriage in the very charming account which she gives, in 1787, of her daughter's wedding : "My heart has never beaten so hard as at the moment I placed her on the *prie-dieu* where she was going to utter that famous *yes* that one can never unsay when once it is said, much as one may sometimes wish it. My own did not produce such an effect upon me; and yet what a difference! I was about to marry an infirm old man, of whom I was to be rather the sick-nurse than the wife, and she a young man full of grace and merit. But it is that then I felt the consequences so little; everything seemed to me equally well, equally good; as I loved nothing, everything seemed to me worthy of being loved, and I felt toward my *bonhomme de mari* very much as toward my father and my grandfather—a feeling very sweet at that time, and that my heart found sufficient. Time has undeceived me; I have lost my faith in happiness; so in spite of myself, during the whole service, I wept a flood of tears." Her married life lasted but a short time; M. de Sabran died of apoplexy, leaving his wife among social ties that might have beguiled an even less consolable widowhood. The Abbé Delille, the horticultural poet, taught her Latin, and the great Turgot prized her conversation. Several years later she made the acquaintance of the Chevalier de Boufflers, and her first letter, in the volume before us, is of the date of 1778. Madame de Sabran was a woman of culture and M. de Boufflers was a patron of arts and letters; he also passed for one of the most agreeable men of his time, and he figures not infrequently in its chronicles. They became intimate, and Madame de Sabran's friendship ripened into a passion of which the present letters are the flickering but always ardent utterance. At a certain moment (apparently in 1781) she begins to address her correspondent with the *thou* and to call him "my child." Up to this moment it had been "my brother." M. de Boufflers was altogether a man of the world, and of the gayest world, and his roving disposition was a constant interruption to his attentions to his friend. In 1785 he was appointed governor of the colony of Senegal, and during his sojourn in Africa Madame de Sabran continued her letters in the form of a journal. He was absent but eighteen months, but after a short visit to France he returned to his post and remained there two years. Madame de Sabran resumed her diary, and M. de Boufflers also kept, for her entertainment, a journal which is hardly less charming than that of his mistress. He married Madame de Sabran in 1797, when he was sixty years old and his bride was forty-seven. This long delay is but insufficiently accounted for by his desire to be able to offer his wife a fortune and a great position. M. de Boufflers enjoyed many of the advantages of matrimony without its encumbrances. The division was not equal, for Madame de Sabran seems to have had all the anxieties of a wife and none of the guarantees. The couple emigrated during the Revolution and their marriage took place in Germany. The Chevalier de Boufflers died in Paris in 1815, and his widow survived him twelve years. A certain reticence on the part of the editors prompts the adventurous reader to wonder whether, in its later stages, this intimacy was not touched by the ravages of time; but the conjecture is almost impertinent, decidedly cynical and, inasmuch as there is no visible answer to the question, utterly vain.

What have we here, then, is something very light—the passionate, unstudied jottings of an amiable and intelligent woman who loves a man whose affection she is conscious of possessing, but whose absences and delays and preoccupations and admirations and social dissipations, and duties of all kinds, are a constant irritant to the impatience, the jealousies, the melancholy, of which her own affection, in its singularly delicate texture, is all indivisibly composed. It is hard to say why we should be interested in these very personal affairs of an obscure French lady of a hundred years ago, and if a stern logician should accuse us of frivolous tastes we should find it difficult to justify our enthusiasm. Madame de Sabran's letters have in the direct way but a slender historical value, for they allude to but few of the important events of the time. They throw no very vivid light on contemporary manners; for there is little in them to refer them to their actual date. Their psychological and dramatic interest cannot be said to be profound; they have none of the dignity of tragedy. Their compass of feeling is not wide, and the persons concerned in them are not, in any very striking way, at the mercy of events. They portray no terrible suffering, no changes of fortune; the most important event related is that Madame de Sabran marries her daughter. If they are passionate, it is passion in the minor key, without any great volume or resonance. Yet for all that they are charming, simply because so far as they go they are perfect. Madame de Sabran had an exquisite talent for the expression of feminine tenderness, and a gift like this has an absolute value. Two appreciable causes throw it here into a sort of picturesque relief. One is the fascination of the background—our sense of the peculiar atmosphere of the eighteenth century; the other is the extremely dramatic form in which, in this case, the usual contrast between the man's life and the woman's is presented to us—the opposition between the heart for which any particular passion was but one of many and the heart for which all passion resolved itself into a single unquenchable flame. As regards the eighteenth century, it is rather late in the day, perhaps, to talk about that; but so long as we read the books of the time, so long will our sense of its perplexing confusion of qualities retain a certain freshness. No other age appeals at once so much and so little to our sympathies, or provokes such alternations of curiosity and repugnance. It is near enough to us to seem to partake of many of our current feelings, and yet it is divided from us by an impassable gulf. For many persons it will always have in some ways an indefinable charm—a charm that they will entertain themselves in looking for even in the faded and mouldering traces of its material envelope—its costumes, its habits, its scenic properties. There are few imaginations possessed of a desultory culture that are not able to summon at will the dim vision of a high saloon, panelled in some pale colour, with oval medallions over the doors, with a polished, uncarpeted floor, with thin-legged chairs and tables, with Chinese screens, with a great glass door looking out upon a terrace where clipped shrubs are standing in square green boxes. It is peopled with men and women whose style of dress inspires both admiration and mistrust. There is a sort of noble amplitude in the cut of their garments and a richness of texture in the stuff; breeches and stockings set off the manly figure, and the stiffly-pointed waists of the women serve as a stem to the flower-like exuberance of dazzling bosoms. As we glance from face to face the human creature seems to be in an expansive mood; we receive a lively impression of vigour of temperament, of sentimental fermentation, of moral curiosity. The men are full of natural gallantry and the women of natural charm, and of forms and traditions they seem to take and leave very much what they choose. It is very true that they by no means always gain by minute inspection. An acute sense of untidiness is brought home to us as we move from group to group. Their velvets and brocades are admirable, but they are worn with rather too bold a confidence in their intrinsic merit, and we arrive at the conviction that powder and pomatum are not a happy combination in a lady's tresses, and that there are few things less attractive than soiled satin and tarnished embroidery.

In the same way we gather an uneasy impression of moral cynicism; we overhear various phrases which make us wonder whither our steps have strayed. And yet, as we retreat, we cast over the threshold a look that is on the whole a friendly one; we say to ourselves that after all these people are singularly human. They care intensely for the things of the mind and the heart, and though they often make a very foolish use of them they strike here and there a light by whose aid we are now reading certain psychological mysteries. They have the psychological passion, and if they expose themselves in morbid researches it is because they wish to learn by example as well as precept and are not afraid to pay for their knowledge. "The French age *par excellence*," an acute French critic has said, "it has both our defects and our qualities. Better in its intelligence than in its behaviour, more reasoning than philosophical, more moralistic than moral, it has offered the world lessons rather than examples, and examples rather than models. It will be ever a bad sign in France when we make too much of it or too little; but it would be in especial a fatal day were we to borrow its frivolity and its corruption and leave aside its noble instincts and its faculty of enthusiasm." A part of our kindness for the eighteenth century rests on the fact that it paid so completely the price of both corruptions and enthusiasms. As we move to and fro in it we see something that our companions do not see— we see the sequel, the consummation, the last act of the drama. The French Revolution rounds off the spectacle and renders it a picturesque service which has also something besides picturesqueness. It casts backward a sort of supernatural light, in the midst of which, at times, we seem to see a stage full of actors performing fantastic antics for our entertainment. But retroactively, too, it seems to exonerate the generations that preceded it, to make them irresponsible and give them the right to say that, since the penalty was to be exorbitant, a little pleasure more or less would not signify. There is nothing in all history which, to borrow a term from the painters, "composes" better than the opposition, from 1600 to 1800, of the audacity of the game and the certainty of the reckoning. We all know the idiom which speaks of such reckonings as "paying the piper." The piper here is the People. We see the great body of society executing its many-figured dance on its vast polished parquet; and in a dusky corner, behind the door, we see the lean, gaunt, ragged Orpheus filling his hollow reed with tunes in which every breath is an agony.

The opening lines of the first of Madame de Sabran's letters are characteristic both of the time and of the woman. The time was sceptical and priests were out of fashion, except for such assistance as they might render at a lady's toilet; but Madame de Sabran's most amiable quality is a certain instinctive moderation. "I really need to talk with you to-day, my brother, to cheer myself up and divert myself from a certain visit I have been making. And what a visit! A visit that one makes only at certain times, to the knees of a certain man, to confess certain things which I won't tell you. I am still very weary and ashamed with it. I don't at all like that ceremony. They tell us it is very salutary, and I submit, like a respectable woman." It is not in our power to say what sins Madame de Sabran had to confess; she gives an account of her life at Anisy, the residence of her uncle the Bishop of Laon, where she regularly spent her summers, which seems to allow a margin for none but venial aberrations: "I get up every morning at eight, and read and write till eleven; then I set myself at painting till dinner time. I am doing a superb oil picture which I have composed for myself and which I will show you. . . . I read in Latin the original letters of Héloïse and Abélard, and I have a good mind to translate some of the most coherent ones—not those of Abélard, for they are most tiresomely dry and pedantic, but those of poor Héloïse." In everything that Madame de Sabran says there is a certain closely personal accent, and at last we have a complete portrait, formed by a multitude of desultory touches. The total is something we like so much that we do not feel disposed to call the weak spots by their specific names. Is it vanity when she frankly pronounces her oil painting " superb " ? " Apropos, I have not yet spoken to you of the portrait of the Countess Auguste that I made while she was staying here; it is a little masterpiece. It is a perfect likeness. It is full length, a table beside her, with books and papers. It is a charming picture, and it will be a pleasure to me to show it to you." Is this vanity, or is it the unaffected frankness of a person who is conscious of genuine talent ? We have no means of taking the measure of Madame de Sabran's talent; but she was a very clever woman, and it is not hard to believe that her pictures were charming and that the musical airs which she is constantly composing and sending to M. de Boufflers were infinitely sweet. But in dealing with people of this race and society, especially at that time, we Anglo-Saxons are constantly reminded of the necessity of weighing virtues and vices in an adjusted scale. Words and things, ideas and feelings, have a different value. There are French vanities that are very innocent and English humilities that are not at all so; French corruptions that, *mutatis mutandis*, are by no means damning. For instance, M. de Boufflers, writing from Africa, tells Madame de Sabran of the condition of her portrait, which she has given him. "As by a special grace, I have been left alone a moment. I have just left my letter to go and kiss you. You are behind certain cross-pieces of wood, intended to fix the picture in its case, and you look like your pretty Delphine in her convent parlour—though if there is a difference, I know very well to whose advantage it is." Here is a gallant gentleman trying to be agreeable to a superior woman by telling her that she is prettier than her own daughter. The inference is, that M. de Boufflers thought he was saying something very charming and that Madame de Sabran received his compliment in a sympathetic spirit. And yet Madame de Sabran was a devoted mother. M. de Boufflers in the next sentence speaks with the tenderest solicitude of Mademoiselle de Sabran, and in the following letter he sends a most graceful message to his friend's children. "Kiss your charming children for me. My heart bleeds when I think that I cannot press them against my breast and prove to them what it is in my eyes to be born of you." The portrait mentioned by M. de Boufflers is apparently not the charming picture by Mme. Vigée le Brun of which a capital reproduction in aqua-fortis is prefixed to the Correspondence. Madame de Sabran was called a beauty, but we should say that, if this picture is to be trusted, this was just what she was not. It is an intensely French physiognomy and quite the one that shapes itself in our mind's eye out of the perusal of the letters. But half its interest is in the way it pleases in spite of its irregularity. It is extraordinarily sympathetic, and offers a singular combination of wit and amiability.

In the letter but one preceding that one which has been mentioned as indicating the moment of expansion, as it were, in Madame de Sabran's friendship, she evidently defends herself against such contingencies. She has been scolding her friend for delay in writing. "You can have no idea what I have suffered, and I am so frightened at it myself that there is nothing I wouldn't do to recover my reason, even to going to the moon in search of it on the back of a hippogriff. But meanwhile I take the firm resolution to trouble myself no more about your silence, your absence, and even your indifference; to live a little for you, a great deal for myself, and to be always gay and contented whatever befalls me. In the midst of all this fine philosophy, however," she adds, "I rejoice in your return"; and her philosophy henceforth was destined to play a very secondary part. There are times when she summons it to her aid—for as regards all things in which M. de Boufflers was not concerned it was very alert and

competent; but when she plays at resignation or
indifference, stoicism or epicureanism, she hardly even
pretends that she deceives herself. She had indeed a
strain of melancholy in her disposition which is constantly cropping up; she was afraid of the deeper
currents of life, and she thought that when one felt
one's feet touching bottom it was the part of wisdom
to stand still. "I don't rejoice as you do in the
discovery of *truth*. I am afraid it will hurt me. All
those people will turn your head and, in conducting you
to happiness, they will spoil this happiness of ours.
We are comfortable; let us rest upon that; what do
we need more? I don't care for a science which is of
no use to our love and which may on the contrary be
injurious to it." M. de Boufflers had sent home a little
blackamoor as a present to a friend who had taken the
interesting stranger to see the aunt of the donor.
Shortly afterward Madame de Sabran called upon this
lady, who denounced the little negro as an ill-bred
monster. "As soon as he saw her he uttered horrible
cries and threw himself upon the ground with signs of
the greatest fright, while he had been caressing every
one else. On his being asked why, he replied that she
made up a face at him. The Maréchale never suspected
that he had reasons for finding her different from other
people, and she has given him no thanks for his

frankness. It makes one shudder to see how little we know ourselves. Is it a good?—is it an evil? I can't decide. But I believe that illusion is useful in all things, and for myself all that I fear in this world is the truth. The truth is almost always sad and she leaves almost no consolation behind her. Happily every individual has a common interest in being cheated, and the human race in this respect doesn't spare itself. What is most to be desired is to be *well* cheated, till one's last day." In one place, however, she relates how her mind has taken a flight into the very empyrean of philosophy. "At the degree of elevation at which my spirit travelled, objects grew so small to my imagination that you also seemed no more to me than a worm, and I was indignant that so little an animal could do me so much harm and make me see things so crookedly."

One feature of this correspondence—and I suppose we may dignify it with the name of historical, for it is probable that in love-letters exchanged in aristocratic circles at the present day such allusions are rare—is the manner in which both Madame de Sabran and M. de Boufflers expatiate on the state of their health and upon their drugs and doses. "Meanwhile," the former writes, "I will take no more pills, since they make *you* so sick at your stomach"; and she adduces this concession as a proof of her lover's empire over her mind.

Could there be a more touching illustration of intimate union than this phenomenon of a lover being acted upon by his mistress's medicine? Madame de Sabran's health was delicate and she paid frequent visits to various healing springs. "These two days," she writes from Spa, "I have been in my bed with fever. I shall get off with a bad cold, which I owe to the Princess of Orange, who did me the honour—I don't know by what fantasy—to choose me out of a thousand to accompany her in a ride on horseback, which she performed throughout at a great gallop, beneath a fearful sun, and with an abominable wind. I came back tired half to death, coughing, with my ribs and thighs broken, cursing all the princesses on earth, who never do anything like other people." On leaving Spa on this occasion Madame de Sabran made an excursion into the Low Countries, of which she gives a most humorous and entertaining account. "We are making this journey like plain goodwives, by the public vehicles, under assumed names; whereby it will cost us almost nothing, we shall be much better, and be restored to Spa within a week. But don't go and speak to any one of this project; I wish to tell it to you alone for a thousand thousand reasons. You must know that I am called Mme. de Jobert, and Mme. d'Andlau Mme. Bertin. We came hither from Brussels in a barge which was quite

like Noah's ark, as regards all that it contained. I amused myself all day with sketching the queer people who were with us, and among others two Capuchins, whom I painted so like life that every one admired them; which gave me a great reputation and success in the assembly. I effected immediately the conquest of a young English merchant, who never left us during the voyage, and who, from time to time, treated my companion and me to beer, to refresh us, almost making us tipsy, for in politeness we were afraid to refuse it."
"The journey to Holland," she writes later, "was not a success [as regards her health], but it vastly amused us. No one knew who we were; we were taken now for saleswomen on their way to the Haarlem fair, now for ladies from Friesland, now for singing-women. We were treated sometimes very well and sometimes very ill; we often dined at the public table. We travelled sometimes on foot, sometimes in a phaëton, sometimes in a sail-boat. We passed one night on the highway and another at the city-gate. It would be impossible to see and do more things in a week. We went as far as Amsterdam, where the sight of the port amazed us; for neither of us had ever seen a ship. They are superb contrivances, but I should be very sorry to be shut up in one, unless it were with you."

Madame de Sabran's letters are so vaguely dated that

we are often in ignorance of her whereabouts; but considering that in theory she led a very quiet life she seems to have spent a good deal of time on the road. She made excursions if not journeys. To meet M. de Boufflers away from home was often the purpose of her wanderings. It would be part of the entertainment afforded by these letters to understand the logic of Madame de Sabran's goings and comings; to know to what extent it was part of her scheme to conceal from the world the extent of her intimacy with her friend. Such intimacies may in those days have been concealable, but they certainly were not generally concealed. Madame de Sabran lived half the year, however, with a great clerical dignitary. She was a bishop's niece, and this doubtless put her somewhat in the position of Cæsar's wife. It is not unfair to M. de Boufflers, however, to imagine that his society was often to be enjoyed only on his own terms, and that there were moments when he would rather go ten miles to meet his friend than thirty. Was it not in his character to commingle a due appreciation of the bird in the hand with a lively attention to the bird in the bush? Madame de Sabran, who professed in general a high relish for illusions, appears to have judged her friend in some points without them. We cannot say whether she was jealous of the past: if she was, she gave a very amiable turn to her jealousy. Writing in 1787 from Nancy, where M. de Boufflers had formerly been in garrison, "I have not stopped thinking of you all day," she says, "and I am tired to death with it. It must be that the air of this place is impregnated with certain little atoms that come and fasten themselves to me by sympathy. I don't pass through a street without thinking how often you have walked there. I don't see a house without imagining it is inhabited by one of the Dulcineas who formerly vied with each other for the happiness of pleasing you. I was present at the session of the Academy on the day of Saint Louis, where I saw all kinds of these same Dulcineas and was greatly entertained. I tried to read in their faces and their eyes some traces of love for you; for at present, contrary to old times, I want every one to love you. But I saw in them the traces of time much more than of love; they were all frightfully old and ugly." Madame de Sabran is generous, and this little scratch at the end is the least possible tribute to human weakness. She saw another indubitable Dulcinea at the theatre at Valenciennes. "Looking at her with other eyes than mine, she has really very few charms. . . . She amused me a thousand times more than the play. She was extremely occupied with two officers, who kept her in continual motion from right to left, to make neither jealous; she laughed and talked louder than the actors. This time I was jealous, not of her successes, but of her happiness, and I said to myself, 'She knew that poor African; she loved him; she did more, and yet she has been able to forget him and love others. How can she do it?' I should like to have her receipt—*pauvre bête* that I am, consuming myself in vain regrets and, a thousand leagues away from him, seeing only with his eyes, hearing him only, able to think of him only, making the past the present for the love of him, and giving up the present to sadness and despair. My life will not be longer than hers; yet she turns hers to profit and I throw mine out of the window."

The reader, as he goes, marks certain passages as signs of the times; the first thunder-growls of the French Revolution affect one as the strokes of the bell that rings up the curtain at a tragedy. "People talk of nothing but taxes and cutting down pensions : it is the paying the piper—*le quart d'heure de Rabelais.* People live with the edge of their teeth." And elsewhere : "The poor Marshal [de Soubise] died this morning. His sister the *dévote* is in despair—all the more that he died without confession and without consciousness to ask pardon of God for his millions of mortal sins. He was the Solomon of our age, minus the wisdom. His whole seraglio is at present in tears and misery, even to the sultana Validé. The King inherits five hundred thousand livres of income; it comes in the nick of time, for in spite of the notables and their sage counsels, he doesn't know where to thrust his head." Madame de Sabran was in the tree that the tempest had begun to shake; she was on an honourable footing of familiarity at court. Her little son Elzéar was at Versailles with his uncle. "He has already," she writes, "great success at court. The Queen found him on her passage and kissed him on his two little pink cheeks. This morning she said to me, 'Do you know that I kissed a gentleman yesterday?' 'I know it, madame, for he boasts of it.'"

The journal kept by M. de Boufflers during his second sojourn in Senegal is appended to these letters of his friend. M. de Boufflers is known on other evidence, but this charming record of homeward thoughts in exile completes his portrait—completes it very favourably. He is not positively an edifying figure, but he is, in his way, a decidedly interesting one. He was an eminent specimen of the "charming man," as this fortunate mortal flourished in favourable social conditions. Those of the last century in France placed him much more in relief, and enabled him to develop on a more imposing scale, than the pre-occupied, democratic, commercial society of our own day. M. de Boufflers was a gentleman in the large picturesque sense; it is striking at what a cost his gentility was kept up—on

what a copious diet it had to be fed. He had an
admirable vigour of temperament and he was thoroughly
at home in the world. He was the son of a king's
mistress and the incumbent of an ecclesiastical living of
forty thousand livres, by the bounty of the king himself (the deposed Stanislaus I. of Poland, to whom as a
comfort for his old age Louis XV.—his son-in-law—
made over the duchy of Lorraine, where the little court
of Lunéville was a vastly less splendid, but an easier
and cosier, Versailles). Boufflers had signalized his
period of probation at the seminary of Saint Sulpice by
the production of certain *contes galants*, which, though
abbés in those days could go far, transgressed even the
ecclesiastical licence. So he turned from priest to
knight of Malta, went to the German wars, amused
himself on a great scale, squandered his money, and at
middle age, to repair his wasted substance, had to
solicit a colonial governorship. In Africa, characteristically, his vigour and vivacity did him service; he
took his duties in hand and really administered his
government. All this time he dabbled in letters and
made love à *l'envi*. There are several anecdotes about
him in Grimm's "Correspondance," but all that I
know of his literature is a short tale in verse, in two
alternating rhymes, quoted by Grimm, and chiefly
remarkable for its frank indecency. On his return from

Africa he went as deputy to the States-General and, after the Revolution, entered the French Academy and completed the circle of his activity by composing a very dull book on Free Will. The Boufflers of these letters is the full-blown Boufflers of middle life, largely versed in men, women and things, and possessed of a great acquired flexibility of sentiment and wit. He strikes one as a shrewd epicurean, with a decided mind to eat his cake and have it. It is nothing new to observe that when men and women spin the web of sentiment together, the finest threads are generally the woman's, and it doubtless cannot be said, in this particular case, that M. de Boufflers abused the lover's usual right to be less exquisite than his mistress. Certain however it is that the reader cannot rid himself of the feeling that not a little of what is exquisite in Madame de Sabran is wasted, given simply to the air, exhaled into the elements. M. de Boufflers balanced his account in the gross, and of a certain proportion of this amiable woman's articulate heartbeats no note was ever made. But probably we make these reflections simply because we are jealous of the extravagant Chevalier. The reader is himself in love with Madame de Sabran and he judges M. de Boufflers but grudgingly. Speaking impartially, these two hundred pages of his journal are delightful reading. His gaiety, his wit, his ardour, his tenderness, his mingled impatience and resignation, his marital invocations and ejaculations, his delicate natural compliments, make the tone of this fragmentary diary a real model of manly grace.

There is a sketch of M. de Boufflers in one of Madame de Sabran's letters which should already have been quoted: "No, my child, I have no use for illusion on your part; our love has no need of it; it was born without it and it will subsist without it; for it was surely not my charms, which had ceased to exist when you knew me, that fixed you near me; neither is it your *manières de Huron*, your absent, surly air, your stinging, truthful sallies, your great appetite, and your profound sleep when one wishes to talk with you, that have made me love you to distraction; it is a certain nameless something that puts our souls into unison, a certain sympathy that makes me feel and think like you. For beneath this rude envelope you conceal the spirit of an angel and the heart of a woman You unite all contrasts and there is no being in heaven or on earth more lovable and more loved than you. Come and see me, *à cause de cela*, as soon as you can." It implies no want of sagacity to imagine that the unflattering lines in this picture are only finer and subtler caresses. M. de Boufflers could at times express himself with an implicit tenderness of which an angel, since Madame de

Sabran would have it so, need hardly have been ashamed. " A thing that no one suspects, not even you, is that I am forty-eight years old to-day. Here is a vast amount of time lost; for there have been nothing but minutes well spent. I leave you to guess them. But, *ma fille*, this number of forty-eight—doesn't it impress you with respect? I let you off of the respect in advance, for it seems to me that I leave half of my years here, as I leave half of my luggage, not wanting it all on my voyage. Besides, I have grown so used to the idea of being loved by you, in spite of youth, in spite of old age, that I think much less of my age as it goes on. You remember, perhaps, that portrait that I loved so before I dared to speak to the original; that widow's dress which I wished you to retain in my honour. My age makes me think of it, but it doesn't make me think of your change; it is only matter that changes in us, and there is so little in you that it seems to me that I have nothing to fear. Farewell, my daughter. I have struck out two or three lines which would have saddened you. Let us love life and not fear death, for souls don't die, but love for ever." This was written on his ship, as he was approaching the shores of France, and he adds the next day: "I see France drawing near, and I am like the little girl of a fairy story when they told her, There is a kingdom; in the kingdom there is a town; in the town there is a house; in the house there is a room. . . . Here are forty days thrown overboard," he says later, recording adverse winds. "Forty days! that is almost the life of a man, if one counts in life only the moments worth counting." It is to be hoped that he found reason to reckon time less wastefully after his reunion with his friend.

These few extracts from Madame de Sabran's letters can have given but an imperfect idea of those things by which she irresistibly pleases. Her grace, her tempered vivacity, her softened intensity, her admirable mixture of passion and reason, her happy, natural, flexible style, are all forcible appeals to our sympathy. It seemed in place just now to say that some of these charming qualities had been squandered; but I must hasten to unsay it when I reflect that, in this foreign land and in this alien age, we restlessly appreciative moderns are almost reverently inhaling their faint, sweet perfume.

MÉRIMÉE'S LETTERS.

THE many readers who take pleasure in clever French books have found themselves of late deploring the sadly diminished supply of this commodity. The past few years have brought forth no new literary names of the first rank in France and have witnessed the decline and extinction of most of the elder talents. It is a long time now since a French book has made a noise on valid grounds. Here, at last, however, is a publication which, in six weeks, has reached a fourth edition and which most people of taste are talking about. But, though new in subject, the two volumes to which we allude belong to the literature of thirty years ago. They are the last contribution to literature of a writer whose reputation was made in the early part of the century. We recently heard it declared by a competent critic that they contain the best writing (as simple writing) that has appeared in France since Voltaire. This is strong language; but the reader of the easy, full-flavoured, flexible prose to which Mérimée treats his correspondent will certainly feel the charm that prompted it. Prosper Mérimée's title to fame has hitherto consisted in a couple of dozen little tales, varying from ten to a hundred pages in length. They have gradually come to be considered perfect models of the narrative art; and we confess our own admiration for them is such that we feel like declaring it a capital offence in a young story-teller to put pen to paper without having read them and digested them. It was a very handsome compliment to pure quality (to the sovereignty of form) when Mérimée, with his handful of little stories, was elected to the French Academy. The moral element in his tales is such as was to be expected in works remarkable for their pregnant concision and for a firmness of contour suggesting hammered metal. In a single word they are not sympathetic. Sympathy is prolix, sentiment is diffuse, and our author, by inexorably suppressing emotion, presents his facts in the most salient relief. These facts are, as a general thing, extremely disagreeable—murder and adultery being the most frequent and the catastrophe being always ingeniously tragical. Where sentiment never appears, one gradually concludes that it does not exist; and we had mentally qualified this frigid artist as a natural cynic. A romancer with whom bloodshed and tears were so abundant and subjective compassion so rare had presumably a poor opinion of the stock from which heroes and heroines spring. Many years ago M. Mérimée ceased to publish stories and devoted himself to archæology and linguistics. We have often wondered how during all these years he employed his incisive imagination. The "Lettres à une Inconnue" inform us.

They consist of a series of familiar—often singularly familiar—epistles, addressed during more than thirty years to a lady of whom nothing is generally known. The letters begin apparently about 1838; the last is written in September 1870, two hours before the anthor's death, in the prime of his country's recent disasters. Love-letters we suppose they are properly to be called; but the reader may judge from a few extracts whether they seem superficially to belong to this category. In his private as well as his public compositions Mérimée was an enemy to fine phrases; and here, instead of burning incense at the feet of his beloved, he treats her to such homely truths as these: "The cakes you eat with such appetite to cure you of the backache you got at the opera surprised me still more. But it isn't that among your defects I don't place coquetry and gluttony in the first rank." "The affection that you have for me is only a sort of *jeu d'esprit.* You are all *esprit.* You are one of those 'chilly women of the North.' You only live by your head." He is forever accusing her of coquetry, heartlessness, duplicity, mendacity. "Why, after we have been what we are to each other so long, do you take several days to answer the simplest question?" After her marriage he tells her it is all nonsense for her to say that she is a better person than she was before. "You seem to me prettier; but you have acquired, on the other hand, a pretty dose of selfishness and hypocrisy." It is true that in the beginning of their acquaintance he disclaims the ambition of being her lover. "Perhaps you'll gain a real friend; and I, perhaps, shall find in you what I have been looking for so long—a woman with whom I am not in love and in whom I can have confidence." One doubts whether he was gratified. "You grow every day more imperious and you have scandalous refinements of coquetry." And yet one wonders, too, whether to attribute to friendship or love this vigorous allusion to a walk with his correspondent: "For myself, contrary to my habit, I have no distinct recollections. I am like a cat who licks his whiskers a long time after drinking milk." We owe our knowledge of these letters to the lady herself, who has published them with a frankness more common in France than among ourselves. She has, however, taken every pains to draw the veil about her identity, and it may be said on her behalf that it is none of our business who she was or what she was. But only a very unimaginative reader will spare his conjectures. There is something extremely provoking to curiosity in the image, however shadowy, of a woman clever enough to have all this cleverness addressed to her. The author tells her early in the book that she has "a nature so *raffinée*"—something more than our "refined"—"as to be for him the summing-up of a civilization." It is not, apparently, without reason that he writes to her: "Between your head and your heart I never know which is to carry the day. You don't know yourself; but you always give the victory to your head." She had a head worth favouring. Constantly busy himself with philological studies, he recommends her to learn Greek as a pastime, and tells her how to set to work. It soon appears that she has taken his advice, and in the course of time we find her enjoying Homer and the tragedians. Later, when, with the privilege of a twenty years' friendship, he utters all the crudities that come into his head—and they grow very numerous as he grows older—he scolds her for being alarmed at what she finds in Aristophanes. The burden of his complaint from the first is her reserve, her calculations, her never obeying the first impulse. She had carried so far refusing to see him, for fear of getting tired of him, that he estimates that they have spent but three or four hours together in the course of six or seven years. This is Platonism with a vengeance and Mérimée makes an odd figure in it. He constantly protests, and begs for a walk in the Champs Elysées or a talk in the gallery of the Louvre. The critic to whom we just alluded and whose impression differs from our own in that these volumes have made him like the writer more than before, rather than less, maintains that we have a right to be very severe toward the heroine. She was cold, he affirms; she was old-maidish and conventional; she had no spontaneous perceptions. When Mérimée is not at hand to give her a cue her opinions are evidently of the flimsiest. When she travels he exhorts her almost fiercely to observe and inquire, to make a note of everything curious in manners and morals, and hé invariably scolds her for the inefficiency of her *compte-rendu*. This is probably true enough. She had not the unshrinking glance of her guide, philosopher and friend. But we confess that our own sentiment with regard to her partakes of vague compassion. Mérimée's tone and general view of things, judged in a vivid moral light, were such as very effectually to corrupt a pliable and dependent nature; and what we perceive in his correspondent's reserve—her reluctance, in common phrase, to make herself cheap—is the natural effort to preserve a certain ideal dignity in her own eyes. "Each time we meet," he declares, in 1843, "it seems as if there were a new formation of ice to break through. Why don't I find you the same as I left you? If we met oftener, this wouldn't happen. I am like an old opera for you, which you need to forget to hear it again with any pleasure." He numbers this annoying self-possession, apparently, among the machinations of what he calls her "infernal coquetry." His conception of the feminine character, though it had sunk a deep shaft in a single direction, was strikingly narrow. In the later letters, where he appears altogether in his dressing-gown and slippers, he is for ever berating his old friend for her "prudery." He can think of no other name for the superficiality of her investigation of certain points of harem-life, during a sojourn in Algiers; and he showers the same accusation upon her when, on his having lent her books unfamiliar to most women, she alludes to their peculiar character in returning them. One is anxious to know where he drew the line between "prudery" and modesty, or whether he really thought the distinction not worth making. And yet it was not that his friendship had not a masculine delicacy of its own. He says innumerable tender things, in which his ardour is anything but cynical. Here is an allusion to a Spanish greeting with which she had begun a letter: "I wish I had seen you when you were writing *amigo de mi alma*. When you have your portrait taken for me, say that to yourself, instead of '*petite pomme d'api*,' as the ladies say who wish to make their mouths look pretty." The nearest approach in the book to the stuff that love-letters are generally made of is an allusion to the pains of the tender passion. "Several times it has come into my head not to answer you and to see you no more. This is very reasonable and a great deal can be said for it. The execution is more difficult."

Gradually, however, sentiment of the tenderer sort disappears—but by absorption, as one may say, and not by evanescence. After a correspondence of ten years the writer's devotion may be taken for granted. His letters become an irremissible habit, an intellectual need, a receptacle for his running commentary on life. The second volume of the "Lettres à une Inconnue" contains less that is personal to the lady, and more allusions to other people and things, more anecdotes and promiscuous reflections. Mérimée became more and more a man of the world. He was member of two Academies, inspector and conservator of national monuments (a very active post, apparently), a senator of the Empire and an intimate friend of his sovereigns. He travels constantly from Moscow to Madrid, makes regular archæological surveys through the length and breadth of France, and pays frequent visits to England. He meets every one and knows most people—most great people, at least. In the midst of these things he despatches constant notes to his correspondent, flashing his lantern fitfully over his momentary associates and over events of the hour. There is a multitude of entertaining opinions, characterizations and anecdotes; but we lack space for quotations. Everything he says is admirably said; his phrase, in its mingled brevity and laxity, is an excellent "fit" for his thought. He tells anecdotes as vividly as Madame de Sévigné and in much fewer words. His judgments are rarely flattering and his impressions rarely genial; and, as proper names have been retained throughout, with unprecedented audacity, many of his opinions must have aroused a sufficiently inharmonious echo. He goes again and again to England; but familiarity seems to breed something very much akin to contempt. "I am beginning to have enough of *ce pays-ci*. I am satiated with perpendicular architecture and the equally perpendicular manners of the natives. I passed two days at Cambridge and at Oxford in the houses of 'reverends,' and, the matter well considered, I prefer the Capuchins. I gave (at Salisbury) half-a-crown to a person in black who showed me the cathedral, and then I asked him the address of a gentleman to whom I had a letter from the Dean. It turned out that it was to him the letter was addressed. He looked like a fool, and I too; but he kept the money." The most interesting thing throughout the later letters is not, however, the witty anecdotes and the raps at the writer's *confrères*, but the development of his scepticism and cynicism. He took his stand early in life on his aversion to florid phrases (one must remember, in palliation, that he was a Frenchman of the so-called generation of 1830), and he fell a victim ultimately to what we may call a dogmatization of his temperament. His dislike for fine names led him at last to a total disbelief in fine things. He had found a great many pretty puppets stuffed with sawdust or nothing at all; so he concluded that all sentiment was hollow and flattered himself that he had pricked the bubble. We have noted but a single instance of his speaking of a case of moral ardour without raillery more or less explicit; and even here it is a question to what extent the ardour is in fact moral. " Since there have been so many romances and poems of the passionate or would-be passionate sort every woman pretends to have a heart. Wait a little yet. When you have a heart in good earnest, you will let me know. You will regret the good time when you lived only by your head, and you will see that the evils you suffer from now are but pin-pricks compared to the dagger-blows that will rain down on you when the time of passions comes." M. Taine, in a masterly preface to these volumes, has laid his finger on the weak spot in Mérimée's character. "For fear of being dupe, he *mistrusted* in life, in love, in science, in art; and *he was dupe of his mistrust.* One is always dupe of something." This latter sentence may be true; but Mérimée's fallacy was, of all needful illusions, the least remunerative while it lasted, for it eventually weakened an intellect which had every reason for being strong. The letters of his latter years are sad reading. His wit loses none of its edge; but what the French call *sécheresse* had utterly invaded his soul. His health breaks down, and his short notes are hardly more than a record of reiterated ailments and contemptuous judgments. Most forms of contempt are unwise; but one of them seems to us peculiarly ridiculous—contempt for the age one lives in. Men with but a tithe of Mérimée's ingenuity have been able, and have not failed, in every age, to make out a deplorable case for mankind.

Poor Mérimée, apparently, long before his death, ceased to enjoy anything but the sunshine and a good dinner. His imagination faded early, and it is certainly a question whether this generous spirit, half-sister, at least, to Charity, will remain under a roof in which the ideal is treated as uncivilly as Mérimée treated it. He was constantly in the Imperial train at Fontainebleau, Compiègne and Saint Cloud; but he does little save complain of the discomforts of grandeur in general and of silk tights in especial. He was, however, as the event proved, a sincere friend of the Emperor and Empress, and not a mere mercenary courtier. He always speaks kindly of them and sharply of every one else except Prince Bismarck, whom he meets at Biarritz and who takes his fancy greatly. The literature of the day he considers mere rubbish. Half a dozen of his illustrious contemporaries come in for hard knocks; but M. Renan and his *paysages* are his pet aversion. The manners of the day are in his opinion still worse and the universal world is making a prodigious fool of itself. The collapse of the Empire, in which he believed as much as he believed in anything, set the seal to his pessimism, and he died, most consentingly, as one may suppose, as the Germans were marching upon Paris. His effort had been to put as little as possible of his personal self into his published writings; but fortune and his correspondent have betrayed him, and after reading these letters we feel that we know him. This fact, added to their vigour, their vivacity and raciness, accounts for their great success. There had been lately a great many poems and novels, philosophies and biographies, abounding in more or less fantastic *simulacra* of human creatures; but here is a genuine, visible, palpable *man*, with a dozen limitations but with a most distinct and curious individuality.

THE THÉÂTRE FRANÇAIS.

M. Francisque Sarcey, the dramatic critic of the Paris "Temps," and the gentleman who, of the whole journalistic fraternity, holds the fortune of a play in the hollow of his hand, has been publishing during the last year a series of biographical notices of the chief actors and actresses of the first theatre in the world. "Comédiens et Comédiennes : la Comédie Française"—such is the title of this publication, which appears in monthly numbers of the "Librairie des Bibliophiles," and is ornamented on each occasion with a very prettily etched portrait, by M. Gaucherel, of the artist to whom the number is devoted. By lovers of the stage in general and of the Théâtre Français in particular the series will be found most interesting; and I welcome the pretext for saying a few words about an institution which—if such language be not hyperbolical—I passionately admire. I must add that the portrait is incomplete, though for the present occasion it is more than sufficient. The list of M. Sarcey's biographies is not yet filled up; three or four, those of Madame Favart and of MM. Fèbvre and Delaunay, are still wanting. Nine numbers, however, have appeared—the first being entitled "La Maison de Molière," and devoted to a general account of the great theatre; and the others treating of its principal *sociétaires* and *pensionnaires* in the following order:

>Regnier,
>Got,
>Sophie Croizette,
>Sarah Bernhardt,
>Coquelin,
>Madeleine Brohan,
>Bressant,
>Madame Plessy.

(This order, by the way, is purely accidental; it is not that of age or of merit.) It is always entertaining to encounter M. Francisque Sarcey, and the reader who, during a Paris winter, has been in the habit, of a Sunday evening, of unfolding his "Temps" immediately after unfolding his napkin, and glancing down first of all to see what this sturdy *feuilletoniste* has found to his hand—such a reader will find him in great force in the pages before us. It is true that, though I myself confess to being such a reader, there are moments when I grow rather weary of M. Sarcey, who has in an eminent degree both the virtues and the defects which attach to the great French characteristic—the habit of taking terribly *au sérieux* anything that you may set about doing. Of this habit of abounding in one's own sense, of expatiating, elaborating, reiterating, refining, as if for the hour the fate of mankind were bound up with one's particular topic, M. Sarcey is a capital and at times an almost comical representative. He talks about the theatre once a week as if—honestly, between himself and his reader—the theatre were the only thing in this frivolous world that is worth seriously talking about. He has a religious respect for his theme and he holds that if a thing is to be done at all it must be done in detail as well as in the gross.

It is to this serious way of taking the matter, to his thoroughly businesslike and professional attitude, to his unwearying attention to detail, that the critic of the "Temps" owes his enviable influence and the weight of his words. Add to this that he is sternly incorruptible. He has his admirations, but they are honest and discriminating; and whom he loveth he very often chasteneth. He is not ashamed to commend Mlle. X., who has only had a curtsy to make, if her curtsy has been the ideal curtsy of the situation; and he is not afraid to overhaul M. A., who has delivered the *tirade* of the play, if M. A., has failed to hit the mark. Of course his judgment is good; when I have had occasion to measure it I have usually found it excellent. He has the scenic sense—the theatrical eye. He knows at a glance what will do, and what will not do. He is shrewd and sagacious and almost tiresomely in earnest, and this is his principal brilliancy. He is homely, familiar and colloquial; he leans his elbows on his desk and does up his weekly budget into a parcel the reverse of coquettish. You can fancy him a grocer retailing tapioca and hominy—full weight for the price; his style seems a sort of integument of brown paper. But the fact remains that if M. Sarcey praises a play the play has a run; and that if M. Sarcey says it will not do it does not do at all. If M. Sarcey devotes an encouraging line and a half to a young actress, mademoiselle is immediately *lancée;* she has a career. If he bestows a quiet "bravo" on an obscure comedian, the gentleman may forthwith renew his engagement. When you make and unmake fortunes at this rate, what matters it whether you have a little elegance the more or the less? Elegance is for M. Paul de St. Victor, who does the theatres in the "Moniteur," and who, though he writes a style only a trifle less pictorial than that of Théophile

Gautier himself, has never, to the best of my belief, brought clouds or sunshine to any playhouse. I may add, to finish with M. Sarcey, that he contributes a daily political article—generally devoted to watching and showing up the "game" of the clerical party—to Edmond About's journal, the "XIXième Siècle"; that he gives a weekly *conférence* on current literature; that he "confers" also on those excellent Sunday morning performances now so common in the French theatres, during which examples of the classic repertory are presented, accompained by a light lecture upon the history and character of the play. As the commentator on these occasions M. Sarcey is in great demand, and he officiates sometimes in small provincial towns. Lastly, frequent playgoers in Paris observe that the very slenderest novelty is sufficient to insure at a theatre the (very considerable) physical presence of the conscientious critic of the "Temps." If he were remarkable for nothing else he would be remarkable for the fortitude with which he exposes himself to the pestiferous climate of the Parisian temples of the drama.

For these agreeable "notices" M. Sarcey appears to have mended his pen and to have given a fillip to his fancy. They are gracefully and often lightly turned; occasionally, even, the author grazes the epigrammatic. They deal, as is proper, with the artistic and not with the private physiognomy of the ladies and gentlemen whom they commemorate; and though they occasionally allude to what the French call "intimate" matters, they contain no satisfaction for the lovers of scandal. The Théâtre Français, in the face it presents to the world, is an austere and venerable establishment, and a frivolous tone about its affairs would be almost as much out of keeping as if applied to the Académie herself. M. Sarcey touches upon the organization of the theatre, and gives some account of the different phases through which it has passed during these latter years. Its chief functionary is a general administrator, or director, appointed by the State, which enjoys this right in virtue of the considerable subsidy which it pays to the house; a subsidy amounting, if I am not mistaken (M. Sarcey does not mention the sum) to 250,000 francs. The director, however, is not an absolute but a constitutional ruler; for he shares his powers with the society itself, which has always had a large deliberative voice.

Whence, it may be asked, does the society derive its light and its inspiration? From the past, from precedent, from tradition—from the great unwritten body of laws which no one has in his keeping but many have in their memory, and all in their respect. The principles on which the Théâtre Français rests are a good deal like the Common Law of England—a vaguely and inconveniently registered mass of regulations which time and occasion have welded together and from which the recurring occasion can usually manage to extract the rightful precedent. Napoleon I., who had a finger in every pie in his dominion, found time during his brief and disastrous occupation of Moscow to send down a decree remodelling and regulating the constitution of the theatre. This document has long been a dead letter, and the society abides by its older traditions. The *traditions* of the Comédie Française—that is the sovereign word, and that is the charm of the place— the charm that one never ceases to feel, however often one may sit beneath the classic, dusky dome. One feels this charm with peculiar intensity as a newly arrived foreigner. The Théâtre Français has had the good fortune to be able to allow its traditions to accumulate. They have been preserved, transmitted, respected, cherished, until at last they form the very atmosphere, the vital air, of the establishment. A stranger feels their superior influence the first time he sees the great curtain go up; he feels that he is in a theatre that is not as other theatres are. It is not only better, it is different. It has a peculiar perfection—something consecrated, historical, academic. This impression is delicious, and he watches the performance in a sort of tranquil ecstasy.

Never has he seen anything so smooth and harmonious, so artistic and complete. He has heard all his life of attention to detail, and now, for the first time, he sees something that deserves the name. He sees dramatic effort refined to a point with which the English stage is unacquainted. He sees that there are no limits to possible "finish," and that so trivial an act as taking a letter from a servant or placing one's hat on a chair may be made a suggestive and interesting incident. He sees these things and a great many more besides, but at first he does not analyse them; he gives himself up to sympathetic contemplation. He is in an ideal and exemplary world—a world that has managed to attain all the felicities that the world we live in misses. The people do the things that we should like to do; they are gifted as we should like to be; they have mastered the accomplishments that we have had to give up. The women are not all beautiful—decidedly not, indeed—but they are graceful, agreeable, sympathetic, ladylike; they have the best manners possible and they are delightfully well dressed. They have charming musical voices and they speak with irreproachable purity and sweetness; they walk with the most elegant grace and when they sit it is a pleasure to see their attitudes. They go out and come in, they pass across the stage, they talk, and laugh, and cry, they deliver long *tirades* or remain statuesquely mute; they are tender or tragic, they are comic or conventional; and through it all you never observe an awkwardness, a roughness, an accident, a crude spot, a false note.

As for the men, they are not handsome either; it must be confessed, indeed, that at the present hour manly beauty is but scantily represented at the Théâtre Français. Bressant, I believe, used to be thought handsome; but Bressant has retired, and among the gentlemen of the troupe I can think of no one but M. Mounet-Sully who may be positively commended for his fine person. But M. Mounet-Sully is, from the scenic point of view, an Adonis of the first magnitude. To be handsome, however, is for an actor one of the last necessities; and these gentlemen are mostly handsome enough. They look perfectly what they are intended to look, and in cases where it is proposed that they shall seem handsome, they usually succeed. They are as well mannered and as well dressed as their fairer comrades and their voices are no less agreeable and effective. They represent gentlemen and they produce the illusion. In this endeavour they deserve even greater credit than the actresses, for in modern comedy, of which the repertory of the Théâtre Français is largely composed, they have nothing in the way of costume to help to carry it off. Half-a-dozen ugly men, in the periodic coat and trousers and stove-pipe hat, with blue chins and false moustaches, strutting before the footlights, and pretending to be interesting, romantic, pathetic, heroic, certainly play a perilous game. At every turn they suggest prosaic things and the usual liability to awkwardness is meantime increased a thousand fold. But the comedians of the Théâtre Français are never awkward, and when it is necessary they solve triumphantly the problem of being at once realistic to the eye and romantic to the imagination.

I am speaking always of one's first impression of them. There are spots on the sun, and you discover after a while that there are little irregularities at the Théâtre Français. But the acting is so incomparably better than any that you have seen that criticism for a long time is content to lie dormant. I shall never forget how at first I was under the charm. I liked the very incommodities of the place; I am not sure that I did not find a certain mystic salubrity in the bad ventilation. The Théâtre Français, it is known, gives you a good deal for your money. The performance, which rarely ends before midnight, and sometimes transgresses it, frequently begins by seven o'clock. The first hour or two is occupied by secondary performers; but not for the world at this time would I have missed the first rising of the curtain. No dinner could be too hastily swallowed to enable me to see, for instance, Madame Nathalie in Octave Feuillet's charming little comedy of "Le Village." Madame Nathalie was a plain, stout old woman, who did the mothers and aunts and elderly wives; I use the past tense because she retired from the stage a year ago, leaving a most conspicuous vacancy. She was an admirable actress and a perfect mistress of laughter and tears. In "Le Village" she played an old provincial bourgeoise whose husband takes it into his head, one winter night, to start on the tour of Europe with a roving bachelor friend, who has dropped down on him at supper-time, after the lapse of years, and has gossiped him into momentary discontent with his fireside existence. My pleasure was in Madame Nathalie's figure when she came in dressed to go out to vespers across the *place*. The two foolish old cronies are over their wine, talking of the beauty of the women on the Ionian coast; you hear the church-bell in the distance. It was the quiet felicity of the old lady's dress that used to charm me; the Comédie Française was in every fold of it. She wore a large black silk mantilla, of a peculiar cut, which looked as if she had just taken it tenderly out of some old wardrobe where it lay folded in lavender, and a large dark bonnet, adorned with handsome black silk loops and bows. Her big pale face had a softly frightened look, and in her hand she carried her neatly kept breviary. The extreme suggestiveness, and yet the taste and temperance of this costume, seemed to me inimitable; the bonnet alone, with its handsome, decent, virtuous bows, was worth coming to see. It expressed all the rest, and you saw the excellent, pious woman go pick her steps churchward among the puddles, while Jeannette, the cook, in a high white cap, marched before her in sabots with a lantern.

Such matters are trifles, but they are representative trifles, and they are not the only ones that I remember. It used to please me, when I had squeezed into my stall—the stalls at the Français are extremely uncomfortable—to remember of how great a history the large, dim *salle* around me could boast; how many great things had happened there; how the air was thick with associations. Even if I had never seen Rachel, it was something of a consolation to think that those very footlights had illumined her finest moments and that the echoes of her mighty voice were sleeping in that dingy dome. From this to musing upon the "traditions" of the place, of which I spoke just now, was of course but a step. How were they kept? by whom, and where? Who trims the undying lamp and guards the accumulated treasure? I never found out —by sitting in the stalls; and very soon I ceased to

care to know. One may be very fond of the stage
and yet care little for the green-room; just as
one may be very fond of pictures and books and yet
be no frequenter of studios and authors' dens. They
might pass on the torch as they would behind the
scenes; so long as during my time they did not let it
drop I made up my mind to be satisfied. And that one
could depend upon their not letting it drop became a
part of the customary comfort of Parisian life. It
became certain that the "traditions" were not mere
catchwords, but a most beneficent reality.

Going to the other Parisian theatres helps you to
believe in them. Unless you are a voracious theatre-
goer you give the others up; you find they do not
"pay"; the Français does for you all that they do
and so much more besides. There are two possible
exceptions—the Gymnase and the Palais Royal. The
Gymnase, since the death of Mademoiselle Desclée,
has been under a heavy cloud; but occasionally, when
a month's sunshine rests upon it, there is a savour of
excellence in the performance. But you feel that you
are still within the realm of accident; the delightful
security of the Rue de Richelieu is wanting. The
young lover is liable to be common and the beautifully
dressed heroine to have an unpleasant voice. The
Palais Royal has always been in its way very perfect;

but its way admits of great imperfection. The actresses are classically bad, though usually pretty, and the actors are much addicted to taking liberties. In broad comedy, nevertheless, two or three of the latter are not to be surpassed, and (counting out the women) there is usually something masterly in a Palais Royal performance. In its own line it has what is called style, and it therefore walks, at a distance, in the footsteps of the Français. The Odéon has never seemed to me in any degree a rival of the Théâtre Français, though it is a smaller copy of that establishment. It receives a subsidy from the State, and is obliged by its contract to play the classic repertory one night in the week. It is on these nights, listening to Molière or Marivaux, that you may best measure the superiority of the greater theatre. I have seen actors at the Odéon, in the classic repertory, imperfect in their texts; a monstrously insupposable case at the Comédie Française. The function of the Odéon is to operate as a *pépinière* or nursery for its elder—to try young talents, shape them, make them flexible and then hand them over to the upper house. The more especial nursery of the Français, however, is the Conservatoire Dramatique, an institution dependent upon the State, through the Ministry of the Fine Arts, whose budget is charged with the remuneration of its professors.

Pupils graduating from the Conservatoire with a prize have *ipso facto* the right to *débuter* at the Théâtre Français, which retains them or lets them go, according to its discretion. Most of the first subjects of the Français have done their two years' work at the Conservatoire, and M. Sarcey holds that an actor who has not had that fundamental training which is only to be acquired there never obtains a complete mastery of his resources. Nevertheless some of the best actors of the day have owed nothing to the Conservatoire— Bressant, for instance, and Aimée Desclée, the latter of whom, indeed, never arrived at the Français. (Molière and Balzac were not of the Academy, and so Mlle. Desclée, the first actress after Rachel, died without acquiring the privilege which M. Sarcey says is the day-dream of all young theatrical women—that of printing on their visiting-cards, after their name, *de la Comédie Française*.)

The Théâtre Français has, moreover, the right to do as Molière did—to claim its property wherever it finds it. It may stretch out its long arm and break the engagement of a promising actor at any of the other theatres; of course after a certain amount of notice given. So, last winter, it notified to the Gymnase its design of appropriating Worms, the admirable *jeune premier*, who, returning from a long sojourn in

Russia and taking the town by surprise, had begun to retrieve the shrunken fortunes of that establishment.

On the whole, it may be said that the great talents find their way, sooner or later, to the Théâtre Français. This is of course not a rule that works unvaryingly, for there are a great many influences to interfere with it. Interest as well as merit—especially in the case of the actresses—weighs in the scale; and the ire that may exist in celestial minds has been known to manifest itself in the councils of the Comédie. Moreover, a brilliant actress may prefer to reign supreme at one of the smaller theatres; at the Français, inevitably, she shares her dominion. The honour is less, but the comfort is greater.

Nevertheless, at the Français, in a general way, there is in each case a tolerably obvious artistic reason for membership; and if you see a clever actor remain outside for years, you may be pretty sure that, though private reasons count, there are artistic reasons as well. The first half dozen times I saw Mademoiselle Fargueil, who for years ruled the roost, as the vulgar saying is, at the Vaudeville, I wondered that so consummate and accomplished an actress should not have a place on the first French stage. But I presently grew wiser, and perceived that, clever as Mademoiselle Fargueil is, she is not for the Rue de Richelieu, but for the

Boulevards; her peculiar, intensely Parisian intonation would sound out of place in the Maison de Molière. (Of course if Mademoiselle Fargueil has ever received overtures from the Français, my sagacity is at fault —I am looking through a millstone. But I suspect she has not.) Frédéric Lemaître, who died last winter, and who was a very great actor, had been tried at the Français and found wanting—for those particular conditions. But it may probably be said that if Frédéric was wanting, the theatre was too, in this case. Frédéric's great force was his extravagance, his fantasticality; and the stage of the Rue de Richelieu was a trifle too academic. I have even wondered whether Desclée, if she had lived, would have trod that stage by right, and whether it would have seemed her proper element. The negative is not impossible. It is very possible that in that classic atmosphere her great charm—her intensely modern quality, her super-subtle realism—would have appeared an anomaly. I can imagine even that her strange, touching, nervous voice would not have seemed the voice of the house. At the Français you must know how to acquit yourself of a *tirade;* that has always been the touchstone of capacity. It would probably have proved Desclée's stumbling-block, though she could utter speeches of six words as no one else surely has ever done. It is true that Mademoiselle Croizette, and in a certain sense Mademoiselle Sarah Bernhardt, are rather weak at their *tirades;* but then old theatre-goers will tell you that these young ladies, in spite of a hundred attractions, have no business at the Français.

In the course of time the susceptible foreigner passes from that superstitious state of attention which I just now sketched to that greater enlightenment which enables him to understand such a judgment as this of the old theatre-goers. It is borne in upon him that, as the good Homer sometimes nods, the Théâtre Français sometimes lapses from its high standard. He makes various reflections. He thinks that Mademoislle Favart rants. He thinks M. Mounet-Sully, in spite of his delicious voice, insupportable. He thinks that M. Parodi's five-act tragedy, "Rome Vaincue," presented in the early part of the present winter, was better done certainly than it would have been done upon any English stage, but by no means so much better done as might have been expected. (Here, if I had space, I would open a long parenthesis, in which I should aspire to demonstrate that the incontestable superiority of average French acting to English is by no means so strongly marked in tragedy as in comedy—is indeed sometimes not strongly marked at all. The reason of this is in a great measure, I think, that we have had Shakespeare to exercise ourselves upon, and that an inferior dramatic instinct exercised upon Shakespeare may become more flexible than a superior one exercised upon Corneille and Racine. When it comes to ranting—ranting even in a modified and comparatively reasonable sense— we do, I suspect, quite as well as the French, if not rather better.) Mr. G. H. Lewes, in his entertaining little book upon "Actors and the Art of Acting," mentions M. Talbot, of the Français, as a surprisingly incompetent performer. My memory assents to his judgment at the same time that it proposes an amendment. This actor's special line is the buffeted, bemuddled, besotted old fathers, uncles and guardians of classic comedy, and he plays them with his face much more than with his tongue. Nature has endowed him with a visage so admirably adapted, once for all, to his rôle, that he has only to sit in a chair, with his hands folded on his stomach, to look like a monument of bewildered senility. After that it does not matter what he says or how he says it.

The Comédie Française sometimes does weaker things than in keeping M. Talbot. Last autumn,[1] for instance, it was really depressing to see Mademoiselle Dudley brought all the way from Brussels (and with not a

[1] 1876.

little flourish either) to "create" the guilty vestal in "Rome Vaincue." As far as the interests of art are concerned, Mademoiselle Dudley had much better have remained in the Flemish capital, of whose language she is apparently a perfect mistress. It is hard, too, to forgive M. Perrin (M. Perrin is the present director of the Théâtre Français) for bringing out "L'Ami Fritz" of M. Erckmann-Chatrian. The two gentlemen who write under this name have a double claim to kindness. In the first place, they have produced some delightful little novels; every one knows and admires "Le Conscrit de 1813"; every one admires, indeed, the charming tale on which the play in question is founded. In the second place, they were, before the production of their piece, the objects of a scurrilous attack by the "Figaro" newspaper, which held the authors up to reprobation for having "insulted the army," and did its best to lay the train for a hostile manifestation on the first night. (It may be added that the good sense of the public outbalanced the impudence of the newspaper, and the play was simply advertised into success.) But neither the novels nor the persecutions of M. Erckmann-Chatrian avail to render "L'Ami Fritz," in its would-be dramatic form, worthy of the first French stage. It is played as well as possible, and upholstered even better; but it is, according to the vulgar phrase, too "thin" for the locality. Upholstery has never played such a part at the Théâtre Français as during the reign of M. Perrin, who came into power, if I mistake not, after the late war. He proved very early that he was a radical, and he has introduced a hundred novelties. His administration, however, has been brilliant, and in his hands the Théâtre Français has made money. This it had rarely done before, and this, in the conservative view, is quite beneath its dignity. To the conservative view I should humbly incline. An institution so closely protected by a rich and powerful State ought to be able to cultivate art for art.

The first of M. Sarcey's biographies, to which I have been too long in coming, is devoted to Regnier, a veteran actor, who left the stage four or five years since, and who now fills the office of oracle to his younger comrades. It is the indispensable thing, says M. Sarcey, for a young aspirant to be able to say that he has had lessons of M. Regnier, or that M. Regnier had advised him, or that he has talked such and such a point over with M. Regnier. (His comrades always speak of him as M. Regnier—never as simple Regnier.) I have had the fortune to see him but once; it was the first time I ever went to the Théâtre Français. He played Don Annibal in Émile Augier's romantic comedy of "L'Aventurière," and I have not forgotten the exquisite humour of the performance. The part is that of a sort of seventeenth century Captain Costigan, only the Miss Fotheringay in the case is the gentleman's sister and not his daughter. This lady is moreover an ambitious and designing person, who leads her threadbare braggart of a brother quite by the nose. She has entrapped a worthy gentleman of Padua, of mature years, and he is on the eve of making her his wife, when his son, a clever young soldier, beguiles Don Annibal into supping with him, and makes him drink so deep that the prating adventurer at last lets the cat out of the bag and confides to his companion that the fair Clorinde is not the virtuous gentlewoman she appears, but a poor strolling actress who has had a lover at every stage of her journey. The scene was played by Bressant and Regnier, and it has always remained in my mind as one of the most perfect things I have seen on the stage. The gradual action of the wine upon Don Annibal, the delicacy with which his deepening tipsiness was indicated, its intellectual rather than physical manifestation, and, in the midst of it, the fantastic conceit which made him think that he was winding his fellow drinker round his fingers—all this was exquisitely rendered. Drunkenness on the stage is usually both dreary and disgusting; and I can remember besides this but two really interesting pictures of intoxication (excepting always, indeed, the immortal tipsiness of Cassio in "Othello," which a clever actor can always make touching.) One is the beautiful befuddlement of Rip Van Winkle, as Mr. Joseph Jefferson renders it, and the other (a memory of the Théâtre Français) the scene in the " Duc Job," in which Got succumbs to mild inebriation, and dozes in his chair just boosily enough for the young girl who loves him to make it out.

It is to this admirable Émile Got that M. Sarcey's second notice is devoted. Got is at the present hour unquestionably the first actor at the Théâtre Français, and I have personally no hesitation in accepting him as the first of living actors. His younger comrade, Coquelin, has, I think, as much talent and as much art; as the older man Got has the longer and fuller record and may therefore be spoken of as the master. If I were obliged to rank the half-dozen *premiers sujets* of the last few years at the Théâtre Français in their absolute order of talent (thank Heaven, I am not so obliged!) I think I should make up some such little list as this: Got, Coquelin, Madame Plessy, Sarah Bernhardt, Mademoiselle Favart, Delaunay. I confess that I have no sooner written it than I feel as if I ought to amend it, and wonder whether it is not a great folly to put Delaunay after Mademoiselle Favart. But this is idle.

As for Got, he is a singularly interesting actor. I have often wondered whether the best definition of him would not be to say that he is really a *philosophic* actor. He is an immense humorist and his comicality is sometimes colossal; but his most striking quality is the one on which M. Sarcey dwells—his sobriety and profundity, his underlying element of manliness and melancholy, the impression he gives you of having a general conception of human life and of seeing the relativity, as one may say, of the character he represents. Of all the comic actors I have seen he is the least trivial—at the same time that for richness of detail his comic manner is unsurpassed. His repertory is very large and various, but it may be divided into two equal halves—the parts that belong to reality and the parts that belong to fantasy. There is of course a great deal of fantasy in his realistic parts and a great deal of reality in his fantastic ones, but the general division is just; and at times, indeed, the two faces of his talent seem to have little in common. The Duc Job, to which I just now alluded, is one of the things he does most perfectly. The part, which is that of a young man, is a serious and tender one. It is amazing that the actor who plays it should also be able to carry off triumphantly the frantic buffoonery of Maître Pathelin, or should represent the Sganarelle of the "Médecin Malgré Lui" with such an unctuous breadth of humour. The two characters, perhaps, which have given me the liveliest idea of Got's power and fertility are the Maître Pathelin and the M. Poirier who figures in the title to the comedy which Émile Augier and Jules Sandeau wrote together. M. Poirier, the retired shopkeeper who marries his daughter to a marquis and makes acquaintance with the incommodities incidental to such a piece of luck, is perhaps the actor's most elaborate creation; it is difficult to see how the portrayal of a type and an individual can have a larger sweep and a more minute completeness. The *bonhomme* Poirier, in Got's hands, is really great; and half-a-dozen of the actor's modern parts that I could mention are hardly less brilliant. But when I think of him I instinctively think first of some rôle in which he wears the cap and gown of a period as regards which humorous invention may fairly take the bit in its teeth. This is what Got lets it do in Maître Pathelin, and he leads the spectator's exhilarated fancy a dance to which the latter's aching sides on the morrow sufficiently testify.

The piece is a *réchauffé* of a mediæval farce which has the credit of being the first play not a "mystery" or a miracle-piece in the records of the French drama. The plot is extremely bald and primitive. It sets forth how a cunning lawyer undertook to purchase a dozen ells of cloth for nothing. In the first scene we see him in the market-place, bargaining and haggling with the draper, and then marching off with the roll of cloth, with the understanding that the shopman shall call at his house in the course of an hour for the money. In the next act we have Maître Pathelin at his fireside with his wife, to whom he relates his trick and its projected sequel, and who greets them with Homeric laughter. He gets into bed, and the innocent draper arrives. Then follows a scene of which the liveliest description must be ineffective. Pathelin pretends to be out of his head, to be overtaken by a mysterious malady which has made him delirious, not to know the draper from Adam, never to have heard of the dozen ells of cloth and to be altogether an impossible person to collect a debt from. To carry out this character he indulges in a series of indescribable antics, out-Bedlams Bedlam, frolics over the room dressed out in the bed-clothes and chanting the wildest gibberish, bewilders the poor draper to within an inch of his own sanity and finally puts him utterly to rout. The spectacle could only be portentously flat or heroically successful, and in Got's hands this latter was its fortune. His Sganarelle, in the "Médecin Malgré Lui," and half-a-dozen of his characters from Molière besides —such a part, too, as his Tibia, in Alfred de Musset's charming bit of romanticism, the "Caprices de Marianne"—have a certain generic resemblance with his treatment of the figure I have sketched. In all these things the comicality is of the exuberant and tremendous order, and yet in spite of its richness and flexibility it suggests little connection with high animal spirits. It seems a matter of invention, of reflection and irony. You cannot imagine Got representing a fool pure and simple—or at least a passive and unsuspecting fool. There must always be an element of shrewdness and even of contempt; he must be the man who knows and judges—or at least who pretends. It is a compliment, I take it, to an actor, to say that he prompts you to wonder about his private personality; and an observant spectator of M. Got is at liberty to guess that he is both obstinate and proud.

In Coquelin there is perhaps greater spontaneity, and there is a not inferior mastery of his art. He is a wonderfully brilliant, elastic actor. He is but thirty-five years old, and yet his record is most glorious. He too has his "actual" and his classical repertory, and here also it is hard to choose. As the young *valet de comédie* in Molière and Regnard and Marivaux he is incomparable. I shall never forget the really infernal brilliancy of his Mascarille in "L'Étourdi." His volubility, his rapidity, his impudence and gaiety, his ringing, penetrating voice and the shrill trumpet-note of his laughter, make him the ideal of the classic serving-man of the classic young lover—half rascal and half good fellow. Coquelin has lately had two or three immense successes in the comedies of the day. His Duc de Sept-Monts, in the famous "Étrangère" of Alexandre Dumas, last winter, was the capital creation of the piece; and in the revival, this winter, of Augier's "Paul Forestier," his Adolphe de Beaubourg, the young man about town, consciously tainted with *commonness*, and trying to shake off the incubus, seemed while one watched it and listened to it the last word of delicately humorous art. Of Coquelin's eminence in the old comedies M. Sarcey speaks with a certain pictorial force: "No one is better cut out to represent those bold and magnificent rascals of the old repertory, with their boisterous gaiety, their brilliant fancy and their superb extravagance, who give to their buffoonery *je ne sais quoi d'épique*. In these parts one may say of Coquelin that he is incomparable. I prefer him to Got in such cases, and even to Regnier, his master. I never saw Monrose, and cannot speak of him. But good judges have assured me that there was much that was factitious in the manner of this eminent comedian, and that his vivacity was a trifle mechanical. There is nothing whatever of this in Coquelin's manner. The eye, the nose, and the voice—the voice above all—are his most powerful means of action. He launches his *tirades* all in one breath, with full lungs, without troubling himself too much over the shading of details, in large masses, and he possesses himself only the more strongly of the public, which has a great sense of *ensemble*. The words that must be detached, the words that must decisively 'tell,' glitter in this delivery with the sonorous ring of a brand-new louis d'or. Crispin, Scapin, Figaro, Mascarille have never found a more valiant and joyous interpreter."

I should say that this was enough about the men at the Théâtre Français, if I did not remember that I have not spoken of Delaunay. But Delaunay has plenty of people to speak for him; he has, in especial, the more eloquent half of humanity—the ladies. I suppose that of all the actors of the Comédie Française he is the most universally appreciated and admired; he is the popular favourite. And he has certainly earned this distinction, for there was never a more amiable and sympathetic genius. He plays the young lovers of the past and the present, and he acquits himself of his difficult and delicate task with extraordinary grace and propriety. The danger I spoke of a while since—the danger, for the actor of a romantic and sentimental part, of being compromised by the coat and trousers, the hat and umbrella of the current year—are reduced by Delaunay to their minimum. He reconciles in a marvellous fashion the love-sick gallant of the ideal world with the "gentlemanly man" of to-day; and his passion is as far removed from rant as his propriety is from stiffness. He has been accused of late years of falling into a mannerism, and I think there is some truth in the charge. But the fault in Delaunay's situation is certainly venial. How can a man of fifty, to whom, as regards face and figure, Nature has been stingy, play an amorous swain of twenty without taking refuge in a mannerism? His mannerism is a legitimate device for diverting the spectator's attention from certain incongruities. Delaunay's juvenility, his ardour, his passion, his good taste and sense of fitness, have always an irresistible charm. As he has grown older he has increased his repertory by parts of greater weight and sobriety—he has played the husbands as well as the lovers. One of his most recent and brilliant "creations" of this kind is his Marquis de Presles in "Le Gendre de M. Poirier"—a piece of acting superb for its lightness and *désinvolture*. It cannot be better praised than by saying it was worthy of Got's inimitable rendering of the part opposed to it. But I think I shall remember Delaunay best in the picturesque and romantic comedies—as the Duc de Richelieu in "Mlle. De Belle-Isle"; as the joyous, gallant, exuberant young hero, his plumes and love knots fluttering in the breath of his gushing improvisation, of Corneille's "Menteur"; or, most of all, as the melodious swains of those charmingly poetic, faintly, naturally Shakespearian little comedies of Alfred de Musset.

To speak of Delaunay ought to bring us properly to Mademoiselle Favart, who for so many years invariably represented the object of his tender invocations. Mademoiselle Favart at the present time rather lacks what the French call "actuality." She has recently made an attempt to recover something of that large measure of it which she once possessed; but I doubt whether it has been completely successful. M. Sarcey has not yet put forth his notice of her; and when he does so it will be interesting to see how he treats her. She is not one of his high admirations. She is a great talent that has passed into eclipse. I call her a great talent, although I remember the words in which M. Sarcey somewhere speaks of her: "Mlle. Favart, who, to happy natural gifts, *soutenus par un travail acharné*, owed a distinguished place," etc. Her talent is great, but the impression that she gives of a *travail acharné* and of an insatiable ambition is perhaps even greater. For many years she reigned supreme, and I believe she is accused of not having always reigned generously. However that may be, there came a day when Mesdemoiselles Croizette and Sarah Bernhardt passed to the front and the elder actress receded, if not into the background, at least into what painters call the middle distance. The private history of these events has, I believe, been rich in heart-burnings; but it is only with the public history that we are concerned. Mademoiselle Favart has always seemed to me a powerful rather than an interesting actress; there is usually something mechanical and overdone in her manner. In some of her parts there is a kind of audible creaking of the machinery. If Delaunay is open to the reproach of having let a mannerism get the better of him, this accusation is much more fatally true of Mademoiselle Favart. On the other hand, she knows her trade as no one does—no one, at least, save Madame Plessy. When she is bad she is extremely bad, and sometimes she is interruptedly bad for a whole evening. In the revival of Scribe's clever comedy of "Une Chaine," this winter (which, by the way, though the cast included both Got and Coquelin, was the nearest approach to mediocrity I have ever seen at the Théâtre Français), Mademoiselle Favart was, to my sense, startlingly bad. The part had originally been played by Madame Plessy; and I remember how M. Sarcey in his *feuilleton* treated its actual representative. "Mademoiselle Favart does Louise. Who does not recall the exquisite delicacy and temperance with which Mme. Plessy rendered that difficult scene in the second act?" etc. And nothing more. When, however, Mademoiselle Favart is at her best, she is remarkably strong. She rises to great occasions. I doubt whether such parts as the desperate heroine of the "Supplice d'une Femme," or as Julie in Octave Feuillet's lugubrious drama of that name, could be more effectively played than she plays them. She can carry a great weight without flinching; she has what the French call "authority"; and in declamation she sometimes unrolls her fine voice, as it were, in long harmonious waves and cadences the sustained power of which her younger rivals must often envy her.

I am drawing to the close of these rather desultory observations without having spoken of the four ladies commemorated by M. Sarcey in the publication which lies before me; and I do not know that I can justify my tardiness otherwise than by saying that writing and reading about artists of so extreme a personal brilliancy is poor work, and that the best the critic can do is to wish his reader may see them, from a quiet *fauteuil*, as speedily and as often as possible. Of Madeleine Brohan, indeed, there is little to say. She is a delightful person to listen to, and she is still delightful to look at, in spite of that redundancy of contour which time has contributed to her charms. But she has never been ambitious and her talent has had no particularly original quality. It is a long time since she created an important part; but in the old repertory her rich, dense voice, her charming smile, her mellow, tranquil gaiety, always give extreme pleasure. To hear her sit and *talk*, simply, and laugh and play with her fan, along with Madame Plessy, in Molière's " Critique de l'École des Femmes," is an entertainment to be remembered. For Madame Plessy I should have to mend my pen and begin a new chapter; and for Mademoiselle Sarah Bernhardt no less a ceremony would suffice. I saw Madame Plessy for the first time in Émile Augier's "Aventurière," when, as I mentioned, I first saw Regnier. This is considered by many persons her best part, and she certainly carries it off with a high hand; but I like her better in characters which afford more scope to her talents for comedy. These characters are very numerous, for her activity and versatility have been extraordinary. Her comedy of course is "high"; it is of the highest conceivable kind, and she has often been accused of being too mincing and too artificial. I should never make this charge, for, to me, Madame Plessy's *minauderies*, her grand airs and her arch-refinements, have never been anything but the odorous swayings and queenly tossings of some splendid garden flower. Never had an actress grander manners. When Madame Plessy represents a duchess you have no allowances to make. Her limitations are on the side of the pathetic. If she is brilliant, she is cold; and I cannot imagine her touching the source of tears. But she is in the highest degree accomplished; she gives an impression of intelligence and intellect which is produced by none of her companions—excepting always the extremely exceptional Sarah Bernhardt. Madame Plessy's intellect has sometimes misled her—as, for instance, when it whispered to her, a few years since, that she could play Agrippine in Racine's "Britannicus," on that tragedy being presented for the *débuts* of Mounet-Sully. I was verdant enough to think her Agrippine very fine. But M. Sarcey reminds his readers of what he said of it the Monday after the first performance. "I will not say"—he quotes himself—"that Madame Plessy is indifferent. With her intelligence, her natural gifts, her great situation, her immense authority over the public, one cannot be indifferent in anything. She is therefore not indifferently bad. She is bad to a point that cannot be expressed and that would be distressing for dramatic art if it were not that in this great shipwreck there rise to the surface a few floating fragments of the finest qualities that nature has ever bestowed upon an artist."

Madame Plessy retired from the stage six months ago and it may be said that the void produced by this event is irreparable. There is not only no prospect, but there is no hope of filling it up. The present conditions of artistic production are directly hostile to the formation of actresses as consummate and as complete as Madame Plessy. One may not expect to see her like, any more than one may expect to see a new manufacture of old lace and old brocade. She carried off with her something that the younger generation of actresses will consistently lack—a certain largeness of style and robustness of art. (These qualities are in a modified degree those of Mademoiselle Favart.) But if the younger actresses have the success of Mesdemoiselles Croizette and Sarah Bernhardt, will they greatly care whether they are not "robust"? These young ladies are children of a later and eminently contemporary type, according to which an actress undertakes not to interest but to fascinate. They are charming—"awfully" charming; strange, eccentric, imaginative.

It would be needless to speak specifically of Mademoiselle Croizette; for although she has very great attractions I think she may (by the cold impartiality of science) be classified as a secondary, a less inspired and (to use the great word of the day) a more "brutal" Sarah Bernhardt. (Mademoiselle Croizette's "brutality" is her great card.) As for Mademoiselle Sarah Bernhardt, she is simply, at present, in Paris, one of the great figures of the day. It would be hard to imagine a more brilliant embodiment of feminine success; she deserves a chapter for herself.

December 1876.

THE END.

PENSACOLA JUNIOR COLLEGE LIBRARY
PQ286 .J3 1972
James, Henry, 1843-1916.   000
French poets and novelist   210101

3 5101 00065888 5